BEN **FORTA** & SHM

CAPTAIN CODE

UNLEASH YOUR CODING SUPERPOWER WITH PYTHON

Many of the designations used by manufacturers and sellers to distinguish their products are claimed as trademarks. Where those designations appear in this book, and the publisher was aware of a trademark claim, the designations have been printed with initial capital letters or in all capitals.

The authors and publisher have taken care in the preparation of this book, but make no expressed or implied warranty of any kind and assume no responsibility for errors or omissions. No liability is assumed for incidental or consequential damages in connection with or arising out of the use of the information or programs contained herein.

For information about buying this title in bulk quantities, or for special sales opportunities (which may include electronic versions; custom cover designs; and content particular to your business, training goals, marketing focus, or branding interests), please contact our corporate sales department at corpsales@pearsoned.com or (800) 382-3419.

For government sales inquiries, please contact governmentsales@pearsoned.com.

For questions about sales outside the U.S., please contact intlcs@pearson.com.

Visit us on the Web: informit.com/

Library of Congress Control Number: 2021947621

Copyright © 2022 Pearson Education, Inc.

All rights reserved. This publication is protected by copyright, and permission must be obtained from the publisher prior to any prohibited reproduction, storage in a retrieval system, or transmission in any form or by any means, electronic, mechanical, photocopying, recording, or likewise. For information regarding permissions, request forms and the appropriate contacts within the Pearson Education Global Rights & Permissions Department, please visit www.pearsoned.com/permissions/.

ISBN-13: 978-0-13-765357-7
ISBN-10: 0-13-765357-3

1 2021

Editor-in-Chief
Mark Taub

Acquisitions Editor
Kim Spenceley

Development Editor
Chris Zahn

Managing Editor
Sandra Schroeder

Senior Project Editor
Lori Lyons

Cover Designer
Chuti Prasertsith

Composition
Kim Scott, Bumpy Design

Copy Editor
Kitty Wilson

Production Manager
Aswini Kumar/
Codemantra

Indexer
Timothy Wright

Proofreader
Donna E. Mulder

Pearson's Commitment to Diversity, Equity, and Inclusion

Pearson is dedicated to creating bias-free content that reflects the diversity of all learners. We embrace the many dimensions of diversity, including but not limited to race, ethnicity, gender, socioeconomic status, ability, age, sexual orientation, and religious or political beliefs.

Education is a powerful force for equity and change in our world. It has the potential to deliver opportunities that improve lives and enable economic mobility. As we work with authors to create content for every product and service, we acknowledge our responsibility to demonstrate inclusivity and incorporate diverse scholarship so that everyone can achieve their potential through learning. As the world's leading learning company, we have a duty to help drive change and live up to our purpose to help more people create a better life for themselves and to create a better world.

Our ambition is to purposefully contribute to a world where:

- Everyone has an equitable and lifelong opportunity to succeed through learning.
- Our educational products and services are inclusive and represent the rich diversity of learners.
- Our educational content accurately reflects the histories and experiences of the learners we serve.
- Our educational content prompts deeper discussions with learners and motivates them to expand their own learning (and worldview).

While we work hard to present unbiased content, we want to hear from you about any concerns or needs with this Pearson product so that we can investigate and address them.

- Please contact us with concerns about any potential bias at https://www.pearson.com/report-bias.html.

Contents at a Glance

Contents

Register Your Book

Register your copy of *Captain Code* on the InformIT site for convenient access to updates and/or corrections as they become available. To start the registration process, go to informit.com/register and log in or create an account. Enter the product ISBN **9780137653577** and click Submit. Look on the Registered Products tab for an Access Bonus Content link next to this product, and follow that link to access any available bonus materials. If you would like to be notified of exclusive offers on new editions and updates, please check the box to receive email from us.

Acknowledgments

Ben Forta

It's hard to believe that I've been writing and publishing for 25 years! Pearson was the publisher for my very first book back in 1996, and since then we've collaborated in creating and publishing over 40 titles. Together we have educated and inspired developers (and future developers) the world over. Looking back over a quarter of a century, I can truly say thank you for all these years of dedication and support. This book is the first I've written for young people, so extra thanks for trusting our vision and giving us authors the freedom and flexibility to create this title as we saw fit.

In particular, thanks to Kim Spencely for shepherding this title from concept to fruition, and to Chris Zahn for (once again) providing his development expertise.

For the past few years I've had the pleasure of leading a Robotics class at Farber Hebrew Day School in Southfield, MI. When COVID wreaked havoc on teaching, we pivoted to online classes and I used the opportunity to improve my students' coding skills by teaching them Python. Those students were my guinea pigs, and those lessons were the impetus for this title. So, thank you FHDS for giving me the opportunity to inspire your students, and thank you students for helping me learn how to best teach you.

Thanks to our son Eli, a super talented designer and up-and-coming architect, for creating the image assets provided with this book.

And finally, thanks to our son Shmuel, a brilliant engineer, passionate educator, and my collaborator on this title. I've worked with co-authors on about half of my books, and, if I'm being honest, I'd much rather write all by myself. This collaboration was an exception. Shmuel's experience helped shape this volume, his insights can be felt on every page, and working with him has been a source of joy and pride. Thank you!

Shmuel Forta

Writing this book was an exciting and humbling experience for me. I am honored to have been given the opportunity to share with the world what I have been teaching seventh and eighth graders for half a decade.

I'd like to give a special thank you to Pearson. Their trust in our writing process allowed us to create this book without compromising our vision. An extra special thanks to Kim Spencely and Chris Zahn, without whom this book would not have been written, edited, or published.

I would also like to thank my wife, Chana Mina, for...well...everything. Thank you for putting up with me in general (a feat in and of itself); I know that writing this book took up a significant amount of my time, but you were always there for me. Without your support (as well as your recommendations for this publication), I don't know where I'd be. Thank you for being you.

A special thank you to my family: Mom, my siblings, and my in-laws for helping me and supporting me through everything, as well as for the encouragement and strength you gave me to compose this book.

Finally, a special (though that word doesn't even start to express it) thank you to my father and co-author. When I was under the age of 10, Dad got me started on coding with Visual Basic. Some of my fondest memories are of me and my Dad huddled over the old laptop that I was using, while my Dad patiently tried to steer me toward finding the bug in my code (an '=' instead of an '=='). I remember the sheer joy of running downstairs to show Dad my number guessing game, my inefficient calculator using drop-down menus, and later my first graphical game (an overhead space shooter). The unbridled excitement of child Shmuel from his creations could only be matched by my Dad's pride and love of my work. Dad's enthusiasm, encouragement, and unparalleled support are responsible for my love of coding. I now have met many talented programmers with a variety of skills, but few actually love coding the way that Dad or I do. And my love for coding was shared with me by my Dad. I can't thank you enough for collaborating on this title with me, but even more importantly, for raising me to be who I am today and sharing your love of programming with me.

About the Authors

Ben Forta is, first and foremost, an educator who has been teaching in some capacity since he was a teenager (many centuries ago). He is Adobe's Senior Director of Education Initiatives, and has over three decades of experience in the technology sector in product development, support, training, and product marketing. Ben is the award-winning author of more than 40 books, some of which have been translated into 16 languages, and many of which have become college textbooks. Through his books, lectures, lessons, and videos, Ben has taught coding skills to over a million people. Ben lives in Oak Park, MI, with his wife Marcy and their children. He welcomes your emails at ben@forta.com and invites you to visit him online at http://forta.com/.

Shmuel Forta is an engineer, coder, maker, tinkerer, and teacher. He is a software developer at General Motors and has years of programming experience, including both writing and instruction of code. He has been teaching Python coding to middle school students for more than five years. Shmuel has a Master's Degree in Biomedical Engineering from the University of Michigan and has published research work in IEEE. Shmuel lives in Oak Park, MI, with his wife Chana Mina. He would be happy to respond to any questions or comments via email at shmuel@forta.com.

INTRODUCTION

We need you to talk in a deep voice, the deepest you can manage. Actually, a deep loud whisper would work well. And talk slowly. Got it? Ok, read the next paragraph:

Legend tells of individuals with astounding powers. Scattered around the globe they have been endowed with the ability to bring the inanimate to life. Issuing instructions in varied languages, they can bend machines near and far to their will, making them do their bidding. These individuals are awesome and powerful, for they are…coders!

<ahem> Sorry!

Ok, so we may have gotten a bit carried away there. But, coders are indeed awesome and powerful. We should know; we're coders, and we think that we're pretty awesome and powerful (if we do say so ourselves). The truth is, for most of us, the closest we'll ever get to being Gandalf, Bruce Wayne, Luke Skywalker, Queen Elsa, Tony Stark, Wonder Woman, or Deadpool is mastering coding and developing the ability to command machines to do our bidding.

Yep, it's pretty heady stuff, we know. But, truthfully, that's what coding is. Which means superpowers are quite attainable.

In this book we'll help you hone these skills. You'll learn coding. But, more importantly, you'll learn how to be a coder.

But first, why? Why learn coding at all? If you ask around or search online you'll find various answers to that question.

The most common answer is that coding is important because it is a future-ready skill. This means that if you can code, you'll have an easier time finding a good job in the future. And while there may be some truth to that assertion, honestly, we don't think that's the best reason to learn to code. Why?

For starters, not everyone needs to work as a coder. That makes about as much sense as everyone being a doctor, or everyone being a chef, or everyone being a teacher, or everyone being a pilot, or everyone being a plumber running through pipes to save a princess...you get the idea. To function properly, society needs lots of different people doing lots of different things. Sorry, but humanity just does not need 8 billion coders.

In addition, the tech space (and that includes coding) changes really quickly. What coders do now is not the same as what they did 10 years ago, and what they'll do 10 years from now will be even more different. So, what you learn today is not what you'll be doing as a coder in the future. The best coders never stop learning, evolving, or developing skills. The basics you'll learn in this book will remain relevant and useful, but the specifics change, and frequently. With coding there's no learn-it-and-done; it'll be a mistake to invest time and energy assuming otherwise.

But most importantly, if you're interested in coding primarily from a future career perspective, it'll feel like work rather than fun. If it's not fun then you won't enjoy it; you'll be unlikely to stick with it, and you definitely won't be motivated to really give it your all. And that would be a shame, because coding really is a lot of fun.

That's not to say there aren't good jobs in coding. There are, and there will be for many decades to come. But a future career should not be the only reason to become a coder.

So, why should you learn to code? And should everyone do so? We believe everyone should learn to code, even if they have no intentions of pursuing careers in coding. We believe this just like we believe that everyone should draw and sketch, and everyone should play an instrument, and everyone should cook, and everyone should take pictures and shoot videos, and more. All of these are creative endeavors, which means that they are ways to actually create stuff, and creating stuff is incredibly rewarding and satisfying. Sure, it's fun to spend hours on your phone looking at what other people have created; but that's nothing compared to the joy and satisfaction of creating stuff that other people consume and use.

And, on top of that, when you learn to code, you develop all sorts of invaluable skills and traits beyond just coding. These include planning, problem solving, communication, logic, empathy, attention to detail, patience, resilience, persistence, and creativity.

Oh, and back to jobs and careers—it turns out that these skills (especially creativity and creative problem solving) are some of the most in demand out there. So, yes, coding will indeed help your future career, even if you don't become a coder.

Great, so you should learn coding. But where to start? In our experience, too many books, videos, and lessons overly focus on the mechanics of coding—things like syntax and exact details of how to use specific language elements. They get caught up in the minute details of specific projects. It all feels a whole lot like being talked to, as opposed to being encouraged to tinker and play. And that's boring. As in really enthusiasm-draining, soul-crushingly, yawn-inducingly boring. It's kinda like spending hours and hours learning dictionary words and grammar and then getting to use those by copying someone else's writing, and not being given the chance to find your own words and voice. That's crazy, right? And yet that's how most people are first introduced to coding.

We've been teaching coding for many years. In fact, we've helped over a million people become coders, including lots of young people your age. And we know how to help you develop these skills—we do it the same way we taught ourselves to code. It's fast, fun, results oriented, and it works.

And that's why we wrote this book, to help you learn to code; and, more importantly, to discover your coding superpower and turn you into a coder.

What's in This Book

In this book we don't just teach you how to code; lots of books do that. Some even do a pretty good job of it, too.

No, learning to code is not enough. Instead, we're going to help you learn how to think like a coder, analyze problems like a coder, plan like a coder, progressively iterate like a coder, craft elegant solutions like a coder ... In fact, when we're done we'll have morphed you into <drumroll> a coder!

To that end, this book is quite different from others you may have read. We built it to help you become a coder quickly while having fun, too.

We divided this book into three sections that build upon each other. Here's how it all works.

Part I: It's All Fun and Games

In this section, we cover some basics (and some not so basics, too). By the time you're done with the section, you will have learned every major coding concept, and you'll have the knowledge you need to write just about any application.

This section is made up of 10 chapters:

- Chapter 1 will help you get up and running, including helping you install needed software and getting it ready to use.
- In Chapters 2 through 7 you'll create small games and other programs, lots and lots of them. Each chapter will introduce new coding concepts that you'll utilize immediately in a new project. And in each chapter you'll get a chance to tweak, tinker, and make the code your own.
- Then things will get a bit more sophisticated, and you'll create a more complex game starting in Chapter 8 and finishing it in Chapter 9.
- In Chapter 10 we'll wrap this section with all sorts of ideas for you to try yourself.

We designed these chapters so that they build upon each other; skills you develop in one chapter will help you in subsequent chapters. But we also designed these chapters to be short and focused, and so you'll mostly write small standalone programs in each.

You'll want to take your time working through this section. Try every lesson and example yourself, tinker, tweak, play. Make changes to the code we provide and see what happens to the program. You can't break it because you can always undo it! The stuff you'll learn here is what you'll use most, be it while working through this book or in any future projects.

Part II: On an Adventure

No more kiddie pool, you're in the deep end now. In this section you'll create a bigger (and more fun) game. We'll start slow, and incrementally add functionality. What kind of game? A cool retro-style text-based adventure game that will seriously impress family and friends, and one that you can make complex enough to make hardcore gamers cry.

This section has 8 chapters:

- Chapter 11 gets you started.
- You'll start creating the game in Chapter 12, and you'll keep adding functionality and sophistication all the way through Chapter 17.
- Chapter 18 will provide all sorts of ideas so you can keep improving your game.

Unlike Part I, in this section we want you to go on your own adventure, tell your own story, write your own game. We'll help you get started, and we'll show you all the techniques you need. You are free to use our code. We'll even tell you how to download other story starters, but then we'll turn things over to you to create your own masterpiece.

Part III: Hit the Road

Just as in Part II, this section is one larger game that you'll build incrementally. This time it's a graphical game complete with images, movement, user interaction, scores, and more.

There are 6 chapters in this section:

- Chapter 19 gets you started using a game engine (and explains what that actually is).
- You'll build a complete working game in Chapters 20 through 23. We'll even give you graphics that you can use (yeah, we're just that nice).
- And Chapter 24 concludes with lots of fun ideas for you to add to the game.

In this section, we'll also give you less code to copy (as you'll be a pro by the time you get here). Instead, we'll tell you how to change and update your code to get it to do what you want.

Oh, one more thing. We should mention Chapter 25, "Tinkering, Testing, and Debugging Revisited." Yep, we love you guys so much that we tossed in a bonus chapter. You'll find it online on the book web page. Use the link or QR code at the end of this introduction to access it.

Watch Out for These

As you work through this book you'll come across boxes and icons. This is what they all mean:

NEW TERM

Title We're not just going to help you code, we're also going to help you talk like a real coder. Whenever we use a new word or phrase, we'll explain it in a box that looks like this.

TIP

Title Coders love saving time. When you see a box with this symbol, you'll know that it contains shortcuts, time-saving ideas, or just stuff we think will make coding easier.

Sidebar

We've included lots of lots of useful notes (and some that are less useful but still kinda fun). You'll see these in boxes like this.

CHALLENGE

When you see this box, you'll know that we are going to be giving you extra work. No, no homework; we're talking fun extra work. As we explained earlier, in this book you won't be learning coding by reading, you'll learn by doing. We'll help you create lots of programs, some small and some more complex. And many of these will be followed by challenges—extra stuff for you to try and figure out yourself. And don't worry, if you get stuck you can use our online tips and solutions.

And finally, watch for QR codes (like this one) throughout the book. They'll take you to web pages that contain useful links, downloadable code, challenge solutions, and more.

Getting Help

As you work through this book, you're going to occasionally need some help. When that happens, here's what you need to do:

- First, check the book web page at https://forta.com/books/0137653573 or scan this QR code. We've posted lots of tips, solutions, and more for you.

- You can also do what most coders do and Google it. Type really specific questions (complete with the exact language problem, for example) and you will find answers.

- And you are always free to contact us. You'll find contact information on https://forta.com/ and in the front of this book.

And with that, welcome, turn the page, and let's get started!

Ben & Shmuel

Figure Credits

Figure	Credit
Cover	HelloSSTK/Shutterstock (female superhero) Maxim Maksutov/Shutterstock (male superhero)
New Term, Tip, Sidebar, and Challenge notes icons	Viktoria Kurpas/Shutterstock
Parts Pages image	Bonezboyz/Shutterstock
Chapter opening images	November_Seventeen/Shutterstock (female superhero) Maxim Maksutov/Shutterstock (male superhero)
Python screenshots	© 2001–2021. Python Software Foundation
FIG01-01	Screenshot of computer microprocessor: Tudor Voinea/Shutterstock
FIG01-02	Screenshot of VS Code screen © Microsoft 2020
FIG01-03	Screenshot of Extensions panel, INSTALLED section © Microsoft 2020
FIG01-04	Screenshot of Windows icons © Microsoft 2020
FIG01-05	Screenshot of Look for the New Folder icon © Microsoft 2020
FIG01-06	Screenshot of Click the New Folder icon © Microsoft 2020
FIG01-07	Screenshot of Locate Finder © 2020 Apple, Inc.
FIG01-08	Screenshot of In the Go menu © 2020 Apple, Inc.
FIG01-09	Screenshot of New Folder © Apple, Inc.
FIG01-10	Screenshot of a new created folder © 2020 Apple, Inc.
FIG01-11	Screenshot of VS Code window © Microsoft 2020
FIG01-12	Screenshot of NO FOLDER OPENED display © Microsoft 2020
FIG01-13	Screenshot of open folder © Microsoft 2020
FIG12-01	Screenshot PYTHON section in VS Code Explorer panel © Microsoft 2020
FIG20-01	Screenshot of folder structure © Microsoft 2020

Part I
IT'S ALL FUN AND GAMES

CHAPTER 1

Getting Started

Hello, and welcome. We love coding, and by the time you're done with this book we think you will, too. We're going to help you learn to code the way that we learned, by doing—no long lectures, no reading lots of instructions, and no drawn-out explanations. In every chapter you'll get to do stuff, and you'll learn while doing.

Except for this chapter, sorry. :-(Before you start developing your coding superpowers it's really important to understand what coding actually is, so we'll spend just a few minutes reviewing that. And then we'll help you install the software you'll need to get started. But, after that, it's all doing. Promise.

Understanding Computer Programming

Let's start by taking a few minutes to understand what computer programming actually is, and to do that we need to talk about computers.

What is a computer?

You've seen computers, and they are all basically the same; they have screens, a keyboard, mouse or touchpad, and some fold in half, like a notebook. Right? No, wrong! The truth is that most of the computers that you've seen and used look nothing at all like that. Really.

For example, your gaming consoles are all computers. So are smartphones, smart-watches, and smart TVs. (Actually, anything with "smart" in the name is pretty much guaranteed to be a computer.) Those video doorbells that show you who's at the door? Those are computers. Vacuuming robots, fancy touchscreen thermo-stats, and display consoles in cars are all computers, too. Drones are computers with propellers, and Tesla cars are computers with seats and wheels. Those cool rovers NASA sent to Mars are computers. ATMs at the bank that you can use to withdraw cash from an account? Those are computers, as are self-checkout machines at your local grocery store. You get the idea. There are lots and lots of computers out there, and most look nothing like what we typically call a computer.

So, what makes all of these devices computers? They are all computers because inside of them is a *microprocessor*, a computer chip that functions as the device's brain. The microprocessor controls everything the device does. The display, motors, inputs, sensors, speakers, and more are all controlled by one or more microprocessors.

So now that you know what computers are, answer these questions: Are computers smart? Is your gaming console actually smart? What about your smartphone or tablet? What do you think?

Well, sorry to be the bearer of bad news, but the answer is no, not at all. Computers are not very smart. In fact, quite the opposite, despite the word "smart" in some of their names, computers are actually rather dumb and useless.

Why are computers not smart? Because as powerful as they are, they themselves don't know how to do anything. They can't display videos on a screen, they can't respond to mouse clicks or joystick controls, they can't connect to the Internet, they can't understand what you type, they can't play your favorite games or let you video conference. By themselves computers can't do anything useful at all... So, yep, not very smart.

But computers do indeed do all sorts of wonderful things, so how do they know how to do them? They can do those things because someone taught the computers how to do them. Someone gave the computers very specific instructions teaching them how to do all things we expect our favorite devices to do. And those instructions are indeed pretty smart.

But the real smarts belong to whomever actually created the instructions. So who does that? Who gets to teach all of the computers around us how to do fun and useful things? That's the job of computer programmers, and computer programming is just that, teaching computers how to do stuff.

How do we talk to computers?

When you talk to your friends, they understand what you are saying (well, hopefully). The reason that they understand you is that you are communicating in the same language, one you both understand. This is obviously important. If you spoke to someone who only understood another language, you'd not really be communicating.

What's in a Name?

Computer programmers are also called *coders*, *software engineers*, *application developers*, and *software developers*. Lots of titles, but they all really mean the same thing.

Communicating with a computer is much the same. If you are going to give a computer instructions, you need to provide those instructions in a language that the computer understands. You are going to use a computer programming language, and much like spoken languages, programming languages have words and rules for how they are used.

There are lots and lots of different computer languages. Some have very specific uses, some are more general purpose. And most programmers learn and use multiple languages; that way they can pick the best one for any particular situation. If the idea of having to learn lots of languages sounds scary, don't worry, we have some good news for you:

- Exact language details, the words you use and how you use them (programmers call this *syntax*) differ from one language to the next. But unlike spoken languages, computer programming languages tend to have very few words and rules, so you'll master them pretty quickly.

> **NEW TERM**
> **Syntax** In spoken languages, the word *syntax* means the rules for how words and phrases are put together to make well-formed sentences. In programming languages the word *syntax* is used similarly: It means the rules for how language elements are to be used.

- In addition, pretty much all programming languages do the same basic things (and we'll cover all of those in this book). This means that once you master one programming language, learning the next one is much easier.
- You never need to memorize a programming language. If you ever need a reminder for how to perform a specific task in a specific language, do what professional programmers do: Google it.
- There is one important difference between spoken languages and programming languages, and that is the listener. When you message a friend, you can misspell words (don't), omit punctuation (don't do that, either), even send incomplete sentences (ugh, no, please), and your friend will still

understand you. Computers are less forgiving (not smart, remember?) and if you miss a . or a }, they'll get upset and not know what you want them to do. This is probably the single biggest source of frustration for beginning coders. So why did we point this out among this list of good news? Because editors (the tools you use to write your code...more on that soon) are really good at catching those typos, and that makes things a whole lot less frustrating.

Now that you know what a programming language is, and why they are similar to spoken languages, we are going to let you in on a secret; well, two secrets, actually. We are going to tell you exactly what computer programming is and what programmers do:

- Imagine that you knew every word in your spoken language. You studied your dictionary backward and forward and mastered every single word, including pronunciations and definitions. Would that make you a best-selling author? Would knowing all the words mean that you could write the next blockbuster movie script? Of course not. Knowing the words is one thing. Knowing how to use those words by creatively combining them in any of infinite combinations, well, that's obviously very different. Computer languages are much the same. Knowing the syntax is easy (especially as computer languages have far fewer words than spoken languages). What makes an experienced and skilled programmer is knowing how to use those language elements to artfully solve problems, and that's exactly what we're going to help you learn. And that is a skill that takes time and practice.

- Once more, think about spoken languages. Is there a single right way to share an idea using words? No, of course not. If that were the case, all movies and books would be the same, and that would be horrible! A language is a tool, and authors get to use that tool to craft all sorts of wonderful and unique experiences. Using a programming language is much the same. There is no single right way to write code or solve any specific problem. Rather, there are as many solutions as there are coders. We'll show you lots of techniques and solutions in this book, and you are free to use them in your own coding. But, over time, you'll find your own creative ways to solve problems, just like professional coders do, because coding is all about creative problem solving.

What is Python?

All of this brings us to Python, which is <make a drumroll sound here please> … a programming language.

Yes, Python is a language, and it is used to provide instructions to a computer. Python is not a new programming language, it's actually been around for 30 years or so. But it is super popular, and even powers some of your favorite sites and apps. Why is Python so popular?

- Python is really easy to use, no complicated tools or setups, just write a few lines of code and off you go. Really! In fact, you'll have written code that works before you finish this chapter!

- Python's creators worked really hard to create a language whose syntax is really easy to read. Reading Python code is a lot like reading English. Most other programming languages are far more complicated to read. (Trust us on that one.)

- Those syntax rules we mentioned before, the ones that frustrate most beginning coders? Python's syntax is one of the easiest of any programming language, and we all like fewer rules, right?

- Simple to use and having less rigid rules are great, but what really makes Python so much fun to work with is all of the libraries it makes available. We'll discuss libraries later in the book, but for now, all you need to know is that libraries are sets of code that other programmers have written for you; just download them and use them. So, tasks that might be complicated (for example, embedding Google maps and directions in an app or detecting when a car hits an obstacle in a game) are so much simpler. You don't have to start from scratch—you get to build on top of what other smart coders have kindly shared.

So we are going to learn Python together. But, as we explained before, what we'll learn are the concepts and techniques that are useful in all languages. Once you're done with this book, you will be able to apply your hard-earned knowledge and expertise to whatever language you decide to use next.

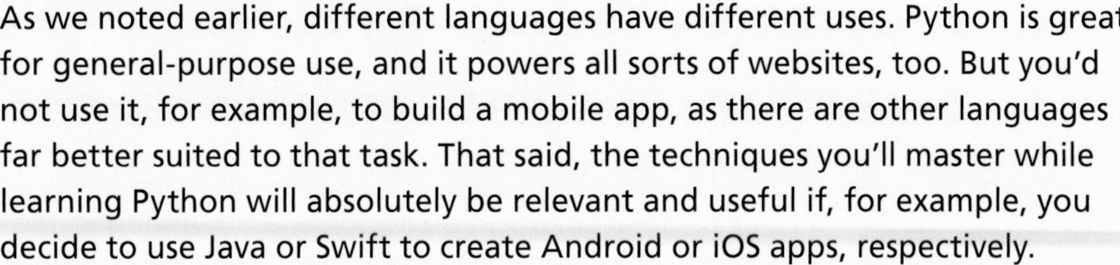

Python and Other Languages

As we noted earlier, different languages have different uses. Python is great for general-purpose use, and it powers all sorts of websites, too. But you'd not use it, for example, to build a mobile app, as there are other languages far better suited to that task. That said, the techniques you'll master while learning Python will absolutely be relevant and useful if, for example, you decide to use Java or Swift to create Android or iOS apps, respectively.

Setting Things Up

Ok, enough talking. Let's get things set up so you can start coding, and to do that you'll need two things: the Python language and an editor. And, yes, we know there are quite a few steps, but you only have to do this once. Promise.

TIP

Watch for the QR Codes All of the links and downloads referred to below can be found on the book web page, at **`https://forta.com/books/0137653573/`** (or just scan the QR code at right). You'll find QR codes throughout the book, scan them for downloads, tips, and more.

Installing Python

Most computers don't come with the Python language installed, so the first thing you'll need to do is to install Python (which is free for the download). To do this:

1. Open your web browser and go to **`https://python.org`**.
2. Click on the **Downloads** link at the top of the screen.

Using a Chromebook?

If you are using a Chromebook, you can still use Python, but the installation steps are a bit more involved. You'll find details on the books web page by scanning this QR code.

3. You'll be presented with an option to download Python. There are different installers for Windows and Mac OSX and the download screen should automatically show the right one (if not, click to select it manually).

   Download the latest version of Python (3.9 something while this book was being written).

4. When the download has completed, double-click on the downloaded file to run the installer. You should be able to just click all the default options and the installer will do its thing.

TIP

Using Windows? During installation, you might see a checkbox that says something like Add Python to PATH. If you see this, be sure to check this box; it'll make things easier for you in the future.

When the installation has completed, you should have Python on your computer ready to use. But, before we start coding, there are two more steps needed.

Installing and Configuring Visual Studio Code

If you want to write a document, you need an editor like Google Docs or Microsoft Word. If you want to create a video, you need a tool to capture and edit video. Right? Coding is much the same—to write code, you need an *editor*, which is an application you use to write and edit code.

There are lots of editors out there, and they let you create and open files, type code, and save the files. Not very exciting, and so most coders use special editors that do a whole lot more. These special editors are called IDEs (which stands for *integrated development environments*). An IDE is an editor in that it lets you open and edit and save files, but it also does other really useful things. It can highlight errors in your code (not that you'll ever make any), it colors your code making it easier to read, and much more. So, yeah, you want an IDE.

Python comes with a built-in IDE called IDLE, and it's ok, kinda. It works, but there are much better options. The one we like a lot is called Microsoft Visual Studio Code (or VS Code, for short). That's what we use, and we recommend that you do, too.

Visual Studio Code

VS Code is the little brother of Microsoft Visual Studio, which is a paid for IDE. If you happen to have access to the full version of Visual Studio, you are free to use that instead of VS Code.

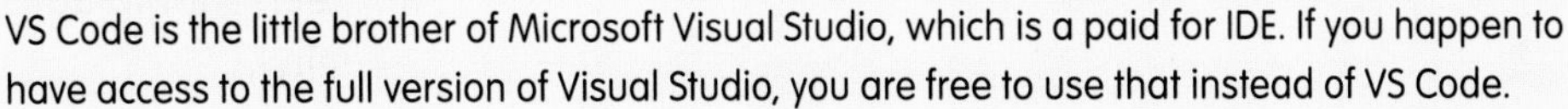

Using a Chromebook?

If you are using a Chromebook, you can use VS Code only if your Chromebook supports Linux. For details on how to check for Linux support and how to install VS Code on Chromebook, go to the book's web page by scanning this QR code.

Why do we like VS Code? Lots of reasons. It's fast. It provides lots of built-in help and syntax support. It supports all sorts of languages, including Python. Oh, and it's free. Thank you, Microsoft!

To install VS Code, follow these steps:

1. Open your web browser and go to `https://code.visualstudio.com/`.
2. Click on the blue **Download** button. Like before, there are different installers for Windows and macOS, and the download screen should automatically show the right one. (If not, click the down arrow next to the **Download** button to select it manually.)
3. Download the latest version of VS Code (it'll probably be called "Stable Build").
4. When the download has completed, double-click on the downloaded file to run the installer.
5. If you are prompted with a checkbox that says **Edit with Code**, check it. Other than that, you should be able to just leave all the default options.
6. When the installer is finished, make sure **Launch Visual Studio Code** is checked and click **Finish**. The installer will close, and VS Code will start.

We're almost done. Remember, VS Code supports all sorts of languages. We are going to use it with Python, so the last thing we need to do is to let VS Code know that. Once VS Code knows that we'll be using Python, it may install extra software so that we'll have all the Python support we'll need.

When VS Code starts, it shows a Welcome screen with links to tutorials, files, and more. On the upper-left edge of the VS Code screen, you'll see these icons:

You'll use these icons extensively, but for now the icon we care about is the bottom one. Click on it. This displays the Extensions panel. What are Extensions? They are additional pieces of software that can be installed into VS Code. That's actually how VS Code can support so many different languages. Each time you need support for a new language, you can just install the right extension, and you're good to go. The Extensions panel will look something like this:

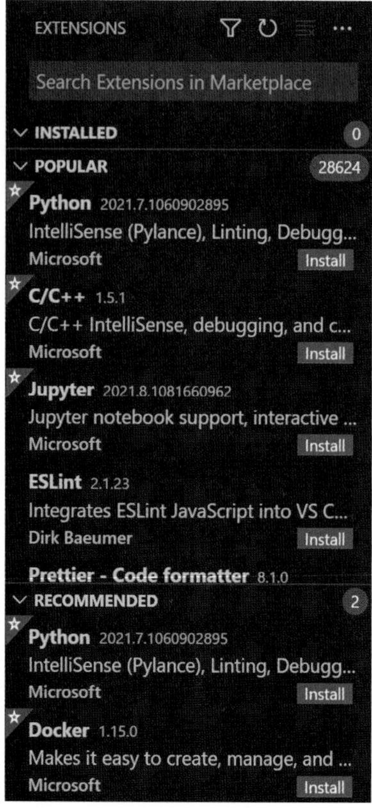

At the top of the Extensions panel is a section named INSTALLED. It'll probably have a 0 next to it, as no extensions are installed yet.

If the number next to INSTALLED is not 0, and if you see Python listed in the INSTALLED section, then the Python extension is already installed. Lucky you!

If the Python extension is not yet installed (it probably won't be), then you'll need to install it. This is super easy to do. In the POPULAR section, you'll see **Python** listed. (Python is indeed very popular.) Just click on the blue Install link to the right of Python, and you'll see it get installed. Python will now be listed in the INSTALLED section, and VS Code may display a new Python Welcome page.

Creating a Work Folder

Programmers organize their code in folders. They usually have a main folder for all of their projects, and create subfolders within it for each specific project or application. So, let's do that now.

Windows users

Windows users have a Documents folder, which is where all work gets stored. This is a great place to store your code, too. Follow these steps:

1. Click the **Windows** button (usually at the bottom-left of your screen).

   You should see a series of icons appear, like this (though the icons may look a little different, depending on what version of Windows you are using):

   The top icon (the one that looks like a piece of paper with the corner folded over) is the Documents icon. Hover your mouse over it, and it'll say **Documents** and you'll know you have the right one.

Using a Chromebook?
Chromebook-specific instructions can be found on the book web page by scanning this QR code.

2. Click the **Documents** icon. This will open the Documents folder in Windows File Explorer.

3. Look for the **New Folder** icon at the top of the window. It should look like this:

4. Click the **New Folder** icon to create a new folder. You'll see the new folder created with a default name:

5. Change the folder's name to **Python** and press **Enter** to save the new folder.

That's it, you've created a new folder. Well done!

Mac users

Mac users have a Documents folder, which is where all work gets stored. This is a great place to store your code, too. Follow these steps:

1. Locate **Finder** (usually at the bottom of your screen):

2. In the Go menu, select **Documents** to open the Documents folder:

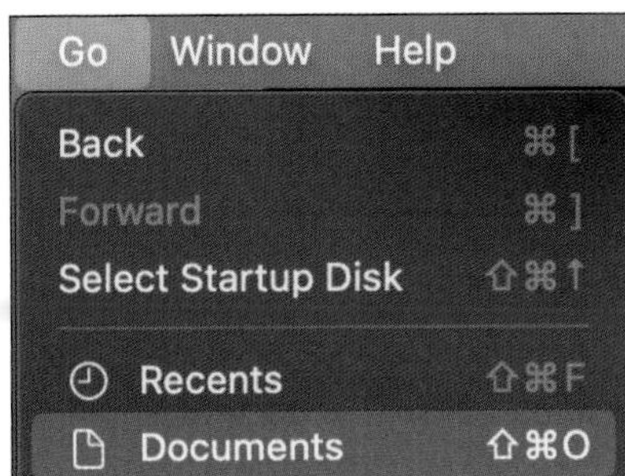

3. Now that Documents is open, you can create your new folder. From the File menu, select **New Folder**:

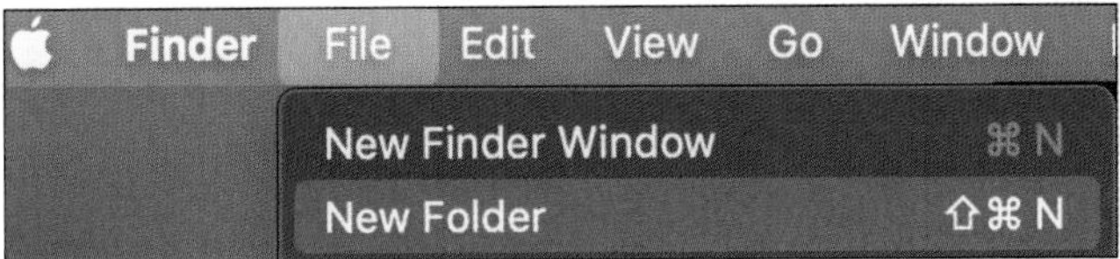

A new folder is created:

4. Name the new folder `Python` and press **Enter** to save the new folder.

That's it, you've created a new folder. Well done!

Writing Your First Python Program

We're going to write a really simple program just to make sure everything is working properly. To do that we're going to create a work folder and then write some code.

Selecting Your Work Folder

As you know, programmers organize their code in folders, which is why you just created one. Now we need to tell VS Code to use your new work folder:

1. Let's go back to the buttons on the top left of the VS Code window:

   The top button opens and closes the Explorer panel, which is where you can see all your files. Click that top button to show the Explorer (if it is not already open).

   As you've not yet told VS Code where your work folder is, you'll see a NO FOLDER OPENED display like this:

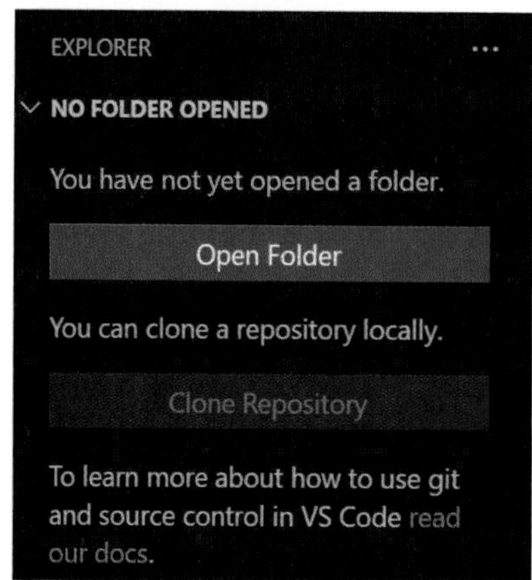

2. Click the **Open Folder** button, and you'll see your regular (Windows or Mac) file folder screen.

3. Navigate to the **Python** folder that you just created and then click the **Select Folder** button.

   You'll now have an open folder with nothing in it:

VS Code now has a work folder, and we're good to start coding.

It's Coding Time!

Now let's create a file and write some code. Remember the steps used to create new files, you'll be doing this over and over (starting right in the next chapter):

1. Move your mouse over the PYTHON box in the Explorer on the left. See those four icons to the right of the word PYTHON? The first one creates a new file. Click it and name your file `Hello.py`. (The .py extension is super important. Every Python file you create must have a .py extension.)

2. Press **Enter**, and the file will be saved. You already know where the Explorer panel is. The next part of the IDE screen you need to know about is the most important one; it is the big box on the upper right, that's the editor, where you type your code. Your newly created file should also automatically be open, ready for you to start coding. If it isn't, just double-click on it in the Explorer panel to open it.

3. Now to start coding, type the following exactly as shown here in the editor part of the screen:

```
Hello.py  ×
Hello.py
print("Yeah, this works!")
```

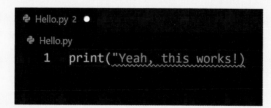

   Let's not worry about the code itself yet. Instead, notice that the file name is shown above the editor. This is really important when you have lots of files open—it's how you can tell them apart.

4. The last important thing to look at is the green arrow above the code, over on the top right. That is used to run your code. (If you hover your mouse over the green arrow, the screen will say *Run Python File in Terminal*. You can hover your mouse anywhere in VS Code to see what buttons will do.)

IDEs Are Awesome!

Notice how VS Code colors the code for you automatically, which makes your code more readable. VS Code also points out errors if there are any. For example, if you remove the second quotation mark, you'll see this (feel free to try this, but put the quote back when you are done):

```
Hello.py 2 ●
Hello.py
print("Yeah, this works!)
```

Red means bad! The filename turns red to let you know the file has errors in it, and VS Code adds a red squiggly line in the code to show you where the error is. See, IDEs are awesome!

Executing Code

You may hear programmers talk about *executing* code. That's not a bad thing; no one is going to hurt the code. *Execute* is another word for *run*, so if you execute code, you run it. Whew!

5. Click the green **Run** button, and Python will run your code. So when you run your code, where do you see the results? The Terminal window, which is right below the editor window. You told Python to print (that means display) some text, and it does just that in the Terminal window, like this:

```
Yeah, this works!
```

   If this text is displayed in the Terminal window, then it means that Python is installed and working properly, VS Code is installed and can talk to your Python installation, and you are ready to code. Congratulations!

Summary

In this chapter, you learned what programming is, what programmers do, and what Python is. You installed Python and Visual Studio Code (and got a short tour of the latter), and wrote your first brilliant (ok, so maybe a little bit less than brilliant) program. We're now ready to really dive into coding with Python.

CHAPTER 2

Mad Libs

Now that you are all set up, we're going to dig into some real coding. In this chapter, we're going to start with an important topic, one that you will use in every single program you ever write: variables. And to do that, you'll also learn about functions and create a simple game. Ready?

Understanding Functions

In programming languages, *functions* are bits of code that perform specific tasks. You've actually seen one function already: the `print()` function you used at the end of Chapter 1. And, as you saw, `print()` does just that, it prints (or displays) text.

In Python, like in most other programming languages, functions are used by referring to their name followed by parentheses. When programmers use functions, they say that they are *calling* the function.

In Chapter 1, you called the `print()` function, like this:

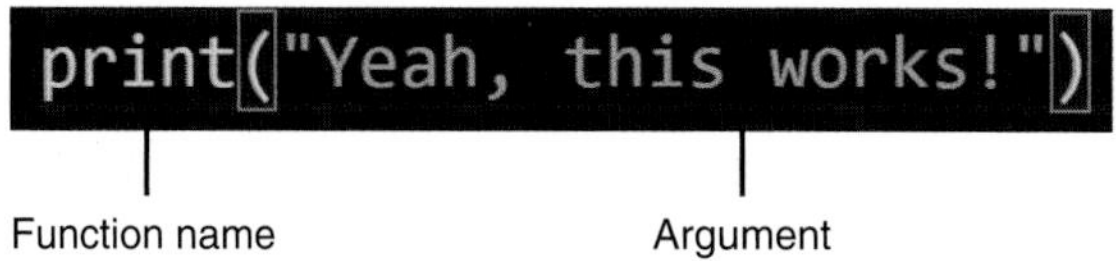

That text that you told `print()` to print is called an *argument*, and arguments always go in between `(` and `)`. Programmers refer to this as *passing* arguments.

How many arguments does a function accept? Well, that depends on the function. Some functions accept no arguments, and others accept one or more arguments, in which case these will be *passed* when calling the function. And whether there are arguments or not, you always need the parentheses.

Let's take a quick look at passing multiple arguments to a function. Create a new file in VS Code. You already have one named `Hello.py`, so name the new one `Hello2.py`.

Now that file `Hello2.py` is open, type this code in it:

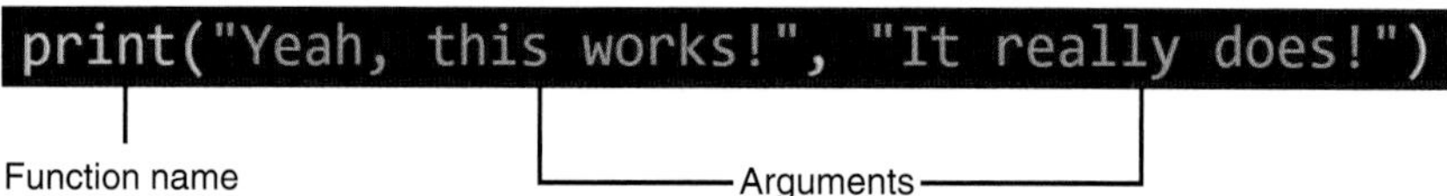

Your Own Functions

For now we'll be using functions that come built into Python. In later chapters, you'll learn how to create your own functions.

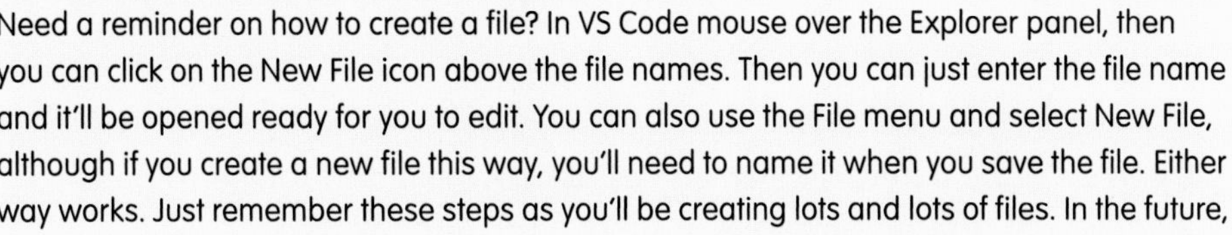

A Friendly Reminder, Just This Once

Need a reminder on how to create a file? In VS Code mouse over the Explorer panel, then you can click on the New File icon above the file names. Then you can just enter the file name and it'll be opened ready for you to edit. You can also use the File menu and select New File, although if you create a new file this way, you'll need to name it when you save the file. Either way works. Just remember these steps as you'll be creating lots and lots of files. In the future, we'll just tell you "create a file named `Hello2.py`," and you'll know what to do.

When you are done, save the file (by selecting the File menu and clicking Save), and run it (by clicking the green arrow above the code on the right). You'll see the results displayed in the Terminal window below.

Look at the `print()` statement you just used. It has two arguments this time, and `print()` displays them both in the Terminal window. Yes, this is not that useful an example. We know, you could have just typed this to get the same results:

```
print("Yeah, this works! It really does!")
```

The reason we had you try it with the quotation marks and comma is to show you something important. When you pass more than one argument to a function, you must separate each argument with a comma. No comma is needed if there is just one argument, but for two or more arguments, make sure there is a comma between each.

So, to summarize, to use a function, you *call* it, and you *pass arguments* if needed; and if you pass multiple arguments, make sure to separate each of them with commas.

Using Variables

Ok, with that out the way, let's move on to the main event: variables. These are really important, so we'll focus on them all the way until the end of this chapter.

Imagine that you are sitting at a desk, working on a project. You're working with lots of information, so you have storage containers that are neatly labeled so that you can put things you need to remember inside of them. Any time you need to get the contents of a container, you just look at the name, and you can access whatever is stored inside of it.

It's a simple analogy, and it is exactly how variables work: You name a variable and put information in it, and then you can get that information out at any time.

Creating a Variable

Let's try this. Create a new file named `Hello3.py`. (You don't need to be reminded how to do that anymore. You are a pro already.)

Then enter this code (putting your own name between the quotes, not mine):

```
firstName = "Shmuel"
```

This code creates a variable named `firstName` and stores the name you specified in it.

Using a Variable

How do you use the variable you just created? You just refer to it by name. Add this line to your code after the line that creates the variable:

```
print(firstName)
```

Now save your code and run it. You'll see your name printed in the Terminal window below.

Now let's make it a bit more interesting. Update your code so that it looks like this (again, use your name, not mine), and then save and run the code:

```
firstName="Shmuel"

print("Hello, my name is", firstName, "and I'm a coder!")
```

Okay, there are a few important things to note here.

Look how many arguments you're passing to `print()`. There are three of them. The first and last arguments contain text you typed. The middle one is the variable `firstName`, but instead of printing `firstName`, Python prints the information you stored in the `firstName` variable.

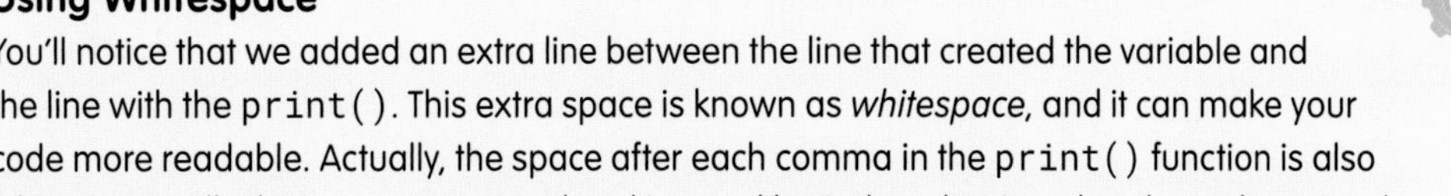

Using Whitespace

You'll notice that we added an extra line between the line that created the variable and the line with the `print()`. This extra space is known as *whitespace*, and it can make your code more readable. Actually, the space after each comma in the `print()` function is also whitespace. All whitespace is optional and ignored by Python, but it makes the code so much easier to read.

Also, notice the code coloring. As we mentioned in Chapter 1, VS Code automatically colors your code for you. Now, the truth is that code is just text, and it doesn't really have colors. But the colored code is really useful. For starters, color makes the code much easier to read. But, more importantly, because all functions are in one color, text in another color, and variables in yet another color, you'll spot mistakes quickly because the colors will be off.

Some Important Variable Rules

Before we go further, there are a couple of important rules you need to know about variables in Python:

- A variable name can contain letters and numbers, but it can't start with a number. So `pet1` is ok to use as a variable name, but `1pet` is not.
- You can't have spaces in variable names. If you want multiple words in a variable name, you can use mixed case (like we did here with `firstName`) or use an underscore (`first_name`, for example).
- And the most important rule to remember is that variable names are case sensitive. What does that mean? It means that if you create a variable named `firstName`, you can't refer to it as `firstname`; they are not the same because one has an uppercase character and the other does not. You can try this if you'd like; change the `print()` statement so that it refers to `firstname` instead of `firstName`. VS Code will realize that you've made a mistake and will put a squiggly line under `firstname`:

```
Hello3.py 1 ●

Hello3.py > ...
firstName="Shmuel"

print("Hello, my name is", firstname, "and I'm a coder!")
```

If you mouse over `firstname`, VS Code will tell you **"firstname" is not defined**, meaning you have tried to use a variable that doesn't exist.

Aside from these rules, you are free to name your variables any way you wish. And, in general, descriptive names are preferred. So `firstName` is a great variable name because the name makes its use really clear. `fn`? That's a far less descriptive name. It could mean "free nachos", "Fortnite", "friendly neighbors"... very confusing indeed. Using clear, descriptive names is one of the hallmarks of a skilled developer (and you always want to look skilled, right?).

Variables, More Variables, and Even More Variables

Take a look at this code? What do you think it does?

```
firstName="Shmuel"
firstName="Ben"

print("Hello, my name is", firstName, "and I'm a coder!")
```

Variable Names Are Case Sensitive

Because variable names are case sensitive, you could actually create multiple variables that only differ by case. For example, you could do this:

```
FirstName="Shmuel"

firstname="Ben"
```

Word of advice: Don't. Keep your variable names nice and distinct. Doing so will prevent you from spending hours trying to figure out why something isn't working.

Actually, why don't you try it? Modify your `Hello3.py` code so that `firstName` gets set twice.

Save your code and run it. What is displayed? Does it do what you expected?

The first line, `firstName="Shmuel"`, creates a variable named `firstName` and puts the name `Shmuel` in it. The second line, `firstName="Ben"`, doesn't create a variable, nor does it add `"Ben"` to the existing variable. Rather, it overwrites the first value, replacing `"Shmuel"` with `"Ben"`.

Ok, one last example. We'll call this one `Hello4.py` (again, use your own name, not mine):

```
firstName = "Shmuel"
lastName = "Forta"
fullName = firstName + " " + lastName

print("Hello, my name is", fullName, "and I'm a coder!")
```

Save the code and run it. What's happening here?

Python processes the code one line at a time. So the first thing it does is create a variable called `firstName` and store a value in it. The next line tells Python to create a variable called `lastName`, and a value is stored in that variable, too.

TIP

Save As Can Save You Time Here's a useful tip. File `Hello4.py` is basically `Hello3.py` with some changes. You can create a new file and type the code as you've done thus far. Or, when you have `Hello3.py` open, use the File menu and select Save As to make a copy named `Hello4.py` and then edit that.

How Many Values Can a Variable Store?

As you can see, variables store one value at a time. Storing a second value? That replaces the first one. One value at a time. But, there are actually special types of variables that can store multiple values. You'll use these in future chapters.

The third line is interesting. It creates a new variable called `fullName` and stores a value in it. What is the value? It is made up of three parts, all joined together using + signs. It uses `firstName`, adds an empty space (that's what `" "` is), and then adds `lastName`. So if `firstName` is `"Shmuel"` and `lastName` is `"Forta"`, `fullName` will be `"Shmuel Forta"`. And that's what is used as the second argument in `print()`.

NEW TERM

Concatenation Joining variables together like this is called concatenation. That's a good word to use when you want to sound really smart.

Getting User Input

You're an expert at using `print()`, so now let's introduce a new function. As its name suggests, `input()` is used to ask the user to input something.

Create a new file named `Hello5.py` and type the following code:

```
name=input("What is your name? ")
print("Hello", name, "nice to meet you!")
```

Save the file and run it.

Your code will run in the Terminal window. It will display **What is your name?** and will wait for you to type a response right there in the Terminal window. When you respond and press Enter, the `print()` function will greet you by name.

As you can see, `input()` accepts text to be displayed, just like `print()`. But `input()` does something else, too: it obtains input from the user. Remember that Python runs your code line by line. When it gets to an `input()`, it stops processing, waits for the user to type something, and then continues. And whatever the user typed at the prompt is provided for you to use. This is called *returning a value*, and the value that `input()` *returns* can be saved to a variable, as we are doing here. This way, the variable `name` contains whatever the user typed in the Terminal window.

Where's the Variable?

Look at this line of code:

```
input("What is your name? ")
```

What do you think is wrong with it? Well, the code is actually valid. Run it, and it'll prompt for input. But this `input()` will prompt the user to type something but not actually save it anywhere probably not what is intended. That's why we used `name=input()`, as that tells Python to save whatever `input()` returns into `name`.

`print()`, on the other hand, doesn't return anything, so there is never a reason to assign it to a variable.

TIP

Watch Where You Click When responding to an `input()` prompt, make sure to click in the Terminal window before typing. Otherwise, your cursor may be in the editor window, in which case you may edit your code by mistake.

CHALLENGE 2.1

The only way to become Captain Code is to write code. The more code you write, the better a coder you'll become. The lessons and examples we'll study together are a good starting point, but you really need to be writing your own code as well. So, throughout this book, you are going to see Challenge sections like this one. These sections will suggest things for you to try, based on the lessons we've already studied together, but we'll not be giving you the solutions; those are all up to you. Don't worry: we've made sure that every Challenge is doable based on what you've already learned.

So, here is your first Challenge. `Hello4.py` created two variables, `firstName` and `lastName`, and then combined them into a new variable, named `fullName`. Modify that code so that it asks the user for a first name and last name instead of using the hard-coded values. Here's a hint: You only need to change the first two lines of code so that each line uses an `input()` function. Can you figure this one out?

Playing Mad Libs

If you've never played Mad Libs before, they are stories that change based on provided words. You get prompted for words (a verb, a noun, an adjective, and so on) which are inserted into the story, changing it in ways that can be funny (or not).

Write Your Story

Let's give it a try. We'll start with a simple story displayed using our familiar friend the `print()` function. You can use our story, or you can make up your own. Actually, scratch that. You're creative, so make up your own story.

Create a new file called `Story.py` and type your story using `print()` functions like this:

```
print("I have a pet iguana named Spike.")
print("He is long, green, and lazy.")
print("Spike eats leaves, flowers, and fruit.")
print("His favorite toy is a small yellow ball.")
```

Save your file and run it. You'll see the text displayed in the Terminal window.

Add Variables

Now let's make things a bit more interesting. We'll replace one word in the story with a variable, like this:

```
animal="iguana"

print("I have a pet", animal, "named Spike.")
print("He is long, green, and lazy.")
print("Spike eats leaves, flowers, and fruit.")
print("His favorite toy is a small yellow ball.")
```

Mad Libs®

This is our take on Mad Libs. The real Mad Libs® is a registered trademark of Penguin Random House LLC.

As you can see, we changed the first `print()`. Instead of displaying the type of animal, it uses a variable and displays that instead.

Save and run your code. The output should be the same as it was before.

Yes, we know this isn't that exciting. Yet. Let's keep going. We'll now change lots of the text to use variables instead of hard-coded words. In our example story, we changed 11 of them, like this:

```
animal="iguana"
name="Spike"
adjective1="long"
color1="green"
adjective2="lazy"
noun1="leaves"
noun2="flowers"
noun3="fruit"
adjective3="small"
color2="yellow"
noun4="ball"

print("I have a pet", animal,"named", name, ".")
print("He is", adjective1, ",", color1, ", and", adjective2, ".")
print(name, "eats",  noun1, ",", noun2, ", and", noun3, ".")
print("His favorite toy is a", adjective3, color2, noun4, ".")
```

Make your changes and save your code.

Run the code, and it should look exactly as it did before.

One interesting thing to note is that the variable `name` is used twice in the story. Once you create a variable, you can use it as many times as you need.

Watch Your Quotes and Commas

Be careful with your quotes and commas. You'll want quotes around text but not around variable names. And be sure to separate all arguments with commas. This is where color coding is super useful: If things aren't the right colors, then you've probably messed up a quote or a comma.

Get User Input

Now that your story uses variables, changing it to display user-provided text is easy. Simply change each variable to use an `input()`, just like we did earlier in this chapter. Here is our example:

```
print("Hello, please answer the following prompts.")
print()
animal=input("Enter an animal: ")
name=input("Enter a name: ")
adjective1=input("Enter an adjective: ")
color1=input("Enter a color: ")
adjective2=input("Enter an adjective: ")
noun1=input("Enter a noun: ")
noun2=input("Enter a noun: ")
noun3=input("Enter a noun: ")
adjective3=input("Enter an adjective: ")
color2=input("Enter a color: ")
noun4=input("Enter a noun: ")

print("Thank you. Here is your story.")
print()
print("I have a pet", animal,"named", name, ".")
print("He is", adjective1, ",", color1, ", and", adjective2, ".")
print(name, "eats",  noun1, ",", noun2, ", and", noun3, ".")
print("His favorite toy is a", adjective3, color2, noun4, ".")
```

You'll notice that we added a `print()` at the top to provide some instructions. We also used a couple of empty `print()` functions. Those add empty lines so that the output is more readable.

Save the code and run it. You'll be prompted for all of your inputs, and the code will then generate a story. Each time you run the code, a new story will be generated based on whatever inputs are provided.

Once you have tested your code, have a friend or family member give it a try. They'll be impressed with your coding skills.

CHALLENGE 2.2

Ready for your next Challenge?

Make your Mad Lib interesting by prompting for at least 15 different words. And then personalize it. At the start, when you provide instructions, ask the user for their name and then use that in the instructions to create a more personalized experience.

Summary

In this chapter, you learned all about variables and how to use them. You also mastered two functions: `print()`, which displays text, and `input()`, which prompts for text. And then you put it all together to create a fully functional app. Congratulations, you're now a real coder!

CHAPTER 3

Roll the Dice

Now that you know how to use functions and variables, we're going to make things more interesting by introducing libraries and a whole lot of randomness.

Using Libraries

We briefly mentioned libraries back in Chapter 1. You can think of libraries as collections of code—usually functions (like the `print()` and `input()` functions you've already used). Libraries are easy to use. You just tell Python what library you need, and you get to use the functions in it. Simple as that. Yes, someone else did the hard work, and you get to just use it. Nice, huh?

Python comes with lots of libraries included. There is one called `datetime` that provides all sorts of functions for working with dates. `math` is used for mathematical operations. There are libraries for working with files on your computer, accessing Internet sites, working with cryptography, and many more. And libraries can contain more than just functions, too, as you'll see.

And if Python doesn't have the libraries you need, they may exist online for you to download and use. We'll look at using 3rd party libraries (which means libraries that come from someone else, as opposed to ones included with Python) in Part III of this book.

The `random` Library

The first library we are going to look at is called `random`, and, as its name suggests, it is used to add randomness to your code. Want to pick a random number between 1 and 100? `random` can help. Creating a game and need enemies to appear at random intervals and with random levels of health? You use `random` for that, too. Even something as simple as simulating a coin toss can be achieved by using `random`.

Ok, so how do you tell Python what library you want to use? You use the `import` statement. Let's try that. Create a new file named `Random1.py` and type the following:

```
import random
```

Get to Know PyPI

The official repository for Python libraries is called PyPI, which is home to more than 300,000 libraries!

The Truth About Random

Here's the truth about computers and randomness: Computers can't do random things. They just can't. Humans can, but computers like to follow instructions methodically, and they have no idea how to do things that make no sense or have no specific order. So, they can't really do random, well, anything. When computers appear to be doing random things, they are actually relying on complex algorithms and factors that constantly change (like the current date and time) to simulate randomness. If that sounds complex, well, it kinda is. Which is why we love libraries like `random`. You just use the library's functions and let the code inside the library do all the hard work for you.

This code tells Python to `import` the `random` library. Save the code and run it.

What happened? Nothing? It may look like nothing, but something big did happen. Remember, Python runs your code one line at a time. When it comes to the line with the `import` statement, it goes and finds the `random` library and pulls it into your code, ready for you to use it. And then you didn't use it. But that's ok. Now you will.

Generating Random Numbers

Update your code, adding two more lines as shown here:

```
import random

num=random.randrange(1, 11)
print("Random number is", num)
```

Save the file and run it. And then run it again. And again. Run it a few times.

What happens? Each time you run your program, a random number is displayed.

Let's look at the code to understand what it is doing. You know what the first line does: `import random` imports the `random` library. And you know what the last line does: It prints some text and the random number.

Put `import` Up Top

As a general rule, put your `import` statement at the very top of your code, and all in one place. This will make it easy to see what you've imported.

So let's focus on the middle line. It calls a function named `randrange()`, you pass it two numbers as arguments which define the range, and it generates a random number between those two numbers. And whatever number gets generated is saved in the variable `num`.

This code is similar to how we used `input()` earlier: You pass it arguments as needed, and whatever gets returned is saved to a variable. But there is one important difference this time.

Look at the code. The function is not called just by the name `randrange()`. Rather, the library name is included, too. `random.randrange()` tells Python to use the `randrange()` function that is in the `random` library. This is important. Skip the library, and Python won't know where to find `randrange()`.

You can try that if you want. Remove `random.` and save and run the code. You'll see that the VS Code puts a squiggly line under `randrange()`, and if you mouse over it, it'll say **`"randrange" is not defined`**. So, just remember that the library name is needed.

Choosing a Random Item

Now you know how to generate random numbers. But what if you want to do something else, like toss a coin? In that case, you'd want to randomly return Heads or Tails, not a number, so `randrange()` wouldn't be able to help you. But worry not; you can do this by using another function in the `random` library.

Careful with Ranges

`randrange(1, 11)` returns a random number between 1 and 10. Why 10? The second argument, which is `11`, means less than 11. It's a bit confusing because the first argument (the `1`) is included in the range, but the second (the `11`) is not. This means that if you want a number between 3 and 8, you'd use `randrange(3, 9)`. The good news is that this behavior is consistent with other Python functions, so you'll get used to it.

Create a new file named Random2.py and type the following:

```
import random

choices="HT"
coinToss=random.choice(choices)
print("It's", coinToss)
```

Save the file and run it. Each time you run the code, you'll see `It's H` (for Heads) or `It's T` (for Tails) displayed in the Terminal window.

So what is this code doing? You know what the first and last lines do.

The code `choices="HT"` creates a variable called `choices` and stores the text `"HT"` in it.

The next line randomly picks `H` (for Heads) or `T` (for Tails). It does this by using the `choice()` function, another function in the `random` library. Unlike `randrange()`, which accepts a range of numbers as an argument, `choice()` accepts a single argument with a list of choices. Here we pass it our `choices` variable, which contains `"HT"`, so `choice()` will return one of those options: `H` or `T`.

Simple, huh?

Ok, so what if you want to display `Heads` or `Tails` instead of `H` or `T`? You can't just pass the text `Heads` and `Tails` as choices, like this:

```
choices="HeadsTails"
coinToss=random.choice(choices)
```

Another Option

We could have written the same code without the `choices` variable. How? By passing `"HT"` to `choice()` directly, like this:

```
coinToss=random.choice("HT")
```

In this example, the end result is the same.

Why? Because `choice()` will treat that as 10 options: the letter `H`, the letter `e`, the letter `a`, and so on. You could end up with a returned value of `i`, not what you'd want.

There are a few ways to do this. We'll show you one option, using a special type of variable.

You'll recall from Chapter 2 that variables contain values. And we mentioned then that there are special variables that can contain multiple values. We'll use these extensively in later lessons, but for now, here's how we can use these special variables to solve the Heads or Tails challenge.

Make just one change to your code. Edit this line:

```
choices="HT"
```

so that it looks like this:

```
choices=["Heads","Tails"]
```

Save the code and run it. Now the output will be `It's Heads` or `It's Tails`.

So what happens when you change that line of code? The `[` and `]` characters are used to create a list in Python. A list is exactly what it sounds like: a list of items. `[10,20,33]` would create a list with three items in it: the three specified numbers. Similarly, `["ant","bat","cat","dog","eel"]` would create a list of five animals.

We'll use lots of lists in future chapters, but for now just know that lists store multiple items, and each item is separated by a comma.

Ok, now back to our code. `choices=["Heads","Tails"]` creates a list with two items in it: the text `Heads` and the text `Tails`. We don't have to change any other code in this case because the `random.choice()` function is pretty smart. Pass it some text, and it knows that you want a random character from that text. But pass it a list, and it'll know that what you want is one random item from the list.

Perfect!

CHALLENGE 3.1

Ok, this one is a little harder, but you can do it, promise! See that list with the five animals? Write code that creates two lists, one with animals, like this:

```
animals=["ant","bat","cat","dog","eel"]
```

You can use your own list of animals, and you can have more than five (the more the better).

Then create a similar list of adjectives, things like `big`, `green`, `smelly`, `cute`, and so on. (Again, the more, the better. And it doesn't matter whether or not your two lists have the same number of items.)

Then pick a random adjective and a random animal and save each to a variable. (You'll need two variables: one for your animal and one for your adjective.) Then `print()` the choices so that the output is something like `I have a cute eel`. Each time you run the app, you'll get a different combination.

"3" Is Not 3

Before we go further, there's an important topic we need to discuss. Did you notice any differences in how we type variable names' values? Here's a reminder: these are all snippets of code that you've already used:

```
lastName = "Forta"
fullName = firstName + " " + lastName
name=input("What is your name? ")
num=random.randrange(1, 11)
choices=["Heads","Tails"]
```

As you can see, sometimes we put double quotes around values and sometimes we don't. Why do we do this?

The reason is because you need quotes to mark a block of text (what coders call a *string*). Numbers don't need quotes around them. Python knows that `1` and `11` are numbers, and they can't be anything else. But `lastName`? It could be text, or the name of a variable (or even the name of a function), and it's up to the coder to specify what it is. Same for `Heads`, sure, it could be a string, but it also could be something else. Computers don't like ambiguity. Things need to be spelled out clearly. So, when you use text and want it to be treated as plain text, then you must surround it with double quotes.

So, to summarize:

- Variables never have quotes around them.
- Numbers never have quotes around them.
- Strings always need quotes around them.

Ok, so let's make this interesting. Is `"3"` a number or a string? And can you multiply it by `5`?

Well, to us humans that's an easy one. Yes, `"3"` is a number, and if you multiply it by `5`, you'll get `15`. But Python doesn't know that `"3"` is a number; it sees the quotes and assumes that it is a string.

So what would happen if you told Python to multiply `"3"` by `5`? This is going to sound crazy, we know, but you'd get `"33333"`! It would multiply the *string* (essentially adding `5` copies of it) instead of the *number in the string*. Seriously!

Strings Need Quotes

If you forget to use quotes around a string, Python will assume that you are referring to a variable, and it will display an error message, telling you the variable doesn't exist.

Testing `"3"` Versus `3`

Want to try this for yourself? In Python, `*` (asterisk) is the multiplication symbol. You can create a file and `print(3 * 5)` and then `print("3" * 5)` to see the difference in output. You will see that `"3" * 5` concatenates five copies of the string `"3"`.

Python Makes Variables Easy

In most languages, you must tell the computer what data type you want when you create a variable. Python is nice that way: It figures it out for you based on the values you provide.

You Can Convert Between Data Types

In future lessons, you'll learn how to convert data from one data type to another so that you can, for example, convert string "3" to number 3.

And now you have been introduced to *data types*. What is a data type? It is simply the type of information that a variable can store. There are lots of data types, but the two you'll use the most are string and numeric. `num=11` creates a variable named `num` with a numeric data type. `lastName = "Forta"` creates a variable named `lastName` with a string data type.

So, are "3" and 3 the same? The answer is no. The first is a string, and the second is a number, and though they look the same, their data types are different.

Commenting Your Code

There's one last important topic we need to cover before we get to our final example in this chapter.

All of the code you've written thus far has been pretty simple—just a few lines. But as you work through the lessons in this book, you'll be writing tens, even hundreds, of lines of code. To make their code easier to read and understand, coders put comments in their code.

How do you add comments? Like this (an example we saw before, but this time with comments added):

```
# Import needed libraries
import random

# Define the choices
choices=["Heads","Tails"]
```

```
# Pick a random choice
coinToss=random.choice(choices)

# And display it
print("It's", coinToss)
```

In Python, comments start with a # symbol. VS Code displays comments in their own color, making it super easy to identify them.

It is important to understand that Python completely ignores comments. When Python sees a #, it ignores anything that comes after it. The comments are for you, the coder, not for Python.

Commenting may seem like a waste of time. But take it from us: It is really important, and good coders comment all of their code. Why?

- Comments will help you read your own code.
- Comments will remind you of what you did and why.
- Comments help others understand what your code does.
- Comments make it easier for other coders to understand and work on your code.
- Comments can explain any assumptions or dependencies, things that are needed for your code to work.

And comments serve another important purpose: They can be used to hide code. For example, earlier you made a change to your code, changing `choices="HT"` to `choices=["Heads","Tails"]`. That was a pretty simple edit, but imagine if it was a more complicated one. You might want to keep the old version while you test the new one. Look at this code:

```
# Import needed libraries
import random

# Define the choices
# choices="HT"
choices=["Heads","Tails"]
```

```
# Pick a random choice
coinToss=random.choice(choices)

# And display it
print("It's", coinToss)
```

Notice that the original line choices="HT" is still in the file. It wasn't deleted or edited, instead it has a # in front of it. That turns the line into a comment so that it is ignored by Python. Want to go back to the prior version? Remove the # symbol from the line and put it in front of the next line; that way, the second choices line becomes a comment instead.

Coders call this *commenting out* code, and it's an invaluable technique to use when revising or testing code.

> NEW TERM
>
> **Commenting Out** Using comments to temporarily hide code, preventing it from being executed.

Ok, so from now on all of our code will be commented.

One Die, Two Dice

Let's look at one last example to review everything we learned so far. Actually, let's make it two examples.

You've rolled dice before; lots of games need them. Dice are cool, but computer dice are way more fun. So we'll create two programs: one that rolls a single die and another that rolls two.

Here's the code for Dice1.py:

```
# Imports
import random

# Roll and print
print("You rolled a", random.randrange(1, 7))
```

This one is pretty simple, and it's all code you've seen before. Save and run the code. You'll see a number between `1` and `6` (remember, the `7` won't be included in the range).

The only real difference here is that the number returned by `random.randrange()` is never saved to a variable. Instead, it is passed directly to `print()` as an argument.

Run this program whenever you need to roll a single die.

Do You Need a Variable?

What is the difference between this code:

```
import random

print("You rolled a", random.randrange(1, 7))
```

and this code?

```
import random

num = random.randrange(1, 7)
print("You rolled a", num)
```

Functionally, there is no difference between these. Both generate a random number and then display it.

The first version generates the random number right inside of the `print()` statement. The return value (the number that `randrange()` generates) is what gets passed as an argument to `print()`.

The second version generates a random number and saves it to a variable named num. It is the variable that gets passed as an argument to `print()`.

The final printed result is the same. The difference is the variable. That's it.

So which version should you use? In this situation, there is no advantage of one version over the other. The difference would only be important if that random number were needed for some other purpose, maybe another `print()` or in some calculations. Then you'd definitely want to save the generated number to a variable so that you could reuse it.

But what about when you need to roll two dice? You could run the program twice and add the numbers yourself. But, nah, that's not what we coders would do. We'd write another program to roll two dice.

This is the code for `Dice2.py`:

```
# Imports
import random

# Roll both dice
die1=random.randrange(1, 7)
die2=random.randrange(1, 7)

# Display total and individual dies
print("You rolled", die1, "and", die2, "- that's", die1+die2)
```

Run the code, and you'll see the values of both dice displayed, along with their sum.

This code should be self-explanatory to a `print()` and `random` expert like you. It creates two variables, and each contains the value for a rolled die. The `print()` statement simply displays the values and then does this:

```
die1+die2
```

This is a simple math operation: `die1` and `die2` are added together, and what gets printed is their sum. Yes, Python can do math on-the-fly.

The + Operator

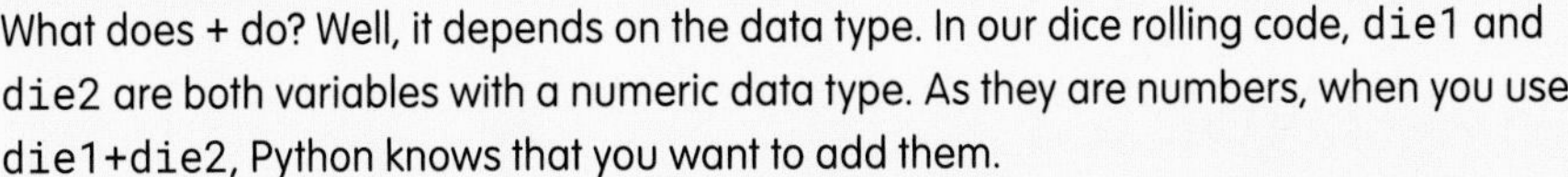

What does + do? Well, it depends on the data type. In our dice rolling code, `die1` and `die2` are both variables with a numeric data type. As they are numbers, when you use `die1+die2`, Python knows that you want to add them.

But if the variables were strings and you used the + operator, Python would concatenate them (as a mathematical addition on strings would make no sense).

Python is smart this way: It tries to figure out what we coders intend to do, and it does that for us.

This seems like a good place to review the math operators you can use in Python:

`+`	The addition operator, so `print(5+5)` will display `10`.
`-`	The subtraction operator. `print(12-7)` will display `5`.
`*`	You saw this one earlier in this chapter: It's the multiplication operator, and `print(10*3)` will display `30`.
`/`	The division operator. `print(10/3)` will display `3.333` (there will be a lot more 3's than this).
`//`	This is also a division operator, but this one returns just the whole number, not the remainder. `print(10//3)` will display `3`.
`%`	The modulus operator, which is used to get the remainder from a division, so `print(10%3)` will display `1`.

Obviously, these operators can be used in all sorts of code and functions. The `print()` statements used as examples here are to help you try the operators, if you are so inclined.

So, why did we use variables to store the dice values in `Dice2.py` but not in `Dice1.py`? Well, truthfully we could have used variables in both. But variables are only needed if the value is to be used more than once. In `Dice1.py`, the value is used only once—when it is displayed—so a variable could have been used but isn't truly necessary. In `Dice2.py`, the dice values are used twice—once when they are displayed and once when they are summed to get their total—and so saving the rolls to a variable is required.

CHALLENGE 3.2

Most dice we use have 6 sides, but some games use dice with more sides. And, actually, ancient Greeks and Romans used dodecahedron shaped dice, which have 12 sides! So, just in case you ever run into an ancient Greek or Roman, write code that rolls a 12-sided die.

Summary

Wow, you covered a lot in this chapter! You learned how to use libraries, and specifically the `random` library and two of its functions. You learned about data types. And you also learned about commenting your code. Next we'll look at teaching your code to make decisions.

CHAPTER 4

Calculate the Day

You now know how to use variables, functions, and libraries. Next up is one of the most important coding tools you'll need: teaching the computer how to make decisions.

Working with Dates

As you have seen, Python processes your code line by line, one line at a time. It starts at the top of a program, and for every line that isn't a comment, it does whatever you have told it to do.

And that's rather boring. If every program written were executed line by line, then every program would do the exact same thing each time it was run. Imagine a website that showed the same content in the same order every single time you visited. Or a game that only ever allowed you to do one thing, and then one more thing, and then one more, always in the same order. Or a chat app that only ever let you enter the same one message to be sent. See what we mean? Boring!

Obviously, any useful programs must be capable of doing lots of different things in lots of different sequences. Which means that you, as the coder, need a way to tell the computer how to make decisions.

Which brings us to the critically important `if` statement, the focus of this chapter (and the next).

The `datetime` Library

Mathematicians love impressing people with a neat trick where they ask someone for their birthday and then, in a few seconds, tell them which day of the week they were born on. When they do this, they aren't guessing (if they did, they'd statistically get it right a mere seventh of the time, and that wouldn't impress at all). They figure it out using math that they do quickly in their heads.

We could learn how to do this just as mathematicians do. But, nah, we're coders. We can impress with our coding skills and make the computer figure it out for us.

To do this let's look at another built-in Python library, the `datetime` library. As its name suggests, this library lets you do all sorts of things with dates. What type of things?

- Getting the current date
- Figuring out future and past date details (like their day of the week)
- Calculating the difference between two dates (which is actually quite tricky when you have to take into account different month lengths and leap years)

Oh, and it does all the same things for times, too.

The `datetime` Library
Part of the reason we picked the `datetime` library as our next library example is that it is really useful. Also, it works a little differently from the last library we used, `random`, and it's good to experience lots of different libraries.

Create a new file named `Date1.py`. Here is the code to type:

```
# Imports
import datetime

# Get today's date
today=datetime.datetime.now()

# Print it
print("It is", today)
```

Save and run the program, and it'll display the current date and time, including milliseconds (really useful, we know).

You know what the `import` and `print()` lines do, so let's focus on that middle line, which, admittedly, looks a little strange.

The code `today=datetime.datetime.now()` gets today's date and saves it to a variable named `today`. `now()` is obviously the function that returns the date and time right now. And unlike the functions you've used thus far, this one doesn't need any arguments. The parentheses are still needed. Any time you call a function, you must provide the parentheses, but you can just leave them empty, with no argument, so nothing in between `(` and `)`.

But what's up with the `datetime.datetime`? Why couldn't we just use `datetime.now()` like we did with the `random` library functions that we used in Chapter 3?

Functions Versus Variables
Just remember that when functions are being executed, they are always followed by parentheses. Variables are not followed by parentheses.

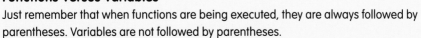

The first `datetime` is indeed the library name. It matches the library referred to in the first line of code: `import datetime`.

The second `datetime` is not a library or a function. It's actually something called a *class*. We're going to look at classes in detail in Part II of this book, where you'll be creating classes of your own. For now, you just need to know that a class is a way programmers can organize their code so that functions and pieces of information can be stored together in one place. Classes have functions in them that you can call, just like any other functions.

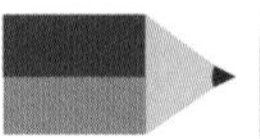

NEW TERM

Methods Functions in a class are called *methods*. But they are still functions, just like the ones you've seen thus far.

The `datetime` library has a class in it named `datetime`. (Yeah, we agree: It would have been simpler if they weren't named the same!) So, `datetime` is the imported library, and `datetime.datetime` refers to the `datetime` class inside of the `datetime` library. Whew!

And then `now()` is the function (in `datetime`) that returns today's date and time, which is then saved in the `today` variable.

The `type()` Function

In Chapter 3, we mentioned data types. So, what is the type of the `today` variable that you just created? It is not a string or numeric type. The type is actually a `datetime` class.

If you ever want to know the type of a variable, you can use the Python `type()` function. All `type()` does is look at the variable so that it can tell you what it is via a return value. `type(3)` will return `int` (for integer) because 3 is a number. `type("3")` will return `str` (for string). And `type(today)` (the variable you created above) will return type `datetime.datetime`.

We'll look at types (and the `type()` function) in greater detail in future chapters.

Using the `datetime` Class

In our first example in this chapter, we just printed whatever was in the `today` variable. But because `today` is a class, it actually has lots of data and functions inside of it that you can use.

Let's try another example. Create a file named `Date2.py`, this is the code:

```
# Imports
import datetime

# Get today's date
today=datetime.datetime.now()

# Print today's year, month, and day
print("The year is", today.year)
print("The month is", today.month)
print("The day is", today.day)
```

Save and run the code, and it will display the current year, month, and day, each on its own line.

`today.year` means the `year` value inside of the `today` class. Same for `month` and `day`.

As you have seen, `today` contains lots of information. Earlier we printed the whole `today` variable (without any specific item in it), like this:

```
print("It is", today)
```

Here Python does us a favor and displays it all in a default readable format. But doing this is not recommended, and in general, you're better off displaying each item you need so that you have more control over the output.

Methods Versus Properties

Why no ( ) after `year`, `month`, and `day`? Because those are not functions (well, methods). They are pieces of data that you can use, kind of like variables inside of the class. These are actually called *properties*. We'll look at properties (and methods) in Part II.

You don't use parentheses when you refer to properties; you do when you use methods (again, functions). You'll see an example of this soon when we use `weekday()` (which is a method).

CHALLENGE 4.1

Modify `Date2.py` to also display the current time. The properties you want are called `hour` and `minute`.

Making Decisions

Now that you know how to use dates, let's return to our main topic, `if` statements, and using these to help your computer make decisions.

The `if` Statement

We know that you'd love to spend every waking moment coding. But you have other responsibilities, things like school. Right? So, let's write a program that figures out what day of the week it is and then displays a useful message for different days. Obviously, this is going to require the computer to make a decision. It can't just go line by line and print stuff; it has to do different things depending on the day of the week.

Create a new file named `Date3.py` and type the following:

```
# Imports
import datetime

# Get today's date
today=datetime.datetime.now()

# Display the right message for different days of week
if today.weekday() == 6:
    print("It's the weekend, no school today!")
    print("We can code all day long!")
```

Save and run the code. What happens? Well, if you happen to be running this on a Sunday, you'll see a message displayed (the two `print()` statements). But if it is any other day of the week, you'll see nothing at all.

The magic here is this line:

```
if today.weekday() == 6:
```

`if` is used to create a condition that goes after the word `if` and before the closing colon (the : symbol). The `today.weekday()` method returns the day of week, `0` for Monday, `1` for Tuesday, and so on. This condition is pretty simple: It tells Python to call the `weekday()` method inside of `today` and then compare what it returns to the number `6` (which means Sunday). So what this is saying is *if today is Sunday*.

Pay special attention to what is between `weekday()` and `6`. That's two equal signs, not one. `==` means check to see if two things are equal. It is not the same as `=`, which saves a value to a variable, as we have seen previously.

The condition passed to an `if` statement must be one that resolves to `True` or `False`. Here, if today is indeed Sunday, then the condition is `True`. If not, then it's `False`.

Python's Weird Week

The Python week starts on Monday. Yes, Monday is the first day of the week, and Sunday is the last.

And, just like pretty much every programming language out there, Python starts counting from `0`. If you have a list of items, for example, they are numbered `0`, `1`, `2`, and so on. The first item is in position `0`, not `1`.

Put both of these points together, and this means that `0` is Monday, `1` is Tuesday, and so on. This means that `5` is Saturday, and `6` is Sunday.

= Versus ==

`=` and `==` are not the same, and many programmers have spent hours trying to figure out why their code is broken, only to discover that they used `=` when they meant `==` or vice versa. So, to be super ultra mega clear:

- `=` is the assignment operator, and it assigns a value, meaning it saves whatever is on the right of `=` into the variable on the left. The code `x = 3` creates a variable named `x` and stores the number `3` in it.
- `==` is the equality comparison operator, meaning it is used to compare two things. The code `x == 3` checks to see if the variable `x` has a value of `3`.

Don't confuse them!

Be Careful with Indentation

Be careful with your indentation. If the prior code had looked like this:

```
if today.weekday() == 6:
    print("It's the weekend, no school today!")
print("We can code all day long!")
```

then the first `print()` would be executed if today is Sunday, but the second `print()` statement would always print for every single day of the week. Why? Because the second `print()` is not inside of the `if` statement, it's just a regular Python line of code that always runs.

How does Python know what code you want to run if the condition is `True`? It looks for any code indented under the `if` statement, and whatever is indented will get processed. When Python encounters a line that is not indented, it knows that it is done processing the `if` statement.

What `else`?

We now have code that prints a message for Sunday. If today isn't Sunday, Python prints nothing. Let's fix that now. Here is the updated code, which adds two lines to the bottom:

```
# Imports
import datetime

# Get today's date
today=datetime.datetime.now()

# Display the right message for different days of week
if today.weekday() == 6:
    print("It's the weekend, no school today!")
    print("We can code all day long!")
else:
    print("It's a school day.")
```

Save and run the code. It'll now display the first two `print()` statements on Sunday and the last one on any other day.

else is used to define code that should run if the if statement is False (in our case, not Sunday). else doesn't need a condition; it's just else: (with the colon after it). And then whatever is indented next will get executed when the if condition is False.

if Revisited

There's a problem with our if statement. It only checks to see if weekday() returns 6 (Sunday). What about Saturday (that would be a 5)?

Let's rewrite the if statement to test for both Saturday or Sunday. Here's the updated code; only one line has changed, the if statement:

```
# Imports
import datetime

# Get today's date
today=datetime.datetime.now()

# Display the right message for different days of week
if today.weekday() == 5 or today.weekday() == 6:
    print("It's the weekend, no school today!")
    print("We can code all day long!")
else:
    print("It's a school day.")
```

Save and run the code.

So, what changed here? The revised if statement has a condition with two parts as it checks for two things: weekday() returning 5 (Saturday) or weekday() returning 6 (Sunday). The or means that either of the tests must be True for the if statement to be True (and the code indented beneath it to be executed). Now the correct messages (the first two print() statements) are displayed for both Saturday and Sunday.

When providing multiple tests to an if statement, you always connect them using and or or. What's the difference? Let's look at some examples of conditions (and we'll use English rather than code):

If lunch is pizza and dessert is ice cream	When would this be True? Only if lunch is indeed pizza and dessert is indeed ice cream. Both condition parts must be True for the whole condition to be True. If lunch is not pizza, then it doesn't matter if dessert is ice cream or not; either way, the condition is False. The *and* means that the whole condition will be True only if every single part of the condition is True. It's all or nothing.
If it is Sunday or school's out for vacation	When would this be True? Here the condition uses *or* to join the two parts, not *and*. So either of the two parts needs to be True for the overall condition to be True. If it is Sunday but school is not out, then the condition will be True. Similarly, if school's out but it is not Sunday, the condition will also be True. And what if it happens to be a Sunday while school's out? That'll make the condition True, too. When using *or*, if any of the individual parts are True, or if they all are True, then the condition is True. An *or* condition will only be False if all the parts are False.
If it is Monday or Tuesday or Wednesday	When would this be True? There are three parts in this condition, with *or* between each part. This condition will be True if it is Monday or if it is Tuesday or if it is Wednesday. If any of the three parts are True, then the overall condition is True.

Our code uses two tests, each testing for equality (meaning what is on the right and left are equal to each other). Here is a summary of the tests you can perform:

`==`	Tests for equality, as you saw above.
`!=`	Tests for non-equality, meaning the two are not the same, which is the exact opposite of `==`.
`>`	Tests for greater than. It will be `True` if the left value is greater than the right value.
`<`	Tests for less than. It will be `True` if the left value is less than the right value.
`>=`	Tests for greater than or equal to. It will be `True` if the left value is greater than the right value or if it is the same as the right value.
`<=`	Tests for less than or equal to. It will be `True` if the left value is less than the right value or if it is the same as the right value.

Don't Confuse `and` and `or`

Obviously, `and` makes no sense in our example, as there would never be a day that is both Saturday (5) and Sunday (6). And if you did use `and` here, like this:

```
if today.weekday() == 5 and today.weekday() == 6:
```

the statement would always evaluate to `False` because no day can be both Saturday and Sunday. That's why we use `or` here. We'll be using `and` a lot later in this chapter.

There are other tests that you can perform, we'll see one in a moment, actually. But the ones in this table are the ones you'll use most.

Testing for Other Options

So, `if` tests for a condition, and if the test is `True`, then the code indented beneath the `if` will be executed. `else` provides the code that gets executed if the `if` statement is `False` (not `True`).

What if you wanted to test for other conditions? For example, our code displays one message for Saturday and Sunday and another for every other day. What if you wanted a special message just for Friday? For that, you can use `elif` (which is short for *else if*).

Here's an example. It's our same code with two lines added between the `if` block and the `else` block:

```
# Imports
import datetime

# Get today's date
today=datetime.datetime.now()

# Display the right message for different days of week
if today.weekday() == 5 or today.weekday() == 6:
    # Display this on Saturday and Sunday
    print("It's the weekend, no school today!")
    print("We can code all day long!")
```

```
elif today.weekday() == 4:
    # Display this on Friday
    print("It's Friday, tomorrow we'll have tons of time to code!")
else:
    # Display this every other day
    print("It's a school day.")
```

Save the code and run it. Now it displays one message for Saturday and Sunday, another for Friday, and another for all other days.

So what changed here? Well, for starters, there are some more comments, just to keep things very clear.

But the important change is the addition of the `elif` line:

```
elif today.weekday() == 4:
```

This line is another `if` statement, but as it is an `elif`, it is only called if the first `if` is `False`. The code tests for `weekday()` returning 4, meaning Friday. If that test is `True`, then the code indented beneath the `elif` is executed.

`if`, `elif`, `else`...let's review:

- If you are writing code to test for stuff, you always start with the `if` statement.
- If you want additional tests, you can use `elif`. `elif` is always optional, so you can have no `elif`, or you can have lots of `elif`s—as many as you need, actually.
- If you want code that gets executed if none of the `if` or `elif` tests are `True`, then you use `else`. `else` is optional; it is never actually needed. `else` doesn't have a condition, it's just `else`, that's it. If you do use `else`, then you can only have one, and it must be the last statement in the sequence.

Using `in`

Before we move on, we want to show you another way to test for one of multiple values. Let's look at the first `if` statement again:

```
if today.weekday() == 5 or today.weekday() == 6:
```

As you know, this if statement tests for two things, and either one can be True for the whole if statement to be True.

There are two tests, and both are comparing values to the same thing. First we check to see if today.weekday() is a 5 and then we check to see if today.weekday() is a 6. As both tests are comparing values against today.weekday() we can write the if statement another way.

Look at this if statement:

```
if today.weekday() in [5,6]:
```

You saw [ ] used in Chapter 3; it creates a list of items. Here we've created a list of two values, 5 and 6. Python lets us use a special test called in, and it returns True if the value we are looking for is anywhere in the list. So, if today.weekday() is 5 or 6, then it is in the list, and the test will return True. If today.weekday() is any other value, it won't be in the list, and the if statement will return False.

Neat, huh? If you'd like to try this, just replace the if statement in your code with this revised one.

So, two ways to accomplish the same task. You can use either technique: in or the or operator. It's really a matter of personal preference.

Beating the Mathematician

You've now learned everything you need to write a program that will ask the user for their birthday and then tell them what day of the week they were born. And as for raw speed? You'll beat the mathematician every time!

Handling Numeric Inputs

But, before we proceed, there's one more thing we should point out. Look at this code:

```
year = input("What year were you born? ")
```

You know what this does. It asks the user for some input and then saves it to a variable named year.

But, there's the problem. As we saw in Chapter 3, strings and numbers are not the same thing. `input()` always returns a string. If the user types `2011` as the year, the `year` variable will be the string `"2011"`, but we need it to be the number `2011` (as that is what `datetime` wants numbers, not strings).

We'll spend more time looking at data types and how to convert between them in later chapters. For now, just know that there is a wonderful function called `int()`. You pass it a string containing a number, and it returns that number as an actual number. So, this code:

```
year="2011"
```

stores the string `"2011"` to `year`, but this code:

```
year=int("2011")
```

stores the number `2011` to `year` (the string `"2011"` is converted to a number).

Putting It All Together

And with that, let's write our program. Create a file named `Birthday.py`. Here is the code:

```
# Import
import datetime

# Get user input
year = input("What year were you born? ")
year = int(year)
month = input("What month were you born? ")
month = int(month)
day = input("What day were you born? ")
day = int(day)

# Build the date object
bday = datetime.datetime(year, month, day)
```

```
# Display the results
if bday.weekday() == 6:
    print("You were born on Sunday")
elif bday.weekday() == 0:
    print("You were born on Monday")
elif bday.weekday() == 1:
    print("You were born on Tuesday")
elif bday.weekday() == 2:
    print("You were born on Wednesday")
elif bday.weekday() == 3:
    print("You were born on Thursday")
elif bday.weekday() == 4:
    print("You were born on Friday")
elif bday.weekday() == 5:
    print("You were born on Saturday")
```

Save and run the program. It will prompt you for a year, month, and day and will then tell you what day of the week you were born on.

So, how does this work?

We need the `datetime` library, so we start with `import datetime`.

Then we ask the user to enter a year, month, and date. Look at these two lines:

```
year = input("What year were you born? ")
year = int(year)
```

The first is an `input()`, it'll prompt for a year and save what the user types as a string in the variable `year`.

The second line then converts that string year value to a number by using `int()` and saves it to the same variable (overwriting the string year with a numeric year).

We could have actually combined those lines into one, like this:

```
year = int(input("What year were you born? "))
```

Here int() surrounds the whole input() function, and so it converts whatever input() returns and saves that to the variable. The end result is the same as when these two functions are executed independently.

Now that we have the year, month, and date, we need to use them to create a Python date. Earlier you saw that this code creates a Python date with today's date in it:

```
today=datetime.datetime.now()
```

How can we create a date using our variables? Instead of using now(), we just pass the year, month, and date values to datetime, like this:

```
bday = datetime.datetime(year, month, day)
```

This way, bday contains our Python date, ready to use.

Then come the if and elif statements, which are much like the ones you saw before:

```
if bday.weekday() == 6:
    print("You were born on Sunday")
elif bday.weekday() == 0:
    print("You were born on Monday")
elif bday.weekday() == 1:
    print("You were born on Tuesday")
```

We are checking Sunday, then Monday, then Tuesday, and so on. So first comes an if statement (it checks for Sunday) and then a series of elif statements (for all the other days). We won't repeat them all here as they should be self-explanatory.

What About else?

There's no else in this if block? Why? Well, there are only seven possible day-of-week options. That's all weekday() can return, nothing else. And we handled all seven in our if and elif statements. We could have included an else, but it would never ever be executed, so why bother?

Remember, else is always optional.

An Alternate Solution

One last thought: In our code, we have seven `print()` statements, one beneath each `if` and `elif`. If you only want a single `print()` statement (so that you don't repeat the same display text over and over), you could have done this (this would replace the `if` block currently in the code):

```
# Calculate the day of week
if bday.weekday() == 6:
    dow="Sunday"
elif bday.weekday() == 0:
    dow="Monday"
elif bday.weekday() == 1:
    dow="Tuesday"
elif bday.weekday() == 2:
    dow="Wednesday"
elif bday.weekday() == 3:
    dow="Thursday"
elif bday.weekday() == 4:
    dow="Friday"
elif bday.weekday() == 5:
    dow="Saturday"

# Display the results
print("You were born on", dow)
```

There are always multiple ways to write code. In this version, the `if` statements don't display anything. Instead, each of them stores a day in a variable called `dow` (for *day of week*). Then that `dow` variable is used in a single `print()` statement. Same result, slightly different way to organize your code.

Summary

In this chapter, you learned one of the most important parts of any programming language. The `if` statement is used to make decisions, and we'll continue to look at `if` in the next chapter.

CHAPTER 5

Rock Paper Scissors

In Chapter 4 you learned how to use `if` statements to create conditions. This is a really important topic, so we're going to dedicate one more chapter to it, this time creating the game of Rock, Paper, Scissors.

More Strings

We've used lots and lots of strings in these past few chapters. As a reminder, strings are simply blocks of text. Code like this should be very familiar by now:

```
name="Ben"
print(name)
```

In this example, `name` is a variable; specifically, it's a string.

But, now that you've seen classes (such as the `datetime` class in the last chapter), we'll let you in on a secret: That `name` string is actually a class, too; it's a `str` class. If you run code like this:

```
name="Ben"
print(type(name))
```

you'll see that the variable `name` is of type `str` (that's what Python calls the string class).

And, as you know, classes have methods that you can use.

Here's something fun you can try: Open a new file, let's call this one `StringTest.py`, and type the following (use your own name, not mine...unless your name happens to be Ben, in which case, awesome name, use it):

```
name="Ben"
name=name
print(name)
```

Yep, that middle line of code is rather useless: It sets `name` to whatever `name` currently is.

But try this. Add a `.` (a period) after the last `name` and wait a moment. You'll see VS Code pop up a display like this:

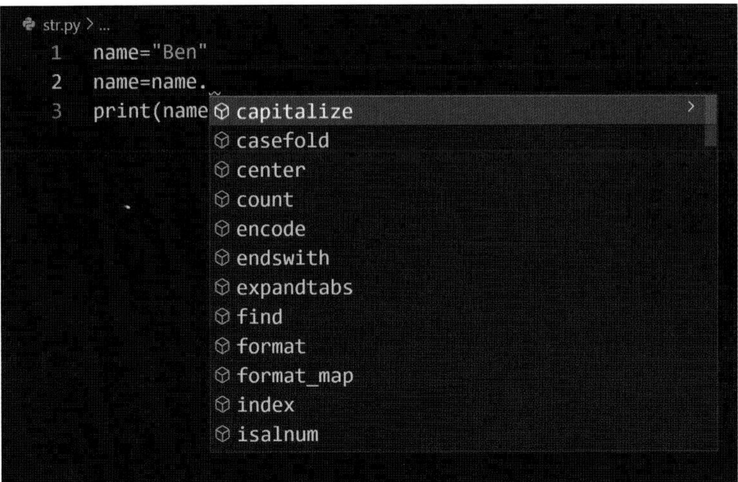

`name` is a string, which is actually a `str` class, right? When you type the period, VS Code helpfully shows you all the methods (remember, methods are functions) available to you. And as you select any method, you'll see help to its right telling you what it does.

Let's try a couple. Change the middle line so that it looks like this:

```
name=name.upper()
```

Save and run the code. You'll see that the value in `name` has been converted to uppercase. That's what the `upper()` method does. There's also a `lower()` method, which converts text to lowercase. And there's a really useful method called `strip()` that removes (strips) any extra characters from before and after text.

If you want to convert your text to uppercase and also strip all extraneous empty space, you can use both functions:

```
name=" Ben "
name=name.upper()
name=name.strip()
print(name)
```

Here, `name` starts off as ` Ben ` (with a space before and after the text). The next line turns it into ` BEN ` (still with those spaces). The next line removes the spaces.

TIP

Stripping Whitespace There are actually three different methods for stripping (removing) extraneous text. `rstrip()` strips extraneous text from the right side of a string (meaning at the end of the text). `lstrip()` strips text from the left of a string (meaning at the start of the string). `strip()` is basically a combination of `rstrip()` and `lstrip()` that removes spaces from both ends of a string.

And, actually, Python lets you use these functions stacked on each other. Look at this code, which is functionally the same, but both methods are in one line:

```
name=" Ben "
name=name.upper().strip()
print(name)
```

We'll use these methods in our game.

Game Time

Now that you know how to use `if` statements, let's create our Rock, Paper, Scissors game. This is usually a hand game played between two people, in which each player simultaneously forms one of three shapes with an outstretched hand. Rock beats scissors, scissors beats paper, and paper beats rock. We'll create a computer version of this game, where you'll pick one of the three, as will the computer, and you'll see who wins (or if it's a tie).

Handling User Input

We're going to do things a little differently this time. Instead of creating multiple programs, we'll create one and incrementally add functionality to it, using everything you've learned thus far.

Create a new file named `rps.py` (`rps` stands for rock paper scissors, duh!). Start with this code:

```
# Imports
import random

# Computer picks one
cChoice = random.choice("RPS")

# Get user choice
print("Rock, Paper, or Scissors?")
uChoice=input("Enter R, P, S: ")

# Test it
print("You:", uChoice)
print("Computer:", cChoice)
```

Save the code and run it. It will prompt you to enter `R`, `P`, or `S`, and then it will display the user choice and the computer choice.

The code starts by importing the `random` library, just as we did in Chapter 3. Next, it uses the `choice()` method to pick one of three options, `R`, `P`, or `S`, again, as we did in Chapter 3.

Then it asks the user to enter `R`, `P`, or `S` using an `input()` function.

At this point, you have the computer's selection (randomly picked) and the user's selection.

The last few lines (from the `# Test it` comment to the end) are temporary. They'll let us test our code before we go any further. As soon as we know the first few lines work we can delete the test code.

Do What the Pros Do: Test as You Work

Incrementally testing your code as you work is a really good idea. It is much easier to find problems when you have less code to work with. And as soon as you know that you got one part working properly, then you can move on to the next. This is what all professional coders do.

Did you try it out? Did it work? The user needs to enter one of three letters, which we'll use in an `if` statement. The code asks for an `R`, a `P`, or an `S`. What if the user types `s` (lowercase) or adds a space after the letter? That would mess up the `if` statements.

You know how to fix this one. Add this line after the line with the `input()`:

```
uChoice=uChoice.upper().strip()
```

Alternatively, because Python lets you stack methods on to each other, you can just change the `input()` line to look like this:

```
uChoice=input("Enter R, P, S: ").upper().strip()
```

The end result is the same thing: `uChoice` will contain uppercase text with no extraneous whitespace.

Test the code again: Type upper- or lowercase text and add some spaces, to make sure the code is doing what it is supposed to do. And when you are satisfied, you can delete the test code (from `# Test it` to the end).

The Game Code

Now you can use `if` statements to see who won the game. Add this code to the bottom of the file:

```
# Compare choices
if cChoice == uChoice:
    print("It's a tie!")
elif uChoice == "R" and cChoice == "P":
    print("You picked rock, computer picked paper. You lose.")
elif uChoice == "P" and cChoice == "R":
    print("You picked paper, computer picked rock. You win.")
elif uChoice == "R" and cChoice == "S":
    print("You picked rock, computer picked scissors. You win.")
elif uChoice == "S" and cChoice == "R":
    print("You picked scissors, computer picked rock. You lose.")
```

```
elif uChoice == "P" and cChoice == "S":
    print("You picked paper, computer picked scissors. You lose.")
elif uChoice == "S" and cChoice == "P":
    print("You picked scissors, computer picked paper. You win.")
else:
    print("Not very good at listening to instructions. Huh?")
```

Save the code and run it. Each time you play, you make a choice that will be compared to the computer's choice, and the display will tell you who won or if there is a tie.

The code should make sense to you, but let's review it a bit.

The first `if` statement checks to see if the user's choice (variable `uChoice`) and the computer's choice (`cChoice`) are the same. If yes, then it's a tie.

Then come six `elif` statements that each check every possible combination of choices. Notice that this time, we used `and` in the condition, not `or`, because each `elif` has to test for both choices matching.

And finally, there is an `else` at the bottom. This will only ever get reached if none of the `if` or `elif` tests are `True`. The only way that could happen is if the user didn't enter `R`, `P`, or `S`, so the message reflects that.

And that's the game!

Users Never Follow Instructions

Our code asked the user to enter R, P, or S, and we added an `else` to our `if` that would only ever get executed if the user entered something other than R, P, or S.

This is generally a good idea. Users tend to be lousy at following directions. You, the coder, should always assume that your users won't follow instructions, expect that, and write code that anticipates and handles the situation. That way, your code won't break due to user error.

One Last Tweak

The game is done. Each time you play you have equal chances of winning, losing, or tying. Well...

Look around, make sure no one is watching for this part. Seriously. We're about to go all super-villain on the code. Ready? Ok. As the coder, you have complete control over the app, and, not that we'd ever condone such behavior, but you can use that control to give yourself an edge.

Let's start by personalizing the game. Add this code after the `import` line, before the computer's choice:

```
# Ask the user for their name
name=input("What is your name?: ")
```

Now update the line before the input to personalize it, like this:

```
print("Hello", name, "let's play Rock, Paper, or Scissors")
```

Now when you run the game, it asks the user for their name and greets them.

So nice and friendly to personalize the game. Or is it?

Now that the code knows who the user is, it can <ahem> *adjust* the computer's choice based on what the user entered. ;-)

Add this code after the user `input()` lines and before `# Compare choices` (and you'll want to use your name there, not mine):

```
# TOP SECRET CODE
if name == "Ben":
    if uChoice == "R":
        cChoice = "S"
    elif uChoice == "P":
        cChoice = "R"
    elif uChoice == "S":
        cChoice = "P"
```

Save the code and run it. Now the odds are firmly stacked in your favor. If you play (your name is entered) you'll win every time. Everyone else? They get the same one-out-of-three odds.

So, what does the code we added actually do? It starts with an `if` statement that checks to see who you are. If your name was entered (that's what gets stored in the variable `name`), Python runs the code that is indented. If not, it skips all of the indented code.

The indented code is interesting. It is another `if` statement, but this one is indented so that it is inside of the first one. It's an `if` statement inside of an `if` statement, and coders call this a *nested if statement*. The `if` and `elif` statements look to see what the user entered (`uChoice`) and then ... well, let's call it a tweak, right? ... it tweaks the computer choice (`cChoice`) so that the computer will always lose, and you'll always win. The program still picks a random choice, we just overwrote it with one that helps you win.

Try this code with family or friends. They'll be amazed at your luck.

> NEW TERM
>
> **Nested** When an `if` statement is inside of another `if` statement, we call it *nested* (kind of like Russian Nesting Dolls). In future chapters, you'll see other commands that can be nested.

CHALLENGE 5.1

You wouldn't want someone else with the same name getting the same advantage. How could you modify this code to make it a little more private? You could require the name to be typed a specific way (all lowercase maybe), or have a space or two at the end. Come up with an option and modify the `if` statement to check for it.

Summary

`if` statements are really important, and you are unlikely to write any code ever that does not use them. And so in this chapter we looked at lots of examples of using `if` statements with different tests and conditions. Which brings us to our next topic, loops.

CHAPTER 6

Secret Codes

Now that you have mastered `if` statements, there is only one major topic left to learn. And so in this chapter we're going to start to explore loops.

Lists

Loops are super important. Different types of loops, and how to properly use them, is the focus of the next few chapters.

But, before we look at loops, let's take a few moments to revisit a special type of variable, the list. We briefly showed you lists already. Back in Chapter 3 you used this code:

```
choices=["Heads","Tails"]
```

As we explained then, variables usually store a single value. Lists are a special type of variable that can store lots of values (as well as 0 values).

The code above is from Chapter 3, and it creates a list named `choices` that has two items in it: the string `Heads` and the string `Tails`.

Creating Lists

So, how do you create a list in Python? Well, as you have already seen, you can simply create a variable to create a list. What makes it a list? If the values you store in the variable are enclosed with `[` and `]` (square brackets), then you've created a list.

So this line of code will create an empty list:

```
animals=[]
```

`animals` is a variable that is a list, but it is empty.

This line of code creates a list with five items in it:

```
animals=["ant","bat","cat","dog","eel"]
```

Lists Can Contain All Sorts of Things

The list you created in Chapter 3 was a list of strings. And to keep things simple, the examples we'll use here will all be lists of strings. But it is worth noting that lists in Python are powerful and flexible. They can store all sorts of things—numbers, dates, even lists. (Yep, you can create a list of lists, and we'll do that in Part II of this book.)

List items must all be enclosed within the square brackets, and they must be separated by commas.

Let's give this a try. Create a file named `List1.py` and type this code:

```
# Create a list
animals=[]
# How many items in it?
print(len(animals), "animals in list")
```

Save and run the code. You'll see the text `0 animals in list` displayed in the Terminal window.

What does the code do? `animals=[]` creates an empty list. The `print()` statement displays how many items are in the list. To do this, it uses the `len()` function. `len()` returns the length of whatever item is passed to it, like the number of items in a list. So `len(animals)` returns the number of items in the list `animals`. Because the list is empty, it returns `0`.

Update your code to look like this (you can use your own list of animals, it doesn't have to be ours):

```
# Create a list
animals=["ant","bear","cat","dog","elephant"]
# How many items in it?
print(len(animals), "animals in list")
```

Save and run this updated code. The output will tell you that the list contains five animals.

The `len()` Function

Here we used `len()` to find out how many items were in a list. But `len()` is not limited to lists. It can return the lengths of other things, too. One common use of `len()` is to get the lengths of strings. For example, `len("hello")` will return 5.

`len()` Versus Index Values

Don't confuse the value returned by `len()` with an index value. As you will recall, Python starts counting at 0, so a list with five elements will have items with indexes from `0` through 4. But `len()` will return 5.

Initializing Lists

Like all data types in Python, lists are actually a class named—you guessed it—`list`. When you use code like this:

```
animals=[]
```

internally Python is creating a list and initializing it with no values. It does this by using a method named `init()`. This means you can do the same thing yourself. The line of code that creates the empty list could be written like this:

```
animals=list()
```

Both of these lines of code do exactly the same thing.

Accessing List Items

Lists are designed to store, well, lists, like our list of animals. For a list to be useful, you need to be able to access the items stored in it. To do this, you once again use square brackets, specifying the item number you want.

Let's try that. Create file `List2.py`. Here's the code:

```
# Create a list
animals = ["ant","bat","cat","dog","eel"]
# Display a list item
print(animals[1])
```

Save and run the code. What animal gets displayed? The position of an item in a list is called an *index*. In the `print()` function, we specified the index `1`, which is `bat`. Why? Because, as you know, Python always starts counting at `0`, so `ant` is in position `0`, and `bat` is in position `1`.

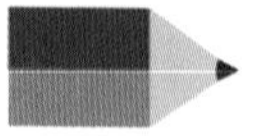

NEW TERM

Index The position of an item (within a list, for example) is its *index*.

Some Lesser-Used Indexes

If you want to return a series of items from a list, you can provide the start and end values for a range, separated by a colon (the : character). Look at this example:

```
print(animals[2:4])
```

This will print cat, which is index 2 (as Python starts counting at 0), and dog, which is at index 3. As usual, the end range number is not included, 2:4 means start at 2 and stop before 4.

If you want to count from the end of a list, you can use a - (the minus sign), like this:

```
print(animals[-1])
```

What will this display? -1 means the last item in the list, -2 is the second-to-last item, and so on. Therefore, this code will display eel.

Try updating and running the code with different index values. Then try using an index that is too high (like 5 if you are using the same example). Python won't like that, it will tell you that list index out of range, which means the index you provided isn't valid.

Changing List Items

You've seen that you can refer to specific items in a list by their index. We used this to get an item from the list, but the same syntax can be used to update an item in the list.

Create a file named List3.py. Here is the code:

```
# Create a list
animals = ["ant","bat","cat","dog","eel"]
# Display the list
print(animals)
# Update item 2
animals[2] = "cow"
# Display the list
print(animals)
```

Save and run the code. It will display a list of animals and then display the list again but with `cat` replaced by `cow`. This line of code:

```
animals[2] = "cow"
```

saves `cow` into the `animals` list in the third spot (once again, starting from `0`, so that `2` is the third item). It does not add an item but overwrites the existing value. Bye bye, `cat`; hello, `cow`!

Adding and Removing Items

All of the lists we've used so far were created and initialized with a set of values. But what if you need to add or remove values on-the-fly?

Let's look at adding an item first. This is the code for `List4.py`:

```
# Create a list
animals = ["ant","bat","cat","dog","eel"]
# How big is the list?
print(len(animals), "animals in list")
# Add an item
animals.append("fox")
# Now how big is the list?
print(len(animals), "animals in list")
```

Save and run the code. It will report five animals in the list and then six animals in the list.

Why? The `animals` list does indeed start with five animals, and so the `len()` in the `print()` statements returns `5`.

But then comes this line:

```
animals.append("fox")
```

The `append()` function adds an item to the end of the list. So the next `print()` statement says there are six animals as that is what `len()` will return.

Adding a List to a List

If you want to append multiple items to a list, you can call the append( ) function multiple times. Or you can use `extend()` to add a list to a list, like this:

```
list2=["goat","hippopotamus","iguana"]
animals.extend(list2)
```

This code creates a second list (called `list2`) and then appends all of the items in `list2` to the end of `animals` by using the `extend()` function.

You'll often find more than one way to accomplish a task, and you, as the coder, get to pick which option works best for you.

How do you remove an item from a list? There are two functions that can do that. If you know the exact index you want to remove, you can use the `pop()` function, like this:

```
animals.pop(5)
```

If you want to remove an item by its value, you can do this:

```
animals.remove("fox")
```

Finding Items

What if you want to check if a value is in a list? There are a couple of ways to do this.

If you just wanted to know if the list contains a value and don't care about exactly where in the list it is, then you can use a simple `if` statement.

Create the file `List5.py` with this code:

```
# Create a list
animals = ["ant","bat","cat","dog","eel","fox"]
# Is "goat" in the list?
if "goat" in animals:
    # Yes it is
    print("Yes, goat is in the list.")
```

```
else:
    # No it isn't
    print("Nope, no goat, sorry.")
```

Save and run the file. The text `Nope, no goat, sorry.` will be displayed. Add `"goat"` to the animals list (on line 2) and then run the code again, this time it'll display `Yes, goat is in the list.`

You saw lots of `if` statements in the previous chapters. Here the `if` uses an `in` clause, which, exactly as its name suggests, returns `True` if the value on the left can be found anywhere in the list and `False` otherwise.

If you want to know exactly where in the list an item is, you can use the `index()` function. Update the code to look like this (the only change is on line 6, in the first `print()` statement):

```
# Create a list
animals = ["ant","bat","cat","dog","eel","fox"]
# Is "goat" in the list?
if "goat" in animals:
    # Yes it is
    print("Yes, goat is item", animals.index("goat"))
else:
    # No it isn't
    print("Nope, no goat, sorry.")
```

Save and run the code. If there is no `goat` in `animals`, it'll behave exactly as it did before. But if there is a `goat` in `animals`, the display will tell you where in the list it is because `animals.index("goat")` returns the index of `goat`.

Sorting

Lists don't have any specific order. They store and display items however they were added.

All of the lists we used in this chapter were alphabetically sorted. They didn't have to be. We did that because it makes it easier for you to read and write the code.

But what if you actually do want the list in order? Imagine you have code like this:

```
# Create a list
animals = ["iguana","dog","bat","eel","goat","ant","cat"]
```

This list is definitely not in alphabetical order. What if it needed to be?

Now, granted, this isn't a great example because you could have just typed the animals in alphabetical order, right? True. But what if the list was not *hardcoded* and the user was typing animals, and then you needed to sort the list when they were done?

NEW TERM

Hard Coding When values (numbers, text, dates, all sorts of stuff) are typed into the actual code, we say that they are *hard coded*. And, as a rule, hard coding anything is bad.

Create file `List6.py`; here's the code (feel free to add more animals than we've done here; the more, the better):

```
# Create a list
animals = ["iguana","dog","bat","eel","goat","ant","cat"]
# Display the list
print(animals)
# Sort the list
animals.sort()
# Display the list
print(animals)
```

Save and run the code. You'll see the complete list of animals displayed twice: first in the order in which they were put into the list and then alphabetically.

The magic in the code is this line:

```
animals.sort()
```

`sort()` is a function that does just that, it sorts the list. By default, it sorts alphabetically, but you can also make it sort in reverse order and more if needed.

Fun stuff, huh? Ok, so what does this all have to do with loops?

You Can Only Sort the Same Type

You can sort lists of strings, as you have seen. And you can sort a list of numbers like this:

```
[98,1,65,43,1]
```

But you can't sort a list with mixed data types. For example, if you try to sort this:

```
[98,"car",1,65,"plane",43,1,"boat"]
```

Python will have no idea how to sort that, and will therefore display an error message.

List Functions Change the Actual List

Did you notice something interesting and different about the list functions? They don't behave exactly like the functions we used previously. Why? Look at this code:

```
name="Shmuel"
name.upper()
```

What does this code do? It creates a variable called `name` and then creates an uppercase version of it. Right? Yes, but `upper()` returns an uppercase copy of `name` and doesn't actually change `name`. You can test this for yourself. Try the above code and then `print(name)`, and you'll see that `name` is not converted. If you really do want to convert `name` to uppercase, you need to save whatever `upper()` returns into `name`, overwriting it, like this:

```
name="Shmuel"
name=name.upper()
```

The list functions don't work this way. For example, `animals.append()` actually adds a value to `animals`.

This is an important difference to remember.

Other Goodies

As you saw before, `len()` will tell you how many items are in a list. If you want to know how many specific items there are, you can use the `count()` function. For example, to find out how many items are equal to cow, you can use `animals.count("cow")`, which will tell you how many items are equal to `cow`.

If you need to make a copy of a list, you can use `copy()`. And to insert an item into the middle of a list (moving all the following items down one place), you can use `insert()`.

We'll see examples of these functions in future chapters.

Loop-de-Loop

Thus far, you have learned that Python executes code line by line. It starts at the top of a file, ignores comments, and processes each line in order. In Chapter 4 we introduced `if` statements, which effectively allow lines of code to be included or excluded in the processing.

But what if you want to repeat a block of code over and over? Perhaps you are writing a game, and you need to allow movements over and over until an obstacle is reached. Or maybe your users can take selfies and send messages over and over until a chat session is closed. Or perhaps it's something as simple as a calculator app that lets users enter numbers over and over until they hit the Calculate button.

All of these examples have one thing in common: They allow the same functionality to be used over and over until the process has completed.

Coding these actions requires the use of loops, and Python supports two types of loops:

- You can loop through a defined set of options. This might be looping from 1 to 10, or looping through a set of uploaded images, or looping through the lines of a file you are reading. In this type of loop, the number of iterations (that means how many times the loop loops) is finite. You are looping through a set of options and the loop ends once the last option has been reached. We'll focus on this type of loop in this chapter.

- You can also loop until a condition changes. For example, allowing a user to move in a game until their character dies, the loop repeats so long as a condition (character is still alive) is `True`, and ends when the condition is not (bye bye, character). Or allowing a user to take selfies until they hit Send, the loop allows the camera to be used and pictures to be taken so long as the condition (user has not clicked Send yet) is `True`; as soon as they click Send, the condition becomes `False`, and the loop ends. In this type of loop, the number of iterations is not known; the loop just keeps going and going and going until the condition changes. We'll look at this type of loop in the next chapter.

Looping Through Items

Let's start with the simplest of loops, looping through a list of items:

```
animals=["ant","bat","cat","dog","eel"]
```

You know what this is: It's a list called `animals` containing five items in it.

Earlier in this chapter, we saw how to access individual list items. But what if you want to loop through the list so as to print each one individually? Tada! Loops to the rescue!

Create a new file named `Loop1.py` and type the following:

```
# List of animals
animals=["ant","bat","cat","dog","eel"]

# Loop through the list
for animal in animals:
    # Display one per loop iteration
    print(animal)
```

Save and run this code. You should see output like this:

```
ant
bat
cat
dog
eel
```

You know what the first line of code does, so let's look at the loop code. This line:

```
for animal in animals:
```

tells Python to loop through `animals` and, in each iteration, to put the next item in a variable named `animal`. Note that there are now two variables used here: `animal` and `animals`. `animals` is the list we created, but what is `animal`? We didn't explicitly create the `animal` variable; the `for` loop code did that for us, and the loop changes the value of `animal` automatically on each iteration. We told the `for` loop what to name the variable by specifying `for animal`. (We could have named the variable anything, but `animal` seemed like a good choice for a variable that holds one animal from a list of animals.)

> **NEW TERM**
>
> **Iteration** Each cycle of a loop is called an *iteration*. You may also hear coders say *the code iterates*, which means it loops.

Just like `if` statements, loops end with a colon (the `:` character), and then whatever is indented beneath the loop is what gets called once per iteration.

So, in our example, how many times does the `print()` statements get called? Five—because there are five items in the list `animals`. Try adding an item or a few, and run the code again. The indented code will always be called once per item in the list.

And just like with `if` statements, you need to be careful with indentation. Mess it up, and the loop won't work as intended. For example, if the loop code looked like this:

```
# Loop through the list
for animal in animals:
    # Display one per loop iteration
    print("Here is the next animal:")
print(animal)
```

the output would look like this:

```
Here is the next animal:
Here is the next animal:
Here is the next animal:
Here is the next animal:
Here is the next animal:
eel
```

Why? The indented `print()` statement will be called once per iteration, so five times. But the last `print()` statement is not indented (coders will say that it is *outside of the loop*), so it isn't processed until loop processing has completed. Therefore, that last `print()` gets called only once, and the variable `animal` then will contain the last value that was put in it (the final item in the list).

Minimum List Size

What is the least number of loop iterations when using a list? The answer is 0. If the list is empty, then the indented code will never be called at all.

Why would you ever want an empty list? You'll see an example of this in a future chapter.

Looping Through Numbers

Next let's look at looping through numbers. This is similar to the list loop we just saw, but instead of looping through a list we specify a set of numbers and loop through them.

Create the file `Loop2.py`. Here is the code:

```
# Loop from 1 to 10
for i in range(1, 11):
    # Display i in each loop iteration
    print(i)
```

Save and run the code, and you'll see numbers `1` through `10` displayed, one per line, in the Terminal window.

`range()` specifies the range of numbers, and just like `randrange()` in Chapter 3, the end number is not included, so `range(1, 11)` means start at 1 and stop before you reach `11`.

`for i` creates a variable named `i`, and inside the loop, `i` contains the next item in the range. On the first iteration `i` will be `1`, then `2`, then `3`, and so on.

Try changing the range values and then run your code. Try that a few times.

CHALLENGE 6.1

`range()` takes an optional third argument—a step. If you specify `range(1, 11, 2)`, the loop counter will increase by `2` each time, so the loop will run 5 times instead of 10 (for `1`, `3`, `5`, `7`, and `9`). Try to create a loop that displays the numbers `10`, `20`, `30`, all the way to `100`.

Nested Loops

Now let's make things more interesting. At the end of Chapter 4 we showed you a nested `if` statement, which is an `if` statement inside of another `if` statement. You can do the same with loops.

Let's try an example that will bring back fond memories of your earliest years in school. Remember studying your multiplication tables? Fun, right? It might have taken you a while to memorize all the way to 12 x 12, but Python can do that for you in just three lines of code!

Nesting and Nesting and...

You can nest loops within loops, `if` statements with `if` statements, loops within `if` statements, `if` statements within loops, and you can nest within nests within nests. However, at some point nesting too deeply makes the code really hard to read and maintain.

Create a file named `Loop3.py` and type this code:

```
# Loop from 1 to 12
for i in range(1, 13):
    # Loop from 1 to 12 within each iteration of the outer loop
    for j in range(1, 13):
        # Print both loop values and multiply them
        print(i, "x", j, "=", i*j)
```

Save and run the code. You'll see 144 lines of output fly by, starting with `1 x 1 = 1` all the way to `12 x 12 = 144`.

Ok, so how does this code work? We have two loops here, so to keep things clear, let's call them *outer loop* and *inner loop*.

The outer loop uses `range(1, 13)`, so everything indented beneath it gets called `12` times, and each time, variable `i` will contain the current outer loop iteration number (first `1`, then `2`, and so on).

The inner loop also uses `range(1, 13)`, and so everything indented beneath it also gets called `12` times, and each time, variable `j` will contain the current inner loop iteration number.

So how many times does that `print()` statement get called? The outer loop makes the inner loop execute 12 times. And each time the inner loop executes, it executes the `print()` statement 12 times. So `print()` gets executed 144 (12 times 12) times in total.

The `print()` statement itself is pretty simple:

```
print(i, "x", j, "=", i*j)
```

The first time this runs, `i` will be `1`, and `j` will be `1`, so this is effectively:

```
print(1, "x", 1, "=", 1*1)
```

`print()` does the math on-the-fly and will display `1 x 1 = 1`.

The next time around, `i` will be `1`, and `j` will be `2`, so the output will be `1 x 2 = 2`. This will continue until `j` is `12` and the displayed text is `1 x 12 = 12`.

Then the inner loop will have finished, and the outer loop will restart the inner loop a second time; this time, `i` will be `2`. So on the next iteration, it will display `2 x 1 = 1` and so on, all the way until `i` is `12` and `j` is `12` and the output is `12 x 12 = 144`.

And all in just three lines of code. (Yes, we know there are six lines above, but three of them are comments. Python ignores them, so we can, too!)

Cracking the Code

Now that you know how to use loops, let's create programs to encrypt and decrypt text. Yes, we'll create two programs. The first will ask the user for some text and will display an encrypted version of that text. The other will ask the user for encrypted text and will decrypt it and display the original text. And so long as the same secret key (more on that in a moment) is used for encryption and decryption, all will work well.

So, if you receive this text:

```
Fphjsp#jw!hxrm%
```

you could decrypt it and it'll say...um, nope, can't tell you, sorry! You'll find out soon....

Ok, a warning. The following code may look complicated. But don't panic: It is using stuff you've already learned. Ready?

Encoding Versus Encryption

Technically, what we're doing here isn't really encryption. Real encryption code is a bit too complex for what we need here, so we're using a process called *encoding*, which replaces characters in text with secret characters. And we're going to use a key to make it a little harder to decode.

If you want to perform real encryption with Python, that's very doable, and there are lots of greater libraries that can help you do it.

Encrypting Characters

Replacing characters with their encrypted version requires doing a little math. Math, you say? Letters aren't numbers, so how can you do math on them?

Well, as it so happens, inside of your computer letters are indeed numbers. Every single letter and character has an internal number. You don't usually care about these; to us, letter `A` is just `A`, `b` is just `b`, and `3` is just `3`. But inside of your computer, the letter displayed as `A` is character number `65`, `b` is `98`, and the character for number `3` is `51`. Every single character has its own number; so `a` and `A` have different numbers because they are different characters.

Yep, this sounds odd, but just accept it for now. Every character has a number (called an ASCII Character Code) that can be used to refer to it.

> **TIP**
>
> **Use Test Files** Every coder has dozens of test files (usually named `test42.py`, or something like that). Sometimes coders have whole test folders (yep, often named `test`). Test files are great places to tinker and try stuff out.

In Python you can get the ASCII code for any character by using the `ord()` function. Run this code. (You have `test` Python files, right? They are perfect for this):

```
print(ord('A'))
```

and it will display 65, the ASCII code for `A`. Change that `A` to a `B`, and it'll display `66`. And so on.

ASCII Character Codes

ASCII (pronounced "ASS-key") stands for American Standard Code for Information Interchange. It is a character encoding standard for electronic communication, and it predates the Internet and all modern devices.

As `ord()` returns a number, you can do math with it. Not that this next example is particularly useful, but this code:

```
print(ord('A') + 1)
```

will display `66`: `ord('A')` returns `65`, and the program adds `1` and you get `66`.

So how do you turn this number back into a character? The opposite of the `ord()` function is the `chr()` function. This code:

```
print(chr(65))
```

will display the letter `A`.

So, if you wanted to add `1` to `A` to get `B`, you could do this:

```
print(chr(ord('A')+1))
```

What does this do? It is easiest to read it from the inside working outward. `ord('A')` returns `65`, as you saw previously. Add `1` and the total is `66`. That sum, `66`, gets passed to `chr()`, which returns `B`.

We can use this technique to encrypt your text. To encrypt the text `HELLO`, we just need to know how much to add to (or subtract from) the ASCII value of each character. If we add `10`, then `HELLO` becomes encrypted as `ROVVY` (`H` becomes `R`, `E` becomes `O`, and so on). Subtract `10` from each letter in `ROVVY`, and you get the decrypted `HELLO`.

Modulus Math

In the example we just saw, `10` is the magic number—the encryption key. It is what we use to change each letter.

But it's not very safe to use a simple number like this for encryption. Users could try `1` and then `2` and then `3` and eventually guess your code. To make this safer, you'd want to use different keys.

For example, what if the key was `314159`? To encrypt `HELLO`, we'd use `3` for the `H`, `1` for the `E`, `4` for the first `L`, `1` for the second `L`, and `5` for the `O`. So `HELLO` becomes `KFPMT`. Guessing this is much harder because a different key is used for each letter.

Longer Keys Are Better

This type of encryption can be broken by looking for patterns and repeats. A short key will result in lots of repeats, and a longer key in fewer ones, so the longer your key, the harder it will be for your nemesis to decrypt your secret plans. You have been warned!

But what if your text is longer than the key? Say you were encrypting the text `Hello World`. The key has `6` digits in it, we need `11` digits (because the space value has an ASCII value, too). What to do?

The answer is reuse the key. If the key is 6 digits long, we use these 6 digits for the first 6 letters to be encrypted. And then we start over: For letter 7, we use the first digit in the key, for letter 8 the second, and keep reusing the key over and over as needed.

How do we figure out which digit to use? We use division and look at the remainder. For the 8th character (we need the second number from the key), we just divide the character index (8, as this is the 8th character) by the key length (6), and the remainder is 2. In Chapter 3 we introduced the modulus operator (`%`), which finds a remainder. It is used like this:

```
print(8%6)
```

Here `8` is divided by `6`, and the remainder is `2`.

Using modulus, we can always divide the character position (`8` for the 8th character, `42` for the 42nd, and so on) by the key length, and the remainder will point to a valid key digit to use.

Encryption Code

Ok, here's the code for file `Encrypt.py`:

```
# ASCII range of usable characters - anything out of this range
could throw errors
asciiMin = 32   # Represents the space character - " "
asciiMax = 126  # Represents the tilde character - "~"
```

```
# Secret key
key = 314159    # Top secret! This is the encryption key!
key = str(key)  # Convert to string so can access individual digits

# Get input message
message = input("Enter message to be encrypted: ")

# Initialize variable for encrypted message
messEncr = ""

# Loop through message
for index in range(0, len(message)):
    # Get the ASCII value for this character
    char = ord(message[index])
    # Is this character out of range?
    if char < asciiMin or char > asciiMax:
        # Yes, not safe to encrypt, leave as is
        messEncr += message[index]
    else:
        # Safe to encrypt this character
        # Encrypt and shift the value as per the key
        ascNum = ord(message[index]) + int(key[index % len(key)])
        # If shifted past range, cycle back to the beginning of the
range
        if ascNum > asciiMax:
            ascNum -= (asciiMax - asciiMin)
        # Convert to a character and add to output
        messEncr = messEncr + chr(ascNum)

# Display result
print("Encrypted message:", messEncr)
```

Save and run this code. It will ask you for a message to encrypt and will then display the encrypted message. It doesn't decrypt; we'll get to that next.

So how does this work?

Not all ASCII characters print well, so to be safe, you define the range of characters you want to use, like this:

```
asciiMin = 32   # Represents the space character - " "
asciiMax = 126  # Represents the tilde character - "~"
```

Next comes the key:

```
# Secret key
key = 314159     # Top secret! This is the encryption key!
key = str(key)   # Convert to string so can access individual digits
```

`key` is the numeric encryption key. This one has six digits, though yours can be longer or shorter. The key here (hee hee, bad pun, sorry) is that you must have the same key to encrypt and decrypt the text.

We need to use each digit in the key individually. Remember? That's how we can encrypt each character with a different key digit. To do this, we convert the key to a string, so `314159` becomes `"314159"` because getting characters from a string is super easy. It's much like getting them from a list. Remember those?

Next, the code asks for the text to be encrypted using an `input()` function. You're very familiar with this one.

Then this code is used:

```
messEncr = ""
```

This creates an empty string variable named `messEncr` (for *message encrypted*). The code is going to encrypt the text one character at a time, and as it does so, the encrypted character will be added to this variable.

`str()` and `int()`

`str()` is the opposite of the `int()` function you saw in Chapter 4. `int()` converts a string to a number, and `str()` converts numbers back to strings. We'll look at `int()` in more detail in Chapter 7.

Now we loop through message:

```
for index in range(0, len(message)):
```

Here we use a for loop that loops from 0 to the length of the text. How does the loop know how long the text is? Once again, we can use the len() function for that. If the text is 10 characters long, len() returns 10, so the range for the loop will be range(0, 10), meaning loop from 0 to 9, exactly what we need. Within each iteration, the variable index will contain the iteration number: 0 the first time, 1 the second, and so on.

The code indented under the for statement will be executed once per character to be encrypted. At the start of each loop, we need to get the ASCII value for the letter being processed, like this:

```
char = ord(message[index])
```

message[index] lets us access a single character. index is 0 on the first loop, so on the first iteration, message[index] will return the first character. On the next iteration, it will return the second. ord() gets the ASCII code for the number, and that code is saved to the variable char.

The next if statement checks to see if the ASCII code for this character is within the safe range. If not, we don't encode it. If yes, this code gets executed:

```
ascNum = char + int(key[index % len(key)])
```

This code does the actual encryption. index is the current character number (set by the for loop). index % len(key) divides the index by the length of the key, giving us a remainder, which is the key digit to use. That gets added to char (the current ASCII code), and the result is saved in ascNum. So if, for example, the loop is currently at index 9, and the key has six digits, index % len(key) will become 9 % 6, which returns 3 (the remainder), and index 3 of the key will be used.

The encoded character then gets appended to messEncr, like this:

```
messEncr = messEncr + chr(ascNum)
```

`chr(ascNum)` converts the newly calculated encoded character to a string, and that gets appended to `messEncr`. (Remember that adding strings concatenates them.)

As we mentioned previously, some ASCII characters don't print, and so we need to make sure to exclude these. This code checks to ensure that the encoded character is within the safe range, and if it isn't, it shifts to a safer value:

```
if ascNum > asciiMax:
    ascNum -= (asciiMax - asciiMin)
```

And finally, a `print()` is used to display the encrypted text.

That does it. Enter text, and the program will encrypt it using the digits in the secret key. If you send someone a message, they'd need the matching key to read it. You can use different keys for different people (that way they won't be able to read each other's messages).

Decryption Code

Great. But how do you decrypt the encrypted messages? The process is actually exactly the same. It's so similar, in fact, that you can use the same `Encrypt.py` file and just make a few changes.

> **TIP**
>
> **Use Save As** If you use the VS Code Save As option (in the File menu) to save `Encrypt.py` as `Decrypt.py`, you have two files that are identical. Try it!

Click on `Decrypt.py` and we'll make a few changes. First, change the `input()` so the prompt is correct:

```
message = input("Enter message to be decrypted: ")
```

Next, find the line that does the actual encryption, which looks like this:

```
ascNum = char + int(key[index % len(key)])
```

Recall that when we encrypt, we add a key digit. To decrypt, all we need to do is subtract the same digit. So, change the code to this:

```
ascNum = char - int(key[index % len(key)])
```

The `+` is changed to a `-`.

Next, look at the `if` statement right below the line you just edited. It checks to see that we haven't gone above the allowed range and subtracts the change, if needed. We need to reverse that so it looks like this:

```
if ascNum < asciiMin:
    ascNum += (asciiMax - asciiMin)
```

In the `if` statement, the `>` gets changed to a `<`, and in the assignment, the `-=` becomes `+=`. Now if the decoding process creates a number below the range, we can fix that.

Some of the comments will be wrong, best to fix those, too.

That's it! Now you can encrypt and decrypt messages, so long as both parties have the same key. And all made possible by some simple `for` loops.

Oh, using the key `314159`, were you able to decrypt the encrypted text we showed you earlier in this chapter?

CHALLENGE 6.2

As you have seen, `Encrypt.py` and `Decrypt.py` are almost identical. In truth, they should have been the same program. We just separated them to make the code a little simpler.

But, you can improve this. Create a program that both encrypts and decrypts. It will need to prompt the user for the action—something like this:

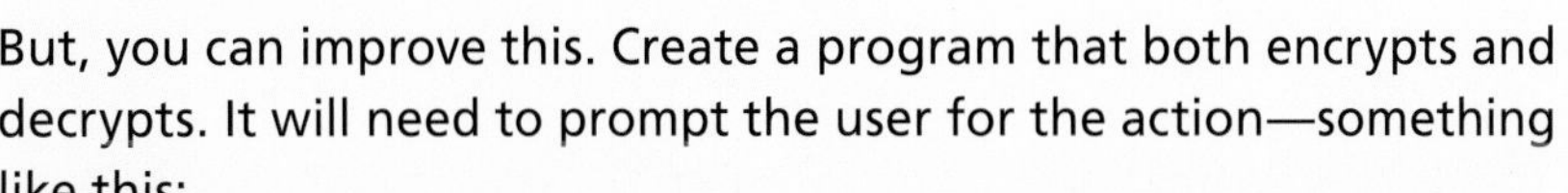

```
action = input("Encrypt or decrypt? Enter E or D: ")
```

Then, in your code, you can use `if` statements to select the encrypt or decrypt versions of the code, based on `action` being `E` or `D`.

Summary

In this chapter, you learned how to use `for` loops to loop over a known set of items. In the next chapter, we'll look at conditional loops (and how to use both loop types together).

CHAPTER 7

Guess the Number

In Chapter 6 we looked at `for` loops. In this chapter, we'll look at conditional loops and use one to build a Guess The Number game.

Conditional Loops

You now know how to use `for` loops. As a reminder, these are used to loop through a finite set of options.

Conditional loops loop based on a condition. They are the more powerful and flexible type of loops, and they also tend to be the one you'll use most.

Let's start with a simple (and useless) example. Create file `Loop4.py` and type the following:

```
# Get some input
userInput=input("Say something, say STOP to stop: ").upper().strip()

# Loop until the user says STOP
while userInput != "STOP":
    userInput=input("Say something, say STOP to stop: ").upper().
strip()
```

Save the file and run it. You'll be prompted to type some text in the Terminal window. Then you'll be prompted to do so again. And again. And you'll keep being prompted until you type **STOP**.

The first line of code is an `input()` much like you've seen already. And like we saw in Chapter 4, it uses `.upper().strip()` to convert the user input to uppercase and strip any extraneous whitespace.

Then comes this line:

```
while userInput != "STOP":
```

`while` creates a loop. But unlike `for` loops, `while` takes a condition (much like the conditions we passed to `if` statements in Chapter 4). This condition checks the `userInput` variable to make sure that it is not equal to `STOP` (`!=` means not equal and is the opposite of `==`).

Just like `if` and `for`, a `while` statement ends with a colon, and whatever is indented beneath it will get called over and over until the loop ends. Here the indented code again asks for input from the user.

And when will the `while` loop end? When the user types `STOP`. Then the `while` condition will be `False` (because `userInput` will no longer be not equal to `STOP`).

while Conditions

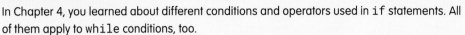

In Chapter 4, you learned about different conditions and operators used in `if` statements. All of them apply to `while` conditions, too.

So, question, what is the fewest number of times that the indented code inside of the `while` loop will run? The answer is 0. If the user types `STOP` right away in response to the first `input()`, the `while` condition will never be `True`—not even once—and the indented code will never be run.

TIP

if and while Here's another way to look at it. `if` statements and `while` statements are very similar in that they both take conditions, which, if `True`, execute the code indented below. The difference is that when the condition is `True`, the `if` statement executes its code once, as opposed to `while` statements which execute the indented code over and over (until the condition is no longer `True`).

We point this out because while this example works, it will make most professional coders cringe (or even puke). Why? Coders hate duplicated code, and here the two `input()` lines are completely and utterly identical. Why is that bad? Well, it's not that big of a deal here, but in bigger and more complex programs, the risk of them going out of sync is really high. At some point, you'll make a change to one and forget to change the other. That's asking for future trouble.

So let's rewrite this code with only one `input()` line. How can we do that? Like this:

```
# Initialize the input variable
userInput=""

# Loop until the user says STOP
while userInput != "STOP":
    userInput=input("Say something, say STOP to stop: ").upper().
strip()
```

Initialize All Variables

Coding best practices recommend that all variables be initialized with some default value. Strings can be empty, numbers can be set to 0, it's your choice. Doing so can prevent a situation where you expect variables to contain something that they don't.

Save and run the code. It should behave exactly as it did before.

So how does this work? The trick is forcing the `while loop` to always run at least once. The code starts by initializing (that is a fancy way of saying *start with an initial value*) the `userInput` variable to be an empty string (that's what `""` is). The truth is, we could have initialized `userInput` to anything other than `STOP`, but an empty string is nice and clean. By doing this, the `while` loop always runs at least once because the very first time `userInput` does not equal `STOP`, it equals empty. Much better!

NEW TERM

Initialize *Initialize* means put a default initial value into a variable.

Let's create another example combining your knowledge of lists with `while` loops. This is the code for file Loop5.py:

```
# Create the empty animals array
animals = []

# Variable for input
userInput = " "

# Give instructions to user
print("I can sort animals for you.")
print("Enter your animals, one at a time.")
print("When you are done just press Enter.")

# Loop until get an empty string
while userInput != "":
```

```
    # Get input
    userInput=input("Enter an animal, leave empty to end: ").strip()
    # Make sure it is not empty
    if len(userInput) > 0:
        # It's not empty, add it
        animals.append(userInput)

# Sort data
animals.sort()

# Display the list
print(animals)
```

Save and run the code. It will display welcome text and then prompt for an animal. Then it will prompt for another animal. And another. And it will keep doing this until you press **Enter** without typing any text. Then the program will display all of your animals in alphabetical order.

The code should be pretty self-explanatory. But we'll highlight a few lines that are of special interest.

The code starts with an empty `animals` list, created like this:

```
animals = []
```

Next we create and initialize the `userInput` variable:

```
userInput = " "
```

This time it is not initialized as an empty string (""). Rather, we put a space in it (" "). Why? You will recall that we initialize the variable to force the subsequent `while` loop to run. What does the `while` loop do?

Download the Code

As a reminder, if you don't want to type all the code, you can grab a copy from the book web page by using this QR code.

```
while userInput != "":
```

This while loop will keep looping until userInput is empty, as that is when we know that the user has finished typing the animals. If we had initialized userInput to "", then the while loop would never run—not even once—because the condition could never be True. By initializing userInput to a value other than the one the loop checks for, we can avoid this problem.

Then comes the very familiar input(). No explanation needed.

Then comes this code:

```
# Make sure it is not empty
if len(userInput) > 0:
    # It's not empty, add it
    animals.append(userInput)
```

We want to add anything the user types to animals by using the append() function. But we need to make sure to not add an empty input (which happens when the user just presses **Enter**). To eliminate empty strings, we use an if statement that checks the length of what the user entered by using the len() function. If the length is greater than 0, the user must have typed something, and it is added. If not, then nothing is added.

Next, the code sorts the list:

```
# Sort data
animals.sort()
```

And finally, the list is displayed.

Infinite Loops

You need to be careful when looping until a condition changes. If you don't write the code properly, you can end up in a situation where the condition never changes, and the code will run forever. This is called an *infinite loop*, and it's one of the mistakes that can cause a program to hang or crash. To borrow a phrase from a really close friend of ours, "With great power comes great responsibility."

CHALLENGE 7.1

Double challenge for you this time.

First, look at the final `print()` statement. It displays the sorted list, but the output doesn't look that good. So change that output to use a `for` loop printing the sorted animals one per line.

Second, make sure the user doesn't type an animal already in the list. How? Refer back to Chapter 6 if you need a reminder of how to check if an item is in a list. Then modify the `if` statement so that in addition to checking for the length of the input, it also checks to ensure that the item is not already in the list. Your condition will have two parts, and you'll want to use `and` to join them.

Game Time

Now that you know all about loops, let's create a number guessing game. The computer will think of a number (well, technically, it'll generate a random number), and then it'll ask the user to guess it. Each time the user guesses, the computer will let them know if they guessed correctly or if they are too high or too low. When they finally guess the number, the computer will tell them how many guesses it took.

The Basic Game

Create a new file named `NumGuess.py`. Here is the code:

```
# Guess the number between a specified range.
# User is told if the number guess is too high or too low.
# Game tells the user how many guesses were needed


# Imports
import random
```

```
# Define variables
userInput = ""  # This holds the user's input
userGuess = 0   # This holds the user's input as a number

# Generate random number
randNum = random.randrange(1, 101)

# Instructions for user
print("I am thinking of a number between 1 and 100")
print("Can you guess the number?")

# Loop until the user has guessed it
while randNum != userGuess:
    # Get user guess
    userInput=input("Your guess: ").strip()
    # Make sure the user typed a valid number
    if not userInput.isnumeric():
        # Input was not a number
        print(userInput, "is not a valid number!")
    else:
        # Input was a number, good to proceed
        # Convert the input text to a number
        userGuess=int(userInput)
        # Check the number
        if userGuess < randNum:
            print("Too low. Try again.")
        elif userGuess > randNum:
            print("Too high. Try again.")
        else:
            print("You got it!")

# Goodbye message
print("Thanks for playing!")
```

Save and run the program. You'll be prompted to guess a number between 1 and 100, and each time you guess, you'll be given feedback until you guess the right number.

There is a lot of code here, so let's look at it.

At the top is a comment block that explains the code. Then comes our `random` library.

Next comes this code:

```
# Define variables
userInput = ""  # This holds the user's input
userGuess = 0   # This holds the user's input as a number
```

This creates and initializes two variables: `userInput` will be used to contain whatever the user enters, and `userGuess` will contain the number they guess. Why do we need both? We'll come back to this one in a moment.

Next, the program generates a random number and stores it in `randNum`. Then come a couple of `print()` statements with instructions for the user. So far so good. This is all code you have seen before.

Then we have our loop, which is the main game code. It is what will run over and over until the user has guessed correctly. The `while` condition is simply defined like this:

```
# Loop until the user has guessed it
while randNum != userGuess:
```

This means that so long as `userGuess` and `randNum` don't match, the loop will keep looping. The game is not over until the numbers match.

We initialized `userGuess` to be `0` and `randNum` to be a number between `1` and `100`, so the while loop will always execute the code indented beneath it.

Comments Revisited
As you can see, comments in your code can be on the same line as the code itself. Python will process the code part of the line and ignore whatever comes after the # symbol.

Next comes the input() prompt, which you've seen before.

Once we have input from the user, we want to make sure they actually typed a number. Why is this important? Well, for starters, we should always give the user useful feedback, and if they were to enter something incorrectly, we should tell them so. But, more importantly, we need to be able to compare numbers later in the code, and the code will break if we compare numbers to strings.

So, we include the following:

```
# Make sure the user typed a valid number
if not userInput.isnumeric():
    # Input was not a number
    print(userInput, "is not a valid number!")
```

Remember those string class methods upper() and strip()? isnumeric() is another string method. It returns True if the string is all numbers and False if not.

And what is that not doing in there? if userInput.isnumric() would check to see if the string is a number, and the not turns that around and checks to see if userInput is NOT a number. if not userInput.isnumeric() checks to see if the user didn't enter a number, and the indented print() tells them so.

Then comes the else statement. Any code indented beneath else gets executed only if the user enters a valid number.

And then we have this code:

```
# Convert the input text to a number
userGuess=int(userInput)
```

What does this do? Remember when we briefly discussed data types back in Chapter 3? Back then, we explained that variables can have types. We also showed you that a string with a number (like "3") is not a numeric type, and it can't be really used for math calculations or operations.

This is a problem for us. input() always returns what users enter as strings. Even if the user types a number, userInput will be a string with that number in it. And we need a number.

not Negates

What does the following code do?

```
if userInput.isnumeric():
```

This code checks to see if isnumeric() returns True. It is actually shorthand for this:

```
if userInput.isnumeric() == True:
```

If you don't tell an if statement what you are comparing to, it'll assume that you are comparing to True.

not changes a condition to its exact opposite. Coders say that it *negates* the condition. So by adding not:

```
if not userInput.isnumeric():
```

the code checks to see that isnumeric() returns False.

That said, there is always more than one way to write a line of code. This code could have been written like this:

```
if userInput.isnumeric() == False:
```

Both versions do the exact same thing.

So what to do? We need to convert the string to a number.

You saw the int() function briefly in Chapter 4. As a reminder, int() turns a string data type into a numeric data type; you pass it a string as an argument, and it returns a number. Here the code userGuess=int(userInput) tells Python to look at the userInput string, get the number that is in it, convert it to a number, and save it to userGuess. This way, userInput remains a string—it does not change at all—and userGuess is the number that was in that string. So if userInput was "3", userGuess will be 3, which is exactly what we need.

By the way, using int() with a string that isn't actually a number would throw an ugly error. We avoided that by validating the input previously.

Next comes a set of `if` `elif` and `else` statements:

```
# Check the number
if userGuess < randNum:
    print("Too low. Try again.")
elif userGuess > randNum:
    print("Too high. Try again.")
else:
    print("You got it!")
```

The first statement checks to see if `userGuess` is less than the number we want. The second one checks to see if it is greater. As for the `else`, if the guess is neither greater nor less than the target number, then it must be right. Right? Right.

We know this is a lot of code, but it should all make sense to you (especially as most is code you've seen before).

Feel free to run the program a few times just to make sure it is working properly.

Putting It All Together

That works well. But we can make a few improvements.

First of all, we need a way to tell the user how many guesses they took.

Also, putting the range (`1` and `100`) in the code as we did is a really bad idea. Why? As we noted earlier, code should be written so that you don't inadvertently break things. If you needed to change the range to `10` and `50` or `1` and `1000`, you'd need to change multiple places. And you are going to make mistakes. What we did? That's hard coding, something we told you about in Chapter 6, and something coders try to avoid.

So, here's an updated version of the code:

```
# Guess the number between a specified range.
# User is told if the number guess is too high or too low.
# Game tells the user how many guesses were needed

# Imports
import random
```

```
# Define variables
guesses = 0      # To keep track of how many guesses
numMin = 1       # Start of number range
numMax = 100     # End of number range
userInput = ""   # This holds the user's input
userGuess = 0    # This holds the user's input as a number

# Generate random number
randNum = random.randrange(numMin, numMax+1)

# Instructions for user
print("I am thinking of a number between", numMin, "and", numMax)
print("Can you guess the number?")

# Loop until the user has guessed it
while randNum != userGuess:
    # Get user guess
    userInput=input("Your guess: ").strip()
    # Make sure the user typed a valid number
    if not userInput.isnumeric():
        # Input was not a number
        print(userInput, "is not a valid number!")
    else:
        # Input was a number, good to proceed
        # Increment guess counter
        guesses=guesses+1
        # Convert the input text to a number
        userGuess=int(userInput)
        # Check the number
        if userGuess < numMin or userGuess > numMax:
            print(userGuess, "is not between", numMin, "and",
numMax)
        elif userGuess < randNum:
            print("Too low. Try again.")
        elif userGuess > randNum:
            print("Too high. Try again.")
```

```
        else:
            print("You got it in", guesses, "tries")

# Goodbye message
print("Thanks for playing!")
```

Most of the code is the same, so we'll just highlight the changes.

At the top, we create three new variables:

```
guesses = 0      # To keep track of how many guesses
numMin = 1       # Start of number range
numMax = 100     # End of number range
```

The first line creates a variable that will keep count of how many `guesses` the user made. We initialize it to `0` for now, and we'll add `1` each time the user makes a guess.

The next two lines define two new variables, which are the range of numbers we want for the game: `numMin` is the minimum (the start of the range), and `numMax` is the maximum (the end of the range). If you want to change the game, you only need to change these numbers, and all the code below (generating the number, giving instructions) will all be correct.

How? Because the number generation code has been changed to this:

```
# Generate random number
randNum = random.randrange(numMin, numMax+1)
```

`numMin` sets the range start, and `numMax+1` sets the range end. You'll recall that `randrange()` does not include the end range number, so if `numMax` were `100`, the greatest randomly generated number would be `99`, not `100`. By adding `1` we make the range end `101`, and that way `100` is included.

The `print()` statements with instructions also use `numMin` and `numMax`; that way they always reflect the right instructions.

Inside the main loop is this code:

```
        # Increment guess counter
        guesses=guesses+1
```

Incrementing Variables

This code increases guesses by 1. It does this by overwriting the variable with the current value + 1:

```
guesses=guesses+1
```

Here is another way to do the same thing:

```
guesses+=1
```

The second example looks a little odd, we know. It's a shortcut that tells Python that guesses is to update itself by 1.

Both lines of code do the same thing.

And you can use this type of shortcut for more than addition. -=5 subtracts 5, *=3 multiplies by 3, you get the idea.

Some coders prefer the second format as it is shorter, it doesn't repeat the variable name, and there are fewer places for typos (as we said, coders hate duplication).

This increments (increases the value of) guesses by 1. If guesses was 0, then after this line of code, it will be 1. And then next time, it will be 2, and so on. This is how we keep track of how many guesses the user made.

We also added a new if statement that checks to see if the user entered a number outside of the range (greater than 100, for example):

```
if userGuess < numMin or userGuess > numMax:
    print(userGuess, "is not between", numMin, "and", numMax)
```

This checks to see if userGuess is too low (less than numMin) or too high (greater than numMax), and if it is, it gives the user instructions with the right numbers.

TIP

Don't Hard Code Values See how useful those variables are? This is exactly why we don't hard code values. We can set the variables once and don't have to change any other code in the game. It just works.

And finally, we updated the `You got it!` `print()` statement as follows:

```
print("You got it in", guesses, "tries")
```

`guesses` stores the number of guesses made, and `print()` displays that number.

CHALLENGE 7.2

This one is tricky, but you can do it. Can you provide more feedback? Instead of always displaying `Too low` or `Too high`, can you display `Too low` or `Too high` if they are close and `Much too high` and `Much too low` if they are way off? Think about it.

Summary

In this chapter we built on the prior chapter and learned about looping based on conditions. In the next two chapters we'll use all of the lessons you've learned thus far to build a more sophisticated app.

CHAPTER 8

Becoming a Coder

You've now learned the three most important programming concepts you'll ever need: variables, conditional processing, and loops. In this chapter (and the next two) we'll review them all, and focus on coding techniques and best practices while we plan a more sophisticated application. And in doing so, we'll help you transition from merely writing snippets of code to actually becoming a coder.

How Coders Code

You now know how to use variables, how to code decisions using `if` statements, and how to create looping code using `for` and `while`. You've learned a lot. And, truthfully, you've learned the most important coding concepts. Yes, all of them. If you stop here (don't, please!), you would have learned all you need to be able to write any program you want. That's not a joke. We mean it. It is possible to write just about any application you need using what you have already learned.

So what else is there to learn? Well, lots. In future chapters, we'll look at user-defined functions, variable scope, classes, dictionaries, additional libraries, and more. All of those concepts will help you write cleaner, better organized, reusable, and more efficient code. So you'll want to learn it all. But, honestly, they are all extras. The fundamentals, what you have learned thus far, that's what powers real coding.

So we are going to spend this chapter reviewing what we've learned so far by building a more complex and sophisticated program. This stuff is important, and the more you practice, the better.

As we noted back in Chapter 1, anyone can learn a programming language. What makes a really skilled coder is how they use that language. We want to help you start to think like a coder, and so we'll use the application we create here to introduce you to *how* coders work. And we'll start with two concepts specifically.

Have a Plan

The programs we've written thus far are all pretty simple. Even the Guess The Number game (which ended up at about 50 lines long) is a pretty simple program. Real programs often have thousands, even hundreds of thousands (or many millions) of lines of code.

Real Programs Can Be Huge

Minecraft has about 150,000 lines of code. The classic game *Doom* has 193,000 lines of code. Modern games like *Overwatch*, *Fortnite*, and *Call of Duty* typically have somewhere between 1,500,000 and 5,000,000 lines of code. The Android operating system (which powers most of the world's smartphones) is about 15,000,000 lines of code. Windows (which may be running on your computer) has about 50,000,000 lines of code. Yep, real programs can be huge!

Experience Design

There is a relatively new and exciting field called Experience Design. People who work as Experience Designers focus on the overall user experience when using an application. They think about the user journey (how users move around the app), flow between screens, and more. This is an important part of planning, too. After all, you'd not want to put time and effort into building an application only to find that no one uses it because the user experience is bad.

When writing smaller apps, it's tempting to just start: Open VS Code, write some code, and figure it out as you go. Right?

Wrong! You can get away with doing that for now, but it won't work as your apps grow in complexity.

Think of it this way: If you were building a house, you'd never start without a plan. Right? You'd need to know in advance how big the house is, what rooms it has, what they are used for, how they are connected, and so on.

Coding is kinda the same. You need a plan. You need to know what the app does, what the user expectations are, what your screens should look like, what the complete user experience is—all of that and more.

There is no right or wrong way to plan. Some developers open a document and write notes. Others map things out on a whiteboard. There are all sorts of apps that are used for planning features and requirements. Exactly how you plan is not that important. What *is* important is actually having a plan.

Think Small

Back to our house construction analogy. When you start building your dream house, you wouldn't obtain clay and make bricks from scratch. Nor would you obtain pieces of wood and start building doors and windows. And you'd definitely not create locks and light switches using individual pieces and components. Instead, you'd source and bring ready-to-use materials to the construction site and install them (perhaps modifying them if needed). Same for tiles, roof shingles, electrical wire, piping, appliances,... The final construction of a house is complex and hard work, but it is made simpler by using lots of ready-made, ready-to-use, proven, and trusted objects.

Again, coding is much the same. You need to start looking for the bits you can create in isolation (meaning outside of your main application).

Why? There are a few advantages:

- Testing your code when it is part of a huge app is really hard. Just running a program until you get to where your code snippet is can be time-consuming. And if there are dependencies (user input, menu selections, and so on), it's even harder. Professional coders try to write whole sections of code independently. This way, they can experiment, test, iterate, perfect, and do it all outside of the main application.

- This type of coding is also great for reuse. As you start to build smaller blocks of code, you'll find that they can be used in other programs, too. This saves time because you are not always starting from scratch. And it also saves time because it's always better to start with code that you know has already been used and tested.

- But most importantly, it is so much easier to solve lots of small problems and challenges than big giant scary ones.

And so that is where we are going to start: thinking small.

Game Components

In this chapter and the next, we are going to create a Hangman game. You know Hangman, right? It's usually played with pen and paper. Someone picks a word and draws marks indicating how many letters long the word is. Someone else guesses letters and tries to figure out the word. Every wrong guess builds part of the hangman's gallows. The game is over when the player correctly guesses the word or when there are too many wrong tries.

Most of the game is inputs and checking letters—stuff we've done before.

But there are a couple of parts of the game that are different and which should be carefully planned. Let's look at a few:

- Players need to guess one letter at a time. As we've seen, `input()` accepts text input from a user, but it doesn't limit text; users can type whatever they want. We'll need a way to handle the inevitable situation where users type too much text (more than a single letter).

- The game needs to remember user guesses so it can figure out what to display and whether the player has won or not. Lists (which we looked at in Chapter 6) are probably a really good way to handle the guesses. We should work out all of the steps we'll need in the final game.
- Speaking of lists...as you've seen, they don't display nicely by default. So we'll need to find a way to display user guesses properly.
- The trickiest challenge is the need to display masked words. What does that mean? Let's say the word is `apple`, and the guesses so far are `a` and `e`. The game needs to display something like `a___e` so that the player knows which letters are correct and how many letters are still to be guessed. We obviously need to hide the letters that haven't been guessed yet, and so we mask them. Here the mask character is an underscore, but it could be anything (`a***e` is a useful mask, too).

These are all pieces of functionality that our application needs; the game won't work without them. And they can (and should) be written and tested before they are ever introduced into the complete app.

Again, the idea is to solve these coding challenges in isolation. Experiment, try, code, unit test, tweak,...and then use the code later in the complete application.

> **NEW TERM**
> **Unit Testing** When professional coders write individual components, they usually write code to test these components, too. And if they were to update the components in the future they'd also update the test code. This test code is never part of any application that eventually uses the components. It is just there to test the component in isolation. Coders call this practice *unit testing*.

Restricting User Input

Let's start with the user input challenge. You've seen code like this before:

```
currGuess = input("Guess a letter: ")
```

This code prompts for input and saves the value to a variable, here named `currGuess` (for *current guess*).

The instruction asks for `a letter`, just one. But what if a user types more than one letter? `input()` won't limit or restrict input; it just accepts text. So, what do we do?

There are many ways to handle this. We could reject the input completely and tell the user to try again. Or we could use just the first character and ignore any extra ones. There are other options, too.

You, as the coder, get to decide how your program works. For this game, let's go with the option that accepts the first letter and ignores any additional letters. So, if the user types `HE`, we'll accept the `H` and ignore the `E`.

How do we do this?

Create a test file and let's experiment with some code. We'll start with a simple `input()`:

```
# Get a guess
currGuess = input("Guess a letter: ").strip().lower()

# Display it
print(currGuess)
```

Test the code. You will be prompted to enter text, which will then be displayed. Simple enough.

This `input()` uses two functions. The `strip()` function, which you used in Chapter 5, removes any extraneous whitespace character. `lower()` converts the input to lowercase (because having all text in the same case will make the code simpler).

So far, so good. But how do we make sure input is limited to a single character? To do this, we need to know exactly how many characters the user typed, and for that we can use the `len()` function. In Chapter 6, we used `len()` to count the number of items in a list. But, as noted there, you can also use `len()` to obtain the length of a string. That will do exactly what we need.

This if statement checks to see if a string is longer than 1 character in length:

```
if len(currGuess) > 1:
```

Easy enough. But then what? If the if statement is True, how do we handle that situation?

In Chapter 6, you saw that you can use [ ] notation to access a specific item in a list by using its index. For example, this next line of code returns the third item in a list named animals (counting starts at 0, as you know):

```
animals[2]
```

We can use the same syntax with strings. Look at this code:

```
text="Coding"
text[2]
```

This creates a variable named text containing the string "Coding". So what does text[2] return? The third letter in the string—the letter d.

This means that [0] will give us the first character of a string. Perfect! We can use this syntax to restrict input. Here is the updated code:

```
# Get a guess
currGuess = input("Guess a letter: ").strip().lower()

# Make sure it's just one character
if len(currGuess) > 1:
    currGuess = currGuess[0]

# Display it
print(currGuess)
```

Save and test the code.

The if statement checks to see if currGuess is longer than it should be. If it is, currGuess (the whole string, as typed by the user) gets updated with currGuess[0] (just the first character). By the time print() is executed, `currGuess` will contain a single lowercase character, which is exactly what we need.

Great. We'll use this snippet in the final game.

Storing User Guesses

Users make guesses while they play. The game needs to remember those guesses, so that on each turn, it can display guesses, update the mask, and check to see if the user has won.

What is a good way to store a gradually increasing set of items? Lists (which we looked at in detail in Chapter 6) are perfect for this. We'd need to start with an empty list, like this:

```
guessedLetters = [] # List to store guesses
```

Then we can use `append()` to add letters as they are guessed.

To test this code in isolation, we can fake the inputs. Create a test program to do just that. Create an empty list, prompt for some letters, add each letter to the list, and then display the result. You can hard code the letters to be added, like this:

```
guessedLetters.append("a")
guessedLetters.append("e")
guessedLetters.append("i")
guessedLetters.append("o")
guessedLetters.append("u")
```

Or you can create a few `input()` statements to ask for letters. Or you can loop to prompt for a few letters, like this:

```
for i in range (0, 5):
    # Get a guess
    currGuess = input("Guess a letter: ").strip().lower()
    # Append to list
    guessedLetters.append(currGuess)
```

Lots of Ways to Test

As you can see, there are lots of ways to test code. You can hard code values, manually add `input()` statements, create temporary loops to simulate user input, and more. How you test is up to you. The key is to actually test, and the more ways the better.

Here the code loops five times, each time prompting for a letter and then appending it to `guessedLetters`.

How do you know that letters are being properly added to the list? You can use a `print()`. And while we are at it, let's sort the list (using `sort()`, as you saw in Chapter 6) as we'll need to do that in the finished game, too. Here is the final code:

```
guessedLetters = [] # List to store guesses

for i in range (0, 5):
    # Get a guess
    currGuess = input("Guess a letter: ").strip().lower()
    # Append to list
    guessedLetters.append(currGuess)

# Sort the list
guessedLetters.sort()

# Display it
print(guessedLetters)
```

Save and test the code. Once you have verified that it works, you'll know that it is ready to use in the complete app.

Displaying Lists

Which brings us to displaying lists. If you added `A`, `E`, `I`, `O`, and `U` in your test and then printed the list, your output would look like this:

```
['a', 'e', 'i', 'o', 'u']
```

This is the correct list, but it is not very pretty looking. So, how can we improve this?

In Chapter 6, you learned how to loop through lists, so you could print your list like this:

```
# Display it
for letter in guessedLetters:
    print(letter)
```

This will work. The output won't have quotes and commas and parentheses in it. Instead, each letter will be displayed on its own line (as each one is displayed by its own `print()` as the loop iterates). But also not quite what we want.

To display all the letters on one line, we'll want to use a single `print()` statement for all the letters. And that brings us back to concatenation, which we first looked at in Chapter 3. As you will recall, you can add text to a string like this:

```
youTried=""
youTried += letter
```

`youTried` will display all the letters the user has tried. It starts off as an empty string. `youTried += letter` will add whatever is stored in the variable `letter` to `youTried`.

Which means we can do something like this:

```
guessedLetters = [] # List to store guesses

if len(guessedLetters) > 0:
    # There are, start with an empty string
    youTried=""
    # Add each guessed letter
    for letter in guessedLetters:
        youTried += letter
    # Display them
    print("You tried:", youTried)
```

Save and run this test code. It will display nothing. Why? Because `guessedLetters` is empty, and the `if` statement there checks to see if `len(guessedLetters)` is greater than `0` (meaning that the user has actually made some guesses).

Add some letters to guessedLetters. You can do this in the initialization, or use append()—your choice. Make sure that print() displays a single line of text, like this:

```
aeiou
```

When you know that the code is working we'll move on to the next component.

Masking Characters

This last component is a bit trickier than the ones you've already tackled. We explained the masking requirement earlier in this chapter. What does it take to mask letters in a word? To achieve this, we need three things:

- The word being used
- A list of all the letters that have been guessed so far
- The character you want to use for the mask

In the actual game, you'd have code that picks a random game word. (You know how to do that.) And the list of guessed letters will be provided by the user with each input().

To write our masking code independent of the game, we'll once again fake it, pretending that we have that information.

Create a test file and type this code:

```
gameWord = "apocalypse"
guessedLetters = ['a','e']
maskChar = "_"
```

This code simply creates three variables. gameWord is hard coded (which by now you know should never be done...except in testing). guessedLetters is a list that contains two items because right now we are pretending that the user guessed an a and an e (starting with vowels is very common when playing Hangman). maskChar is the character we'll use for our mask. Again, in the real app, these would be created differently, but for writing and testing our code, these will suffice.

Now add this to your code:

```
# Start with an empty string
displayWord = ""
# Loop through word
for letter in gameWord:
    # Has this letter been guessed?
    if letter in guessedLetters:
        # This one has been guessed so add it
        displayWord + letter
    else:
        # This one has not been guessed so mask it
        displayWord + maskChar

# Display results word
print("Original word:", gameWord)
print("Masked word:  ", displayWord)
```

This code creates a variable named `displayWord`, which will hold the masked word. It then uses a `for` loop like the one we saw in Chapter 6:

```
for letter in gameWord:
```

This code loops through `gameWord` one letter at a time. For each letter, it calls an `if` statement:

```
    if letter in guessedLetters:
```

The `if` statement checks to see if this letter is in the `guessedLetters` list, meaning that it has already been guessed. If it has been guessed, we'll want to display it and add it to `displayWord`. If not, we need to hide it, and so the mask character is added instead.

The two `print()` statements at the bottom are test code. They'll not be part of the finished components, but they will tell us if the code is working. The first prints the game word (which you obviously wouldn't want printed in the real game, as that would kinda ruin things), and the second prints how the word looks when masked.

In this example, the `gameWord` we are testing with is `apocalypse`. The letters already guessed are `a` and `e`, both of which are in the word `apocalypse`. So when you run the code, it should display this:

```
Original word: apocalypse
Masked word:   a___a____e
```

Save the code and run it. The output will look like this:

```
Original word: apocalypse
Masked word:
```

Uh oh! Something is broken.

But this is exactly why we write and test code in isolation. To figure out what is wrong, we need to know what is happening inside of the loop and `if` statements. And to do this, we can add `print()` statements throughout the code to show us what is going on. Here we add four `print()` statements:

```
# Start with an empty string
displayWord = ""
# Loop through word
for letter in gameWord:
    print(letter)
    # Has this letter been guessed?
    if letter in guessedLetters:
        print("This one is guessed")
        # This one has been guessed so add it
        displayWord + letter
    else:
        print("This one is not guessed")
        # This one has not been been guessed so mask it
        displayWord + maskChar
    print("displayWord is", displayWord)
```

Added print() for debugging

Save and run the code. You'll see lots of printed output fly by. This output makes it clear that the `if` statement is working, as it correctly identifies which letters have been guessed and which have not.

The output also shows that displayWord never changes. This tells us that the problem is in the code that updates displayWord. What is that code? There are two lines that update displayWord():

```
        displayWord + letter
```

and

```
        displayWord + maskChar
```

Ugh, we have a bug in our code! There's a problem with those two lines. They are technically valid code; they are indeed adding a letter or a mask character to displayWord. But the result is never being saved, and displayWord is never being updated. Why? We made a teeny weeny little typo: Those two + signs should be +=.

> **NEW TERM**
>
> **Bug** When code is not working, coders say that it has a *bug*. If code has lots of bugs, they may even call it *buggy*. Looking for bugs is called *debugging*. And sometimes coders looking for bugs will use a tool called a *debugger* to help them debug.

Update both lines of code by replacing + with +=. You can also remove all of those test print() statements we just added.

Then test the code again. This time, the masked output should be correct.

But, to be safe, test it further. Add more letters to the guessedLetters list. Try it with an empty list, like this:

```
guessedLetters = []
```

Then try a different gameWord. Test as many different combinations as you can think of. And when you are satisfied that all is good, you'll confidently know that this masking code is ready to be included in your finished application.

But we can probably make one improvement. What happens when the user has made no guesses? guessedLetters will be an empty list, right? The code will loop through every letter in gameWord and check each one to see if it is in the empty list, which it obviously isn't as nothing is in the list.

The masking code works if guessedLetters is empty, but that looping and the if statement tests are completely unnecessary. The end result will always be a completely masked displayWord. Right?

So, when the game first starts and there are no guessed letters, let's skip the whole for loop and just create a completely masked displayWord. That is cleaner code (and coders always want the cleanest, tightest code possible).

We can do this simply. Back in Chapter 3, you learned that 3 * 5 is not the same as "3" * 5. The former returns 15 (it multiplies 3 by 5), and the latter returns "33333" (it repeats the string "3" five times). Back then we didn't want to make a repeating string, but now we do.

Here is some test code:

```
maskChar = "_"
gameWord = "hello"
displayWord = maskChar * 5

print(displayWord)
```

Save it and test it. It will display displayWord, which contains five underscore characters.

maskChar specifies the character to use as the mask; here it is underscore, but you can change it to anything you'd like (but best not to use an actual letter, duh!).

The gameWord is hello, which is five letters long, so we use maskChar * 5 to create a masked string of that length.

That works, but not all game words will be five letters long. The masked displayWord needs to be whatever length the gameWord is. Right? No problem, we can just use len() to get the length of gameWord. Here is the updated code:

```
maskChar = "_"
gameWord = "hello"
displayWord = maskChar * len(gameWord)

print(displayWord)
```

Debugging Using Output

Here we debugged our code using temporary `print()` statements. These statements allowed us to peek into the code to see what it was doing. This is a very popular form of debugging and has been used for as long as coders have been coding. Debugging tools, mentioned previously, are another way to do this and allow coders to look at individual lines of code and variable values while the program is being executed.

Test the code. Try changing the `gameWord` to words of different lengths. You can also try different mask characters. Make sure the code is working before we plug it into the final app.

Summary

In this chapter, we planned the game mechanics and unit tested specific components. In the next chapter, we'll construct this game.

CHAPTER 9

Hangman

In Chapter 8 we planned our Hangman game. Now let's create the game as per the plan.

Game Time

We now understand how our Hangman game will work. We've planned and tested individual bits of code. Now we can put it all together.

Create a new file named `Hangman.py`. Here is the code (and yes, this is a longer one, close to 100 lines of code):

TIP

You Don't Have to Type It All That's a lot of code to type. If you'd like to do so, go for it. But if not, use this QR code to find the code on the book website. Then you can just copy and paste it into VS Code into your `Hangman.py` file.

```
# Imports
import random

# Variables
maxLives = 7          # Maximum allowed tries
maskChar = "_"        # Mask character
livesUsed = 0         # Try counter
guessedLetters = [] # List to store guesses

#Game words
gameWords = ["anvil", "boutique", "cookie", "fluff",
            "jazz", "pneumonia", "sleigh", "society",
            "topaz", "tsunami", "yummy", "zombie"]

# Pick the word for the game
gameWord = random.choice(gameWords)

# Start the display with a fully masked word
displayWord = maskChar * len(gameWord)

# Actual game starts here
# Loop until guessed word correctly or out of lives
```

```
while gameWord != displayWord and livesUsed < maxLives:

    # First display the masked word
    print(displayWord)

    # Next we need to display any letters already guessed
    # Lists don't display nicely, so let's create a string
    # Are there any guessed letters?
    if len(guessedLetters) > 0:
        # There are, start with an empty string
        youTried=""
        # Add each guessed letter
        for letter in guessedLetters:
            youTried += letter
        # Display them
        print("You tried:", youTried)

    # Display remaining lives
    print (maxLives-livesUsed, "tries left")

    # A little space to make it more readable
    print()

    # Get a guess
    currGuess = input("Guess a letter ").lower()
    # Make sure it's just one character
    if len(currGuess) > 1:
        currGuess = currGuess[0]

    # Don't allow repeated guess
    if currGuess in guessedLetters:
        print("You already guessed", currGuess)
    else:
        # This is a new guess, save to guessed letter list
        guessedLetters.append(currGuess)
        # And sort the list
        guessedLetters.sort()
```

```
        # Update mask
        # Start with an empty string
        displayWord = ""
        # Loop through word
        for letter in gameWord:
            # Add letter or mask as needed
            # Has this letter been guessed?
            if letter in guessedLetters:
                # This one has been guessed so add it
                displayWord += letter
            else:
                # This one has not been guessed so mask it
                displayWord += maskChar

        # Is it a correct guess?
        if currGuess in gameWord:
            # Correct answer
            print ("Correct")
        else:
            # Incorrect answer
            print ("Nope")
            # One more life used
            livesUsed += 1

    # A little space to make it more readable
    print()

# Game play is finished, display results
if displayWord == gameWord:
    # If won
    print ("You win,", gameWord, "is correct!")
else:
    # If lost
    print ("You lose, the answer was:", gameWord)
```

Yes, this a lot of code. We warned you.

Save the code and try it out. You'll see the masked display showing how many letters are in the word. You'll be told how many lives you have left. And you'll be able to guess letters and will be told if each guess is right or wrong.

Play the game a few times. See what happens when you win and what happens if you lose.

So How Does It Work?

Once you have a feel for what the game does, we'll look more closely at the code. Fortunately, you have already seen much of it. But let's walk through the main parts together.

It starts by importing the `random` library:

```
# Imports
import random
```

Next it creates a whole bunch of variables:

```
# Variables
maxLives = 7          # Maximum allowed tries
maskChar = "_"        # Mask character
livesUsed = 0         # Try counter
guessedLetters = [] # List to store guesses
```

`maxLives` stores the number of lives (wrong guesses) before the game is over. You already know what `maskChar` is. `livesUsed` keeps track of how many bad guesses the player has made, and we initialize it to `0`. `guessedLetters` is the list that will store user guesses.

TIP

Use Comments to Explain Variables Here we've added a comment next to every single variable. This is a good thing to do, as it'll make things so much easier when you (or someone else) have to come back to the code in the future.

NEW TERM

Syntax In spoken languages, the word *syntax* means the rules for how words and phrases are put together to make well-formed sentences. In programming languages, the word *syntax* is used similarly: it means the rules for how language elements are to be used.

Next comes the words that the computer can pick. We've started with a dozen hard ones, as shown here, and you can add to or change this list as you see fit:

```
#Game words
gameWords = ["anvil", "boutique", "cookie", "fluff",
             "jazz", "pneumonia", "sleigh", "society",
             "topaz", "tsunami", "yummy", "zombie"]
```

Then the program randomly picks one of those words and saves it in a variable named `gameWord`. Again, you know how this works:

```
# Pick the word for the game
gameWord = random.choice(gameWords)
```

As we planned in the last chapter, the code remembers two versions of the word being used. `gameWord` stores the actual word, and `displayWord` stores the version that gets displayed (masked as needed).

Multiline Lists

All of the lists created thus far have been on a single line. The list of `gameWords` here is spread out over multiple lines, which makes it easier to read. Python allows this because it doesn't use line breaks to mark the start and end of a list; as you know, it uses `[` and `]`. So long as each list item is separated by a comma and all are enclosed with `[` and `]`, the list will work properly.

Jazz Is Hard

Did you know that the word `jazz` is considered the hardest word in Hangman? Well, it is, which is why we included it in our list. <evil chuckle goes here>

The masked word obviously needs to be updated during game play as the user makes guesses. Before there are any guesses, the entire word is masked, like this, using the optimized code we created in Chapter 8:

```
# Start the display with a fully masked word
displayWord = maskChar * len(gameWord)
```

The code `maskChar * len(gameWord)` creates a string of mask characters with the exact same length as the game word, as we previously planned.

Then the actual game starts by defining this loop:

```
while gameWord != displayWord and livesUsed < maxLives:
```

This `while` loop ensures that the game keeps playing so long as two conditions are `True`: The word has not been guessed, and there are still lives left. We used an `and` to join the condition parts, and so as soon as either condition becomes `False` (the word has been successfully guessed or there are no lives left), the loop will end.

Inside the indented code the program first masks the display using the code we wrote (and fixed) earlier.

On each loop iteration, the first thing we do is display the masked word. It will be fully masked the first time around and will gradually unmask as the user makes correct guesses:

```
# First display the masked word
print(displayWord)
```

The player needs to know what guesses were already made. This `if` statement checks to see if there are any guesses:

```
    if len(guessedLetters) > 0:
```

If there are, they are concatenated and displayed exactly as we planned and tested.

Next, we tell the player how many lives are left by using simple subtraction:

```
# Display remaining lives
print (maxLives-livesUsed, "tries left")
```

Then the program prompts the user for a guess and restricts input to one character.

Next, we need to check to see if the user has guessed this letter before or not. We can do that with this `if` statement:

```
if currGuess in guessedLetters:
```

If the player made this guess before, the program tells them so. If not, the guess is added to the `guessedLetters` list, and the list is sorted as we planned:

```
    # This is a new guess, save to guessed letter list
    guessedLetters.append(currGuess)
    # And sort the list
    guessedLetters.sort()
```

Now that we have a new letter in `guessedLetters`, the masked `displayWord` must be updated. We tested the code for this thoroughly in Chapter 8, so we know it works.

The main game loop ends with this code:

```
    # Is it a correct guess?
    if currGuess in gameWord:
        # Correct answer
        print ("Correct")
    else:
        # Incorrect answer
        print ("Nope")
        # One more life used
        livesUsed += 1
```

This code uses an `if` statement to check if the guessed letter is in the `gameWord`. If yes, it prints `Correct`. If not, it prints `Nope` and uses the code `livesUsed += 1` to increment the lives used counter. Why do we need to do this? Because the `while` loop relies on that counter to know when the player is out of lives—and thus game over.

Inline `if` Statements

As you know, coders like nice tight code—the more concise and precise, the better.

With this in mind, there is one optimization we could make to our code. Look at this code:

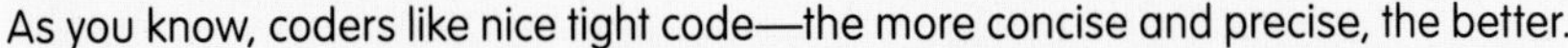

```
for letter in gameWord:
    # Has this letter been guessed?
    if letter in guessedLetters:
        # This one has been guessed so add it
        displayWord += letter
    else:
        # This one has not been guessed so mask it
        displayWord += maskChar
```

As you know, this code loops through each letter in `gameWord`, and on each iteration, an `if` statement checks to see if the letter is already in the `guessedLetters` list. Depending on that `if` statement, either the letter or the mask character is added to `displayWord`.

Now look at this next line of code. It does the exact same thing as the `if` statement—but all in one line:

```
# Add letter or mask as needed
displayWord += letter if letter in guessedLetters else maskChar
```

This code can be read like this: *Add something to `displayWord`. What do we add? `Letter` if it is not already in `guessedLetters`; otherwise, add `maskChar`.*

The end result is the same as with the original code. This version simply replaces a four-line `if` statement with a single line of code that is inline, which is why this is called an *inline `if` statement*. Feel free to use this version if you'd like.

But a word of advice: If you want to use inline `if` statements like this, first test your code using a regular multiline `if` statement. Once you know that it works, you can shorten it. Doing it this way will make it easier to test your code.

The program ends with this code:

```
# Game play is finished, display results
if displayWord == gameWord:
    # If won
    print ("You win,", gameWord, "is correct!")
else:
    # If lost
    print ("You lose, the answer was:", gameWord)
```

This code is outside of the `while` loop, so it'll get executed only when the game is over.

Once the program reaches this code, the user has either won or lost. How do we know which it is? The `if` statement simply compares `displayWord` to `gameWord`. If any of the letters in `displayWord` are still masked, then `displayWord` and `gameWord` won't match, and the `You lose` message is displayed. If `displayWord` and `gameWord` match (which means no letters remain masked), then the user won, and the `You win` message is displayed.

Whew. That's a lot of code. Writing and testing that all at once would have been really complicated. But we had a plan, and we broke the task into smaller steps and wrote and tested key components first. That way, the game worked perfectly the first time. And that's how coders code!

CHALLENGE 9.1

On second thought, we handled the user input badly in this code. Why? If the user entered too many characters, we opted to use the first of them and ignore the rest. That works. But what if the user enters no characters at all? That's a situation we didn't plan for! Oops!

No worries, that's why coders write version 2 (or version 1.1, you get the idea) of their apps. So, update the code so that it catches all invalid input lengths (too long or too short). You can do this with a `while` loop, like this:

```
currGuess = ""
while len(currGuess) != 1:
```

CHALLENGE 9.2

This one is a fun one. In the current game, we display the number of lives left, like this:

```
# Display remaining lives
print (maxLives-livesUsed, "tries left")
```

Can you replace that code to actually display a Hangman picture? You can use simple characters like | and / to draw one. For example, this code would print the picture at the start of the game, with no incorrect guesses yet:

```
print(" |---------")
print(" | /       |")
print(" |/        |")
print(" |")
print(" |")
print(" |")
print(" |")
print(" |")
print(" |")
print("---")
```

Start with this and create the pictures needed for each wrong guess.

You'll need an `if` statement to decide which picture to show.

And, here's a tip. If you plan your `print()` and `if` statements carefully, you can do this without having to create a different picture for each number of lives. You can have one picture and change what gets shown on each line based on the number of lives left.

Oh, watch for backslash characters (the \ character). That's a special character in Python. If you actually want to display \ as part of your hangman, you'll want to type \\ instead (you type two backslashes, but Python will display just one).

Escape Characters

If you want to add a tab to your string you can use \t and Python will know that you want a tab, like this:

```
# Print with a tab
print("Hello\tcoders!")
```

This will display text with a tab in it, like this:

```
Hello	coders!
```

Here's another special character you can use. \n inserts a line break:

```
# Print on two lines
print("Hello\ncoders!")
```

Here is what the output would look like.

```
Hello
coders!
```

You can also use this technique to insert quotes (use \') and double quote (use \") characters in your string.

These are all called *escape characters*, and all start with a backslash.

Do you see a problem with that? The \ is used to create a Python escape character. So, how can you ever display a backslash?

The answer is to use a special escape character for backslashes, and that is the \\ that we mentioned previously.

Summary

In this chapter, we implemented all of the code we planned in Chapter 8 and built a far more complex application. And, more importantly, we looked at how coders plan and build applications. In the next chapter, you'll get the chance to try all this a bit more.

CHAPTER 10

Keep Going

We're going to give you a break in this chapter, no new topics or code. Instead, we'll present a few application ideas for you to try. (Hey, we said "break," not "vacation"!)

Birthday Countdown

We all love our birthdays (until we are adults...and then not so much). Let's write a program that calculates how many days until your next birthday.

We're not going to give you the code. Rather, we are going to help you understand the problem. And we'll give you some tips and pointers.

Program Requirements

We always start by clearly defining what the program needs to do. This program has few requirements, but let's list them anyway:

- You need the current date.
- You also need the upcoming birthday date.

Simple enough.

Program Flow

Next, we define the program flow, meaning, what it does, and in what order. This one is pretty simple:

- Get the birthday (not date of birth, you need the date of the next birthday).
- You'll also need today's date.
- Then you can use simple math to calculate the days between those two dates.

No Cheating, but...

There is no single right way to write this program (or any of the programs in this chapter). You should create your own solution.

But, if you need help or want to see one way to solve each problem, you'll find our solutions on the book website by using this QR code.

Some Tips

As you will recall, you'll want to import `datetime` if you are going to use dates.

How do you get today's date? We did that back in Chapter 3:

```
today=datetime.datetime.now()
```

In this example, `today` is now a variable of type `datetime`.

So how do you create your own `datetime` variable with your own date? You can do this:

```
piday=datetime.datetime(2022, 3, 14)
```

You pass year, month, and day as arguments to `datetime`, and it will create the variable for you.

You can use `print(piday)` to verify that it worked.

We should point out that here we hard-coded the date. If you prompt the user for year, month, and day, you'd pass the variables with those values instead, like this:

```
birthday=datetime.datetime(yy, mm, dd)
```

As for the math, calculating the difference between dates? Python makes this super easy. Assuming you have two variables, `today` (containing today's date) and `birthday` (containing your next birthday), you can calculate the days in between by using simple math, like this:

```
daysUntilBirthday = birthday - today
```

Initializing Dates

When you create a `datetime` variable, you pass it the year, month, and day, as you saw here. These values are required. A date obviously isn't a valid date without year, month, and day.

If you need to work with times, you can also optionally pass hour, minute, and second. If you don't pass time values, then hour, minute, and second will all be `0` (meaning midnight).

CHALLENGE 10.1

Want to make this a bit more interesting? Asking the user for year, month, and date (or hard coding those values) makes the math easier. But, in truth, you only need month and day, as you can figure out the year yourself: It is either this year if the birthday has not occurred yet or next year if it has.

So update the code to prompt for a month and day and do the math to figure out the year.

Tip Calculator

Good service at your favorite restaurant warrants a tip. Calculating tip amounts involves a little math. And because some people hate math (what is wrong with them?), some restaurants print tip amounts on their bills. But that's the easy way to do it, and easy is for wimps, not for coders like us.

So, your next application will calculate tip amounts based on the bill amount and tip percentage.

Program Requirements

As always, we start with the requirements:

- Obviously, you need the amount of the bill.
- You also need the tip percentage. Do you want to hard code this to 15% or 18% or 20%? Or do you want to ask the user how much they want to tip? Either way works, but decide ahead of time.

That's really all we need. The rest is simple math.

Program Flow

As for program flow:

- The first thing you need is the bill amount. You also want to make sure that the user enters a valid number (or else the math will get ugly).
- If needed, prompt for the tip percentage.
- Once you have the amounts you can do the math. You can actually do this right in the `print()` statements, but to make sure the numbers are right, you'll probably want to save them to variables.
- And finally, print all the information.

Some Tips (Pun Intended)

You'll want to build this one incrementally. First, test it with values that are hard coded in variables, like this:

```
billAmount = 53.76
tipPercent = 18.5
```

You'll also want to do your calculations and save the results to variables, something like this:

```
tipAmount = billAmount / 100 * tipPercent
total = billAmount + tipAmount
```

`print()` those values to make sure the math is correct.

And then add the `print()` statements to display the results. You'll probably want to display the bill amount, the tip amount, and the total.

Once you know it is working, add your `input()` statements to set the `billAmount` and `tipPercent`. And make sure that the users actually enter numbers. This will involve the use of `if` statements at a minimum and possible loops (if you want to keep prompting until a user enters a valid numeric value).

CHALLENGE 10.2

Want to make it more interesting? Here are some ideas:

- Ask the user to rate the service and pick a tip amount for them based on the reply. You can use 15% for average service, 20% (or more) for great service, and 10% (or less—maybe even 0%) for poor service.
- Another enhancement would be to help the user split the bill. Ask them how many diners there were and then tell the user how much each needs to pay.

Password Generator

You need passwords. Lots of passwords. And, no, `password123` is not a safe password. Your name is not a safe password, either. Nor are your pet's name, your birthday, or anything with consecutive numbers.

You are super security conscious, and you always use really safe passwords like `4E@:3x&12)PLsx`. Right? Good! But creating all those unique passwords is a pain. So, like any good coder, you are going to write a program that will generate passwords for you.

Program Requirements

Again, let's start by clearly defining what the program needs to do:

- The user should be able to specify a length.
- What types of characters should the password use? All passwords have letters. Should the user be able to specify if they want uppercase and lowercase letters? Or should you assume that you'll always use letters of any case? Either option is ok, but decide that as part of your planning.
- You should ask the user if they want digits (numbers) in their password.
- You should also ask them if they want special characters (things like `&` and `^`).

The World's Worst (and Most Used) Passwords

Do you know what the most commonly used passwords are? Unfortunately they are:

- 123456 (this one is used in over 25,000,000 sites!)
- 123456789
- qwerty
- password
- 1234567

Ouch!

Program Flow

Now let's define the program flow:

- Start by displaying welcome text and any instructions.
- Prompt the user with a series of questions to find out exactly what type of password they want (length and types of characters).
- Start with an empty string for the password.
- Loop as many times as the needed password length, and each time generate a random letter (or digit or symbol) and add it to the password string.
- When done, show the user their newly generated password.

Simple, huh? This is all stuff you've done before.

Some Tips

You know how to pick a random letter from a string. You've done that many times, like this:

```
letter=random.choice("ABCDEFGHIJKLMNOPQRSTUVWXYZ")
```

Well, here's a really useful shortcut. There's a library that comes with Python called `string`. It contains stuff you'll find useful when working with strings. And it also defines constants (much like variables, but they can't change; they are read-only) that you can use.

NEW TERM

Constant A *constant* is a value that can never be changed by the program (unlike variables, which, as you have seen, can be changed as needed). Some constants, like the ones used here, come built into Python. And you can create your own constants, too, if needed.

For example, try this code (use a test file):

```
import string
print(string.ascii_uppercase)
```

This code imports the `string` library (just like we did with `random` and `datetime`). And then it prints `string.ascii_uppercase`. What is that? `ascii_uppercase` is a constant in the `string` library that contains all the uppercase characters from `A` to `Z`.

Another constant is `ascii_letters`, which contains all the letters from `A` to `Z` in both uppercase and lowercase. To pick and display a random letter, you can use this:

```
import string
import random

letter=random.choice(string.ascii_letters)

print(letter)
```

What other constants are there? In VS Code, type **`string.`** and wait a moment, and you'll see a pop-up that lists them all:

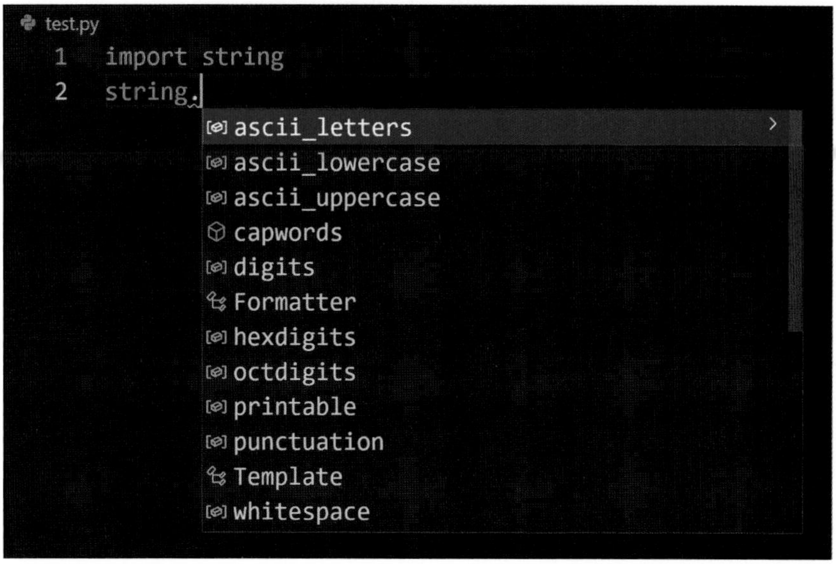

```
test.py
1   import string
2   string.
        ascii_letters
        ascii_lowercase
        ascii_uppercase
        capwords
        digits
        Formatter
        hexdigits
        octdigits
        printable
        punctuation
        Template
        whitespace
```

Some useful ones are:

`ascii_letters`	All letters from `A` to `Z`, uppercase and lowercase. `ascii_letters` is actually a concatenation of `ascii_lowercase` and `ascii_uppercase`.
`ascii_lowercase`	All lowercase letters from `a` to `z`.
`ascii_uppercase`	All uppercase letters from `A` to `Z`.
`digits`	All digits from `0` to `9`.
`punctuation`	All punctuation characters: !"#$%&'()*+,-./:;<=>?@[\]^_`{|}~

You don't have to use these constants, but Python provides them, so if they can help, why not?

As for incrementally adding letters to a string, you've seen that before, but just to remind you:

```
myString = "abc"
myString += "def"
print(myString)
```

You can add to a string by using +=. In this example, the string starts off as `abc`, and then `def` gets added.

What will the `print()` display? `abcdef`

CHALLENGE 10.3

Ok, heads-up, this one is tricky. But, we have faith in you.

Have you ever seen websites that give you password rules? They'll say something like "Passwords must be at least 8 characters in length and have at least 1 digit and 1 special character."

So, suppose the user says *yep, I want uppercase, lowercase, digits, and special characters in my password*. Easy, you pick random characters and build a password. Right?

Well, if you pick random characters from all the options, there is no guarantee that you'll get a digit or a special character. Actually, you may not even get letters at all. You could end up with just digits or special characters.

Ideally, if the user says they want digits, you'll make sure that there is at least 1 digit. Same for special characters.

So, how could you modify the code to do this?

Want to See Our Solutions?
As a reminder, if you want to see our solutions for these three challenges, scan this QR code to access the book web page.

Summary

If you want to be a great coder, you need to code and code and code. There is no shortcut. The more code you write, the better you'll be. And so in this chapter we gave you three applications to build yourself. These were not designed to be super difficult, and all can be written using what you've learned thus far.

And with that, you've finished Part I of this book. Congratulations! In Parts II and III, we'll change how we do things. Instead of lots of little programs, each section builds a complete and more comprehensive one. Ready?

Part II
ON AN ADVENTURE

CHAPTER 11

Getting Func-ky

Welcome to Part II. In this section you are going to build a retro-style text adventure game. Along the way, you'll learn lots of new techniques for creating powerful applications. But first we need to revisit functions, and this time you'll learn how to write your own functions.

Functions Revisited

You know what functions are. You've seen and used lots of them: `input()`, `print()`, `int()`, `now()`, `upper()`, `choice()`, and many others.

As a reminder, a function is made up of three parts:

Part	Description	Required	Example
Name	The unique function name	Yes	An example is `print()`. The name is how you call the function when you want to use it. The function name must always be followed by parentheses. This is required.
Arguments	One or more values passed into the function	No	If you write `print("Hello", firstName)`, then `print()` is being passed two arguments: a string containing the text `Hello` and a variable named `firstName`. Not all functions accept arguments; `print()` and `input()` do as you have seen, but `upper()` and `now()` do not.
Return	Value sent back to whatever called the function	No	One example you've used many times is `input()`, which prompts the user to type something and then returns what the user typed to you. `firstName=input("What is your name?")` prompts for a value, which is returned and saved into a variable (here `firstName`). Some functions return results; others (like `print()`) don't.

Remember this. We'll frequently be referring to function names, arguments, and return values, so don't mix them up.

Methods Are Functions

As you learned in Chapter 4, functions in a class are called *methods*. So, technically, `now()` is not a function but a method within the `datetime` class. But, methods are indeed functions, so to keep things simple, we're just going to refer to functions here. Just keep in mind that the rules and best practices for creating functions apply to methods, too.

Arguments and Return Values

Here's another way to look at it. Arguments go into a function, return values come out of a function. Whatever you pass as an argument goes into the function for processing. What the function sends back to your code when it has finished executing is the return value.

Arguments go in, return values come out.

Using Python to Write Python

Most of the libraries included with Python are themselves written in Python. And just about every third-party Python library is also written in Python.

But there are exceptions, as you'll see in Part III of this book.

Writing Your Own Functions

All of the functions we've used thus far come included with Python. Some are always available, others require you to import libraries as you have seen. But all are part of Python and are ready for you to use.

Like just about every single programming language out there, Python lets you create your own *user-defined functions*. And you write them in Python! Yep, you use Python functions to create Python functions!

> **NEW TERM**
>
> **User-Defined Function** A *user-defined function* (or *UDF*) is just that: a function defined by the user, you, the coder.

Creating a Function

So, how do you create your own function? Let's start with a simple (and rather useless) example. Create a new file named `Func1.py` and type the following:

```
def sayHello():
    print("Hello")

sayHello()
```

Save and run the code. It'll display `Hello`. Yes, we told you it was a rather useless program. But wait, it gets better quickly—promise.

So, what does this code do? Let's start at the bottom this time with this line of code:

```
sayHello()
```

This calls a function called `sayHello()`. Just like calling `print()` or `input()`, to call a function, you just specify its name followed by parentheses.

But there is no `sayHello()` function in Python. So what code gets executed when the function `sayHello()` is called? The answer is that a new function called `sayHello()` is being created right inside the same file, like this:

```
def sayHello():
    print("Hello")
```

In Python you define a function with the statement `def` (for *define*) followed by the name of the function. Here the name is `sayHello`.

The name is followed by parentheses, which is where function arguments are defined. The parentheses are empty here as this function has no arguments. Even if your function accepts no arguments, you must still specify the parentheses after the name.

Just like `if` and `while` statements, the line that defines a function ends with a colon (the : character). And just like `if` and `while`, the code that makes up the function itself is indented under the function definition statement.

`def` Doesn't Execute

It is important to note that defining a function is not the same as executing a function. If your code looked like this:

```
def sayHello():
    print("Hello")
```

then when you executed it, nothing would be displayed. Why? Because you'd have only defined the function but never executed it. If you want to use your defined function (assumedly you do, otherwise why write it?), then you must execute it.

Functions Must Be Defined Before They Can Be Used

In our simple example, we used `def` to define the `sayHello()` function and then called `sayHello()`. What would happen if the `sayHello()` call were before the `def`? You can modify the code to try that if you'd like. You'll see an error message:

```
'sayHello' is not defined
```

This simply means that Python saw your `sayHello()` call and didn't know what to do with it. Why? Remember, Python processes your code line-by-line, starting at the top. If `sayHello()` is called before the function `sayHello()` is defined, it'll have no idea what `sayHello()` is.

So, in Python functions must always be defined before they are used.

Incidentally, this is also why you always put `import` statements at the top of your code. When you import a library, Python sees all the functions in it, essentially defining them on-the-fly right where the `import` statement is. Any code after the `import` can then use the imported functions.

Passing Arguments

Our `sayHello()` function accepted no arguments (and returned no values). That's why it was rather useless.

So let's create a more interesting example. Look at this code:

```
multiply(12, 8)
```

There is no Python function named `multiply()`, so you can't run this code yet. What this code should do is allow you to pass any two numbers to a function named `multiply()`. That function will do just that: It'll multiply whatever two numbers you pass to it, and it will also display the multiplication and result.

Unlike `sayHello()`, which accepts no arguments, `multiply()` obviously needs to accept two arguments—the two numbers to be multiplied.

So, what would the `multiply()` function look like? This is the code for file `Func2.py`:

```
# Function to multiply and print two numbers
def multiply(n1, n2):
    print(n1, "x", n2, "=", n1*n2)

# Test the function
multiply(12, 8)
```

Save and run the code. It'll display `12 x 8 = 96` (unless you used different numbers, which you are obviously free to do...actually, go for it and try running the code with different numbers).

This function definition is a little different:

```
def multiply(n1, n2):
```

This creates a function named `multiply` and tells Python that `multiply()` will accept two arguments. How does it do this? By listing the needed arguments in between the parentheses. The code `(n1, n2)` tells Python to accept two arguments and to also create two variables named `n1` and `n2` to contain whatever values are passed as arguments.

In our test code, we passed `12` and `8` as arguments to `multiply()`. Python puts the first argument (the value `12`) into the first variable, which is named `n1`, and the second argument (`8`) into the second named variable, which is `n2`.

Within the `multiply()` function itself we can use those variables just like any other variables. As such, this line of code:

```
    print(n1, "x", n2, "=", n1*n2)
```

prints the two passed arguments and their multiplication. As we passed `12` and `8`, this becomes `print(12, "x", 8, "=", 12*8)`, as you've seen previously.

Argument Names

The rules for naming arguments are the same as the rules for naming variables that you saw in Chapter 2.

Arguments Are Required by Default

What would happen if you tried to call `multiply()` with no arguments? Or, for that matter, what if you passed one argument—or three?

If you don't pass the right number of arguments, Python will throw an error (just as it does when you pass incorrect arguments to built-in functions). That's because the two arguments defined in `multiply()` are required.

That said, it is possible to create optional arguments. We'll see examples of this in future chapters.

Understanding how to pass (and use) arguments is really important, so let's try another example. This is the code for `Func3.py` (replace the name `Ben` in the last line with your own name):

```
# Function to display text within a border
def displayWelcome(txt):
    borderChar = "*"                     # Border character
    print(borderChar * (len(txt) + 4))   # Top line
    print(borderChar, txt, borderChar)   # Middle line
    print(borderChar * (len(txt) + 4))   # Bottom line

# Test it
displayWelcome("Welcome, O Great Coder Ben!")
```

Save and run the code. It will display something like this:

```
*******************************
* Welcome, O Great Coder Ben! *
*******************************
```

So how does this work? We define a function named `displayWelcome()`, which accepts a single argument, which we've called `txt`.

When the function is called, the entire string (everything between the double quotes) gets passed to `displayWelcome` and is stored in variable `txt`.

The `displayWelcome()` function itself is pretty simple. It first creates a variable named `borderChar`, which contains the character we want to use for the border around the text. We've used an asterisk, but you can change that to any character you want.

The first `print()` statement prints the top border. How many border characters does it need to print for the top line? Well, the answer is it depends. All three lines must be exactly the same length, and the length depends on how long the passed text is. The middle line displays the text surrounded by a border and space. If the text is `Shmuel` (which is 6 characters long) the middle line will be `* Shmuel *` (10 characters long). This means that all of the lines must be exactly 4 characters greater than the passed text. Therefore, to display the right number of border characters, we can do this:

```
print(borderChar * (len(txt) + 4))
```

`len(txt)` returns the length of the passed text. `(len(txt) + 4)` returns the length of the passed text plus 4. And as you've seen previously, multiplying a character by a number returns a string of repeating characters. If the text were `Shmuel`, this `print()` statement would return `**********` (10 border characters).

The next `print()` statement displays the middle line, which is made up of border character, space, text, space, and border character, as we just explained.

The final `print()` statement is the bottom border and is the same as the top border.

Arguments Are Local

Within the `displayWelcome()` function there is a variable named `txt`. This was created by the function, and it contains the argument value—so whatever gets passed to the function will be stored in `txt`.

This variable is special in that it only exists inside the `displayWelcome()` function. This type of variable is called a *local* variable, and it is local to the function that created it.

What does this mean? Try adding a `print(txt)` at the very bottom of the code. You'll see an error message saying `txt is not defined`. This is because outside `displayWelcome()`, the variable `txt` is indeed not defined; it is created when the function starts, and it is destroyed when the function finishes executing.

If the function were to be called again, a new local `txt` variable would be created (possibly with a different value) and would exist until the function finishes executing.

And Python does this all automatically: creating the variable when you need it and destroying it when you are done.

Returning Values

Now you know how to create a function and how to pass it arguments. The last thing we need to look at is how to return values from a function.

Functions can return values. Think about how you used `input()`. It interacted with the user and then returned whatever the user typed as the result. `upper()` returns the uppercase version of a string. `now()` returns today's date and time.

Your own functions will frequently need to be able to return values, too, and you can do this with the (very conveniently named) `return` statement.

Let's look at an example—and a very useful example at that. You know what this code does, right?

```
num=input("Enter a number: ")
```

This code asks the user to `Enter a number:` and then stores whatever they typed into a variable named `num`.

So, if the user typed `abc` (which is definitely not a number), that will be saved into variable `num`. Not good.

So, here's a better version of the code:

```
num=inputNumber("Enter a number: ")
```

This version calls a function named `inputNumber()` instead of `input()`. Unlike `input()`, which will accept any text, `inputNumber()` is smart and makes sure the user actually types a number. Cool, huh?

Well, it would be if the `inputNumber()` function actually existed. But, alas, it doesn't.

But, there's a solution. We can create the function ourselves. Here's the code for `Func4.py`:

```
# Numeric input function
def inputNumber(prompt):
    # Input variable
    inp = ""
```

```
    # Loop until variable is a valid number
    while not inp.isnumeric():
        # Prompt for input
        inp = input(prompt).strip()
    # Return the number
    return int(inp)

# Get a number
num=inputNumber("Enter a number: ")
# Display it
print(num)
```

Save and run the code. It will prompt you for a number, which will then be displayed. If you don't type a number, it'll keep asking you to `Enter a number`, and won't stop until you actually enter a number.

The last two lines of code are pretty simple. `inputNumber()` works just like `input()`. It accepts a prompt and returns a value. Here the value is saved to a variable named `num`, which is then printed.

The real magic is the `inputNumber()` function itself. We start by defining it:

```
# Numeric input function
def inputNumber(prompt):
```

Just like `input()`, `inputNumber()` accepts a prompt—the text that is displayed to the user—and the prompt is passed as an argument.

Next, the code defines a variable that will store the user input:

```
    # Input variable
    inp = ""
```

Then comes the actual prompt inside of a loop:

```
    # Loop until variable is a valid number
    while not inp.isnumeric():
        # Prompt for input
        inp = input(prompt).strip()
```

This is code you've seen before. It uses a `while` loop with a condition that ensures that the loop will keep looping until `inp` is a number.

The actual `input()` is the same one we've been using throughout this book. What text does `input()` display as a prompt? Whatever gets passed to `inputNumber()` as an argument. `prompt` is a *passthrough variable*: You pass it to our UDF `inputNumber()`, which passes it to the built-in function `input()`.

> **NEW TERM**
>
> **Passthrough** A *passthrough* is a variable that is passed to a function, which then just passes it on, untouched and unchanged.

The loop won't end until the user has entered a number, much like we saw when we looked at `while` statements previously.

Then comes the last line of code:

```
# Return the number
return int(inp)
```

`return` specifies the value to be returned from a function. `return inp` would return the user input as a string. Here we are using `int(inp)` to turn the inputted numeric string into an actual number and return that instead.

Perfect!

Now, it is worth noting that if your program needed numeric input, you could have stuck all of this code right where you needed it (kind of like what we did previously). But creating a function to do this is preferable. Why?

- For starters, it makes your code much cleaner. Replace `input()` with `inputNumeric()`, and it just works, without any clutter.
- Functions like this can be cleanly isolated. Any variables inside them are local. There is no chance of overwriting variables of the same name because the function has its own *scope*. Code like this is much safer and reduces the chance of accidentally breaking things.

- Functions like this promote reuse. Write the function once, test it, and then use it all over the place. That saves time.
- But, more importantly, a function like this is easier to maintain. If you had to fix a bug, or needed to add a feature, you'd just change the function itself, and all of your code that uses the function would benefit from the changes.

NEW TERM

Scope Earlier we mentioned that arguments passed to a function create local variables, meaning variables that only exist within the function itself.

The truth is that this doesn't just apply to arguments; it's also true of all variables. The `inp` variable we created in `inputNumber()` only exists while that function is being executed—not before and not after.

This is referred to as *scope*, meaning the visibility of a variable. A variable with local scope can only be seen inside of the function to which it is local. And, yes, there are other scopes, as we'll see in future chapters.

CHALLENGE 11.1

Superheroes often need to travel great distances, and depending on where they go they'll need to measure those distances in miles or kilometers. Create two functions:

- `miles2km()` accepts a distance in miles and returns that distance in kilometers.
- `km2miles()` does the reverse, accepting a distance in kilometers and returning it in miles.

Each of these functions can be written in just two lines of code. The first is the `def` that defines the function and argument, and the second performs the calculation and returns it.

And to save you time, there are 1.6 kilometers in a mile, and .6 miles in a kilometer (rounded to keep things simple).

Summary

In this chapter, you've learned how to create your own functions and how to pass arguments and return results. You'll be creating functions in just about every upcoming chapter.

CHAPTER 12
Exploring

Now that you know how to create your own functions, we're ready to work on our game.

We're going to do things a little differently from now on. In Part I you created lots of small programs, each a single `.py` file. That's a great way to get started, but you're a pro now, so it's time to work like the pros do. In this part of the book (and in Part III), you'll create a single application—a larger and far more comprehensive one. This application will be made up of lots of files, and we'll incrementally add functionality chapter by chapter.

So, what are we going to create? In this section you are going to build a basic retro-style text adventure game.

Game Concept

Now that you know how to create functions and how to accept arguments and return values, let's start working on our game.

Most modern games feature stunning graphics and animation, sound effects, video sequences, and sophisticated interaction using controllers, touch, and motion. This wasn't always the case. The earliest computer games were all text: You typed what you wanted to do in text, and the computer responded in text.

You'll work on a graphics-based game in Part III of this book. In this section, we're going to go all retro and create a text-based adventure game.

Our own game takes place somewhere in space. It starts with the player stranded and trying to understand where they are. We're going to start with a very simple game structure and will add functionality and complexity in the next chapters.

Text-Based Adventure Games

The very first text-based adventure game was called *Colossal Cave Adventure*, and it was created way back in 1976 (at about the same time that the Internet was being invented). The game was all text, and started with:

```
YOU ARE STANDING AT THE END OF A ROAD BEFORE A SMALL BRICK
BUILDING. AROUND YOU IS A FOREST. A SMALL STREAM FLOWS OUT OF
THE BUILDING AND DOWN A GULLY.
```

The player would then type what they wanted to do—for example, `look` or `go east`—and the game would respond with more text. Players would need to find items, solve puzzles, and more, to win.

One year later, Zork (which was inspired by Colossal Cave Adventure) was released by Infocom. Zork was the first commercial (as in sold) text-based game, and it was so popular that it became a series of 10 titles. Yep, sequels are nothing new! Infocom went on to create dozens of text-based adventure games, including *The Hitchhiker's Guide to the Galaxy* (which we authors happen to be super fond of).

Text-based adventure games went out of style when computers were given the ability to display graphics and images. But they are still lots of fun to play, and even more fun to create.

We're Getting You Started

We should point out that the game we'll create together will be very simple; players could complete it in just a few minutes. But, by using the techniques you'll learn in this section (and by completing the Challenges), you'll have all the tools and skills you need to complete this game—or create one of your own. And, actually, we'll wrap up this part of the book with ideas about where to go next so you can really take your game to the next level.

Story Starters

If you are struggling to come up with a good story idea for your game, visit the book web page by scanning this QR code. We've created a few (deliberately incomplete) story starters that you can use as, well, a starting point.

TIP

Write Your Own Game We really want you to write your own game, not just copy ours. If it helps, feel free to use ours as a starting point. But this will be a whole lot more useful (and fun) if you go crazy and invent your own storyline.

A text-based adventure game is usually a series of locations. Each location has a description and things the player can do.

So, to start things off, we need a way to display locations, and a way to prompt users for what they want to do. And, fortunately, we know how to do both. Right?

Game Structure

We're not going to start coding just yet. Before we do so, let's look at how the game will be structured.

The foundation of our game will be functions. Every location is a function. For now our functions will just display text, but we'll add functionality (get it?) soon enough.

When the game starts we'll display a welcome message using the function `doWelcome()`:

```
# Welcome the player
def doWelcome():
    # Display text
    print("Welcome adventurer!")
    print("You wake in a daze, recalling nothing useful.")
    print("Stumbling you reach for the door, it opens in
anticipation.")
    print("You step outside. Nothing is familiar.")
    print("The landscape is dusty, vast, tinged red, barren.")
    print("You notice that you are wearing a spacesuit. Huh?")
```

As you can see, it's a lot of `print()` statements. Simple enough. When your code calls `doWelcome()`, all of those `print()` statements will execute, and the text will be displayed.

Actual game play starts with a function called `doStart()`, which looks like this:

```
# Location: Start
def doStart():
    # Display text
    print("You look around. Red dust, a pile of boulders, more
dust.")
    print("There's an odd octagon shaped structure in front of
you.")
    print("You hear beeping nearby. It stopped. No, it didn't.")
```

Again, this is a pretty simple function (for now), with no arguments and no return values. The code simply displays text using the very familiar `print()` functions.

Here's another example, showing what happens if the player decides to run away:

```
# Player ran
def doRun():
    # Display text
    print("You run, for a moment.")
```

```
    print("And then you are floating. Down down down.")
    print("You've fallen into a chasm, never to be seen again.")
    print("Not very brave, are you?")
```

Again, a simple function and just `print()` statements.

You'll want to create a series of these—one for each location in your game. You can name the functions as you wish. We've started them all with `do` to keep things organized, but you can use any naming convention you want.

TIP

Don't Reuse Function Names Don't use the same name for multiple functions. This is actually allowed, so Python won't display an error message if you do so. But what will happen is the second function will overwrite the first one—probably not what you want. So, keep all function names unique.

Prompting for Options

The locations in the game are all functions...lots and lots of functions. Your code will execute a function, which displays text and then prompts the player for what they want to do next. Once the player makes a choice, you'll execute another function, which displays text and then prompts the user for an action. And so on.

Which means we need to display options and prompt for a choice.

Prompting users for options is easy enough. You're an expert in that by now. We can use a `while` loop with `input()`. For example, at the start of the game, the user has a few choices. They can choose `P` to look at the pile of boulders, `S` to go to the structure, `B` to walk toward the beeping, or `R` to run. We can do something like this:

```
# Prompt for user action
choice=" "
while not choice in "PSBR":
    print("You can:")
    print("P = Examine boulder pile")
```

```
    print("S = Go to the structure")
    print("B = Walk towards the beeping")
    print("R = Run!")
    choice=input("What do you want to do? [P/S/B/R]")
```

This code is much like code you've seen before. It initializes a variable named `choice`. Then it uses a `while` loop to display options and only accepts a valid choice. The condition checks to see that `choice` is in the allowed options (here `P`, `S`, `B`, or `R`).

Easy enough. But what do we do with `choice` once it has been made?

Processing Options

The above while loop will only end once the user has made a valid choice. Once a choice has been made, we just need to call the right function, like this:

```
# Perform action
if choice == 'P':
    doBoulders()
elif choice == 'S':
    doStructure()
elif choice == 'B':
    doBeeping()
elif choice == 'R':
    doRun()
```

Here we have a series of `if` and `elif` statements. Depending on the choice made, we send the user to the right function.

So, the complete `doStart()` function would look something like this:

```
# Location: Start
def doStart():
    # Display text
    print("You look around. Red dust, a pile of boulders, more
dust.")
    print("There's an odd octagon shaped structure in front of
you.")
```

```
    print("You hear beeping nearby. It stopped. No, it didn't.")
    # Prompt for user action
    choice=" "
    while not choice in "PSBR":
        print("You can:")
        print("P = Examine boulder pile")
        print("S = Go to the structure")
        print("B = Walk towards the beeping")
        print("R = Run!")
        choice=input("What do you want to do? [P/S/B/R]").strip().
upper()
    # Perform action
    if choice == 'P':
        doBoulders()
    elif choice == 'S':
        doStructure()
    elif choice == 'B':
        doBeeping()
    elif choice == 'R':
        doRun()
```

Display text, show available options, prompt for input, and then go to the next function. Simple as that.

Create a Work Folder

Unlike all of the code we've created thus far, the text-based adventure is going to be comprised of many files. To keep them all nicely organized together, we'll create a new folder for this project.

Move your mouse over the VS Code Explorer panel. Hover over the **PYTHON** section, and you'll see this toolbar displayed at the top:

The second icon from the left is the **New Folder** icon. Click it, and you'll be prompted for a folder name. Type `Adventure` and press **Enter** to create a new folder for the game.

More Code Online
As already mentioned, you don't have to type all this code. You'll find this and other starters online if you just scan this QR code.

When you create new code files, make sure you have clicked on the new folder in the Explorer panel first. That way, the file you create will be in the right folder.

TIP

Multiple Work Folders You may want to create more than one work folder. That way, you can have one for the example code we provided and will work on together and one for your own game.

Game Time

Okay, now that you understand the game structure and have a work folder, let's start coding. The first file in the game will be called `Main.py` (and it goes in your new `Adventure` folder). Here's the code:

```
##########################################
# Space Adventure
# by Ben & Shmuel
##########################################

# Welcome the player
def doWelcome():
    # Display text
    print("Welcome adventurer!")
    print("You wake in a daze, recalling nothing useful.")
    print("Stumbling you reach for the door, it opens in
anticipation.")
    print("You step outside. Nothing is familiar.")
    print("The landscape is dusty, vast, tinged red, barren.")
    print("You notice that you are wearing a spacesuit. Huh?")
```

```
# Location: Start
def doStart():
    # Display text
    print("You look around. Red dust, a pile of boulders, more
dust.")
    print("There's an odd octagon shaped structure in front of
you.")
    print("You hear beeping nearby. It stopped. No, it didn't.")
    # Prompt for user action
    choice=" "
    while not choice in "PSBR":
        print("You can:")
        print("P = Examine boulder pile")
        print("S = Go to the structure")
        print("B = Walk towards the beeping")
        print("R = Run!")
        choice=input("What do you want to do? [P/S/B/R]").strip().
upper()
    # Perform action
    if choice == 'P':
        doBoulders()
    elif choice == 'S':
        doStructure()
    elif choice == 'B':
        doBeeping()
    elif choice == 'R':
        doRun()

# Location: Boulders
def doBoulders():
    # Display text
    print("Seriously? They are boulders.")
    print("Big, heavy, boring boulders.")
    # Go back to start
    doStart()

# Location: Structure
def doStructure():
```

```
    # Display text
    print("You examine the odd structure.")
    print("Eerily unearthly sounds seem to be coming from inside.")
    print("You see no doors or windows.")
    print("Well, that outline might be a door, good luck opening
it.")
    print("And that beeping. Where is it coming from?")
    # Prompt for user action
    choice=" "
    while not choice in "SDBR":
        print("You can:")
        print("S = Back to start")
        print("D = Open the door")
        print("B = Walk towards the beeping")
        print("R = Run!")
        choice=input("What do you want to do? [S/D/B/R]").strip().
upper()
    # Perform action
    if choice == 'S':
        doStart()
    elif choice == 'D':
        doStructureDoor()
    elif choice == 'B':
        doBeeping()
    elif choice == 'R':
        doRun()

# Location: Structure door
def doStructureDoor():
    # Display text
    print("The door appears to be locked.")
    print("You see a small circular hole. Is that the keyhole?")
    print("You move your hand towards it, it flashes blue and
closes!")
    print("Well, that didn't work as planned.")
    # Prompt for user action
    choice=" "
```

```
    while not choice in "SR":
        print("You can:")
        print("S = Back to structure")
        print("R = Run!")
        choice=input("What do you want to do? [S/R]").strip().
upper()
    # Perform action
    if choice == 'S':
        doStructure()
    elif choice == 'R':
        doRun()

# Location: Explore beeping
def doBeeping():
    pass

# Player ran
def doRun():
    # Display text
    print("You run, for a moment.")
    print("And then you are floating. Down down down.")
    print("You've fallen into a chasm, never to be seen again.")
    print("Not very brave, are you?")
    # Dead, game over
    gameOver()

# Game over
def gameOver():
    print("Game over!")

# Actual game starts here
# Display welcome message
doWelcome()
# Game start location
doStart()
```

There's a lot of code here, but most of it should be self-explanatory.

The code first defines lots of functions. doWelcome(), doStart(), doStructure(), etc. are all locations in the game. As explained before, each is its own function. doWelcome() introduces the game with a series of print() functions. doStart() is the game starting location; it displays text and also prompts for a user choice and then sends the user to the appropriate function.

Defining functions doesn't execute them. When you use def, you are creating and naming a new function for future use. But Python will do nothing with the new function until you actually call it. That's why the code ends with:

```
# Actual game starts here
# Display welcome
doWelcome()
# Game start location
doStart()
```

Once all the functions have been defined, doWelcome() calls the doWelcome() function, which welcomes the user, and doStart() starts the actual game play.

Oh, there is one new statement here that we should mention. Look at this code:

```
# Explore beeping
def doBeeping():
    pass
```

What does pass do? Python does not like empty functions. If you use def to create a function, then something must be indented beneath it. If you have nothing indented, Python will display an error message. pass does, well, absolutely nothing at all. It's a placeholder. You can put it in your code so that Python stops displaying error messages until you are ready to actually write the function code. pass is thus really useful while you are working (but useless in your finished code).

Test It

If you were to run `Main.py`, you'd see this is in the Terminal window:

```
Welcome adventurer!
You wake in a daze, recalling nothing useful.
Stumbling you reach for the door, it opens in anticipation.
You step outside. Nothing is familiar.
The landscape is dusty, vast, tinged red, barren.
You notice that you are wearing a spacesuit. Huh?
You look around. Red dust, a pile of boulders, more dust.
There's an odd octagon shaped structure in front of you.
You hear beeping nearby. It stopped. No, it didn't.
You can:
P = Examine boulder pile
S = Go to the structure
B = Walk towards the beeping
R = Run!
What do you want to do? [P/S/B/R]
```

The code executed `doWelcome()`, which displayed the welcome message, and then executed `doStart()`, which displayed the start location and prompts.

If you select `S` to go to the structure, the function `doStructure()` is executed, and this is displayed:

```
What do you want to do? [P/S/B/R]s
You examine the odd structure.
Eerily unearthly sounds seem to be coming from inside.
You see no doors or windows.
Well, that outline might be a door, good luck opening it.
And that beeping. Where is it coming from?
You can:
S = Back to start
D = Open the door
B = Walk towards the beeping
R = Run!
What do you want to do? [S/D/B/R]
```

And so on.

One function worth noting is `doBoulder()`. This will be an important location in the future (it's where the player can find a key, shhhh!), but for now it just displays text and has no options. So how does the game proceed if there are no options to choose from? Look at the code:

```
# Location: Boulders
def doBoulders():
    # Display text
    print("Seriously? They are boulders.")
    print("Big, heavy, boring boulders.")
    # Go back to start
    doStart()
```

`doBoulder()` displays text and then right away sends the player back to the start by executing `doStart()`. That'll suffice for now. We'll add functionality to `doBoulder()` shortly.

TIP

You Can Stop Execution When you test, you don't have to run the entire program. You can stop execution at any time. You do this by clicking on the garbage can icon to the right of the Terminal window. This terminates the Terminal session, which stops your program from running. Then, when you are ready, you can just start execution again.

You Can Space Your Output

When you run the game, you'll see lots of text, all bunched together. You can space things out by adding empty lines to the output. To do this, just add an empty `print()` function, like this:

```
print()
```

Extra spacing will make the text much more readable.

Oh, and in Chapter 17, we'll add color, which will make things even more readable.

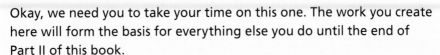

CHALLENGE 12.1

The challenges in Part I were all optional—kind of a nice-to-have. That's not the case anymore. You'll want to do them all as you'll build on them in subsequent chapters.

Okay, we need you to take your time on this one. The work you create here will form the basis for everything else you do until the end of Part II of this book.

So, before going on to Chapter 13, you need to plan your game. And we mean plan, not code. At least not yet. You can base your game on ours or use our story starters. (But, truthfully, we'd rather you come up with your own idea.) Make sure you have at least 10 locations—more are preferable. And have paths that allow the player to go from one location to another.

Think through the flow. Not every location will always be available. Users might have to go to one location to be able to get to another. You may want to draw a map. (Yep, draw...old school, as in pencil or pen on paper. We did say we're going all retro.)

Once you have a plan, start to write your location functions. Make sure that every function can be reached and that every function has options. And it is perfectly ok to make your user go around and around and around.

Then test your code. Try every option. Move from location to location. Verify that everything works as expected.

Summary

In this chapter, you've used your knowledge of functions to create the basic structure of a text-based adventure game. The game doesn't do much yet: It just lets the player wander around. We'll add functionality throughout the rest of this part of the book.

CHAPTER 13

Cleanup Time

In Chapter 12 you created the beginnings of your text-based adventure game. While very incomplete, players can launch your game and move around by making selections. The code works, but you're probably already seeing ways to improve it. That ongoing improvement process is the subject of this chapter and the next.

Optimizing Your Code

As we've previously discussed, before you start coding, you plan your application. The planning is critical, and the more you plan, the easier it'll be to actually write your code. But, even with the best planning, once you start coding, you are inevitably going to discover ways to improve your code.

What type of improvements? Things like:

- Processing that can be moved elsewhere to make your code cleaner and simpler
- Removing duplicated code
- Identifying functionality that can be isolated from your main code so that it can be reused
- Improving specific processing for simplicity or performance

These are just a few types of improvements, and there are many more.

With time and experience, coders learn to write better code in the first place. But, the truth is that even the most experienced coders are continuously looking for ways to improve their code.

For now, let's look at an example of the first type of improvement we mentioned: moving code elsewhere to make everything clearer and simpler.

`Main.py` is the main file of our game. As you've seen, it is made up of lots of functions. But what are those functions made up of? Let's look at a couple starting with the `doWelcome()` function:

```
# Welcome the player
def doWelcome():
    # Display text
    print("Welcome adventurer!")
    print("You wake in a daze, recalling nothing useful.")
    print("Stumbling you reach for the door, it opens in anticipation.")
    print("You step outside. Nothing is familiar.")
    print("The landscape is dusty, vast, tinged red, barren.")
    print("You notice that you are wearing a spacesuit. Huh?")
```

What do you notice about this function? It's all `print()` statements, right? Lots and lots of text.

Let's look at part of the `doStart()` function:

```
# Location: Start
def doStart():
    # Display text
    print("You look around. Red dust, a pile of boulders, more
dust.")
    print("There's an odd octagon shaped structure in front of
you.")
    print("You hear beeping nearby. It stopped. No, it didn't.")
```

Lots of `print()` statements and text, too. Same for `doRun()`:

```
# Player ran
def doRun():
    # Display text
    print("You run, for a moment.")
    print("And then you are floating. Down down down.")
    print("You've fallen into a chasm, never to be seen again.")
    print("Not very brave, are you?")
```

Actually, if you look at all of the code in `Main.py`, you'll probably find that displayed text by `print()` functions makes up a significant part of it.

Is having all of this text right inside the core code a problem? Consider the following:

- Story text spread all over the place is hard to maintain. Keeping spelling consistent and ensuring a common voice and tone is challenging if text is scattered all over the place.
- Making changes is harder. Renaming a character, tweaking descriptions and adjectives, and so on...if you need to do this in multiple places, you'll inevitably miss some.
- Imagine that your program is so popular that you decide to release it in other languages. Translating text that is broken into little bits in different places is difficult.

- And, most importantly, all that text gets in the way. When you want to focus on game functionality, you don't want to be scrolling up and down past hundreds of lines of text.

For all these reasons, and more, developers like to externalize their text. This means that they take the text out of the main code and put it into another dedicated file.

> **NEW TERM**
> **Externalize** The term *externalize* means to move content out of a main program into an external file that can be easily managed and maintained.

String Externalization

String externalization is an important part of code optimization for all the reasons we mentioned. How can you do this? There are lots of ways, but one simple option is to move all of the text into another file and create a function that returns the text you need when you need it.

Creating the Strings File

Let's externalize our text starting with the `doWelcome()` function:

```
# Welcome the player
def doWelcome():
    # Display text
    print("Welcome adventurer!")
    print("You wake in a daze, recalling nothing useful.")
    print("Stumbling you reach for the door, it opens in
anticipation.")
    print("You step outside. Nothing is familiar.")
    print("The landscape is dusty, vast, tinged red, barren.")
    print("You notice that you are wearing a spacesuit. Huh?")
```

We can turn it into something like this:

```
# Welcome the player
def doWelcome():
    # Display text
    print(functionThatGetsTheString())
```

Obviously, this doWelcome() function can't be executed as is; it calls a function that doesn't exist. But, conceptually, this is how things could work. Instead of using lots of print() statements with hard-coded text, we can have a single print() statement that calls a function and prints whatever that function returns.

Incidentally, when coders are thinking through ideas, they often use dummy code like this—fake code meant for them during development. They call this *pseudocode*.

NEW TERM

Pseudocode *Pseudocode* is fake code. It's not actual code that a computer can understand but text meant for humans to read and understand while they think through their code.

Create a new file (in the Adventure folder) named Strings.py. Here's the code:

```
############################################
# Strings.py
# Externalized strings
############################################

def get(id):
    if id == "Welcome":
        return ("Welcome adventurer!\n"
                "You wake in a daze, recalling nothing useful.\n"
                "Stumbling, you reach for the door, it opens in "
                "anticipation.\nYou step outside. Nothing is "
                "familiar.\nThe landscape is dusty, vast, tinged "
```

```
                "red, barren.\nYou notice that you are wearing "
                "a spacesuit. Huh?")
    elif id == "Start":
        return ("You look around. Red dust, a pile of boulders, "
                "more dust.\nThere's an odd octagon shaped "
                "structure in front of you.\nYou hear beeping "
                "nearby. It stopped. No, it didn't.")
    elif id == "Boulders":
        return ("Seriously? They are boulders.\n"
                "Big, heavy, boring boulders.")
    elif id == "Structure":
        return ("You examine the odd structure.\n"
                "Eerily unearthly sounds seem to be coming from "
                "inside.\nYou see no doors or windows.\nWell, that "
                "outline might be a door, good luck opening it.\n"
                "And that beeping. Where is it coming from?")
    elif id == "StructureDoor":
        return ("The door appears to be locked.\nYou see a small "
                "circular hole. Is that the keyhole?")
    elif id == "StructureDoorNoKey":
        return ("You move your hand towards it, it flashes blue "
                "and closes!\nWell, that didn't work as planned.")
    elif id == "Run":
        return ("You run, for a moment.\n"
                "And then you are floating. Down down down.\n"
                "You've fallen into a chasm, never to be seen "
                "again.\nNot very brave, are you?")
    elif id == "GameOver":
        return "Game over!"
    else:
        return ""
```

There is only one function in this file, defined like this:

```
def get(id):
```

Function get() accepts an identifier (a variable named id). So when get() is called, an id must be passed to it.

The rest of the code is a big if elif else statement. It first checks:

```
if id == "Welcome":
```

If Welcome was passed to get(), then that condition will be True, and the code indented beneath it will be executed. What does that code do? It simply returns a block of text:

```
return ("Welcome adventurer!\n"
         "You wake in a daze, recalling nothing useful.\n"
         "Stumbling, you reach for the door, it opens in
anticipation.\n"
          "You step outside. Nothing is familiar.\n"
          "The landscape is dusty, vast, tinged red, barren.\n"
          "You notice that you are wearing a spacesuit. Huh?")
```

The remaining elif statements do the same thing: check the id and return text.

The final else statement is just to be safe:

```
else:
    return ""
```

If an invalid id gets passed to get(), the function will return an empty string.

get() doesn't display text—there is no print() in there—but simply returns it to your code. It's up to your code to decide what to do with the text, and the code could indeed print it if so desired.

If the function is called with get("Welcome"), it will return the Welcome message. Same for any other needed strings. Want to test that it's working? Add this to the bottom of Strings.py:

```
print(get("Welcome"))
```

Multiline Text

Two comments about multiline text.

First, long blocks of text can be broken over multiple lines. Just put quotes around the text on each line. Python will treat the text as if it were one long block of text.

Second, notice the `\n` in the middle of some of the text. That's a newline character (which we mentioned previously). It forces a line break in the Terminal output.

If you run the code, the test associated with `Welcome` will be printed. How? `get("Welcome")` returns the text, and `print()`, ...well, it prints.

You can try other `id`s just to make sure it's working. And then remove the test `print()` when you are done testing.

Each time a new block of text is needed in the game, a section can be added to this function. Each section has a unique `id`. Call `get()` with that `id`, and the right text is returned.

Oh, notice the `return` statements. Most functions have a single `return` statement at the end of the function. Here we have a `return` for each string, and each `return` stops function processing and returns the result. This way, we don't have to save the text to a variable and then return that. But, within the `if` statements, you could indeed save the text to a variable and return that. Either way works.

Using Externalized Strings

So, how do we use this new `Strings` file and `get()` function? We `import` it as a library. Yes, our `Strings.py` file is a Python library.

Add this to the top of `Main.py`:

```
# Imports
import Strings
```

Careful with Library Naming

We called the file `Strings.py`, so the library is named `Strings`. As you will recall, Python has a built-in library named `String`. If we had named the file `String.py`, we'd have overwritten the built-in library, but `Strings.py` is safe.

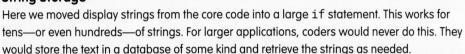

String Storage

Here we moved display strings from the core code into a large `if` statement. This works for tens—or even hundreds—of strings. For larger applications, coders would never do this. They would store the text in a database of some kind and retrieve the strings as needed.

Using a database is conceptually similar to using a Python file. Strings are externalized and retrieved as needed. You can pick a storage option based on your specific needs.

To use the `get()` function, we replace the hard-coded text with the function call. Let's start with `doWeclome()`. Remove all of the `print()` statements and replace them with this code:

```
# Welcome the player
def doWelcome():
    # Display text
    print(Strings.get("Welcome"))
```

`Strings.get()` is our `get()` function in `Strings.py`. As this is the `doWelcome()` function, we use `Strings.get("Welcome")`, which tells `get()` to return the `"Welcome"` text, as you saw previously. That text is passed to `print()`.

`doWelcome()` is now a single line of code. As you can see, this is much cleaner and tighter.

CHALLENGE 13.1

Externalize all of the strings in your application. At a minimum, externalize the display text. If you'd like, you can even externalize option prompts and any other displayed text.

Summary

In this chapter, we introduced string externalization as a way to clean up code. Our application now is made up of two files, and in the next chapter, we'll add a third as we introduce another really important optimization.

CHAPTER 14

Reduce, Reuse, Recycle, Refactor

In Chapter 13 we took a break from coding our game to clean up our code. We are going to continue doing that in this chapter.

Understanding Refactoring

In Chapter 13 we talked about continuously finding ways to improve our code. After all, code is never really done. It can always be further refined and optimized—which is why coders regularly dedicate time to *refactoring* their code. Refactoring is the process of improving how code functions. When you refactor your code, you change how it works without changing what it does.

NEW TERM

Refactoring *Refactoring* is the process of improving how your code functions. When you refactor your code, you change how it works without changing what it does.

The important thing about refactoring is that it is not about adding features or making any functional changes. When you refactor, you are not changing *what* your code does, just *how* it does it. Making lots of changes at once is never a good idea; it increases the chances of breaking things and makes it hard to find exactly what broke. When you refactor your code, your application will do exactly what it did beforehand, which means you can easily verify that things still work properly.

Refactoring may sound complicated, but—surprise!—you've already started refactoring your code. Our string externalization exercise is an example of refactoring. By the time we wrapped up Chapter 13, the code was functionally identical to the code at the end of Chapter 12. We didn't change what the code did, we changed how it did it by reorganizing and improving it. That's exactly what refactoring is all about.

So, let's continue refactoring. And, yes, that means that by the time we've finished this chapter, the code will still be functionally identical to what it was in Chapters 12 and 13. Functionally identical, but reworked—or, rather, refactored.

We previously discussed identifying and eliminating duplicated code. As we've noted, duplicating code is never a good idea. As you write code, you will inevitably discover that you have pieces of code that are repeated, either identically or with minor changes. Eliminating these duplications is an important part of refactoring your code.

Identifying Refactoring Opportunities

There is no rule as to exactly what to refactor. How and where to optimize your code is up to you, the coder. But let's look at one example together.

You now have a simple working text-based adventure. You've created a series of locations, and players can move around through them.

Look at your code. Do you see any parts that look repetitive? There's one very obvious example. At every location, we need to do the following:

1. Display a series of options to the player.
2. Prompt them for what they want to do.
3. Make sure they make a valid selection, and if they don't, send them back to step 2.

While the exact options vary at each location, the flow is the same. Compare these two examples (from our code in Chapter 11...your own story will likely have different options).

This is our `doStart()` function:

```
# Location: Start
def doStart():
    # Display text
    print(Strings.get("Start"))
    # Prompt for user action
    choice=" "
    while not choice in "PSBR":
        print("You can:")
        print("P = Examine boulder pile")
        print("S = Go to the structure")
        print("B = Walk towards the beeping")
        print("R = Run!")
        choice=input("What do you want to do? [P/S/B/R]").strip().
upper()
    # Perform action
    if choice == 'P':
        doBoulders()
```

```
    elif choice == 'S':
        doStructure()
    elif choice == 'B':
        doBeeping()
    elif choice == 'R':
        doRun()
```

The code uses our `Strings.get()` function to display text and then displays options and prompts for a choice.

And this is a snippet from our `doStructure()` function:

```
def doStructure():
    # Display text
    print(Strings.get("Structure"))
    # Prompt for user action
    choice=" "
    while not choice in "SDBR":
        print("You can:")
        print("S = Back to start")
        print("D = Open the door")
        print("B = Walk towards the beeping")
        print("R = Run!")
        choice=input("What do you want to do? [S/D/B/R]").strip().
upper()
```

Compare the code in the two `# Prompt for user action` sections. Obviously, they are not 100% identical; the options differ, but the flow is exactly the same. Right?

They print options, one per line. They prompt for `input()` within a `while` loop. And if you have 10, 15, or more functions, then you've got very similar code repeated over and over. This is an obvious candidate for refactoring.

Creating a User Choice Component

We need to display choices and prompt for one over and over. This needs to be refactored.

We could easily create a function to prompt the user to choose an action. Actually, we could reuse the code and do something as simple as this:

```
def startChoice():
    choice=" "
    while not choice in "PSBR":
        print("You can:")
        print("P = Examine boulder pile")
        print("S = Go to the structure")
        print("B = Walk towards the beeping")
        print("R = Run!")
        choice=input("What do you want to do? [P/S/B/R]")
    return choice
```

This creates a function named `startChoice()`. It contains code copied from our `doStart()` function. It displays options, prompts for an `input()`, and ensures that the input is valid. The only difference is the last line, `return choice`, which returns what the user decided to do.

Using this function, we can change our `doStart()` function to look like this:

```
# Location: Start
def doStart():
    # Display text
    print(Strings.get("Start"))
    # Get user choice
    choice=startChoice()
    # Perform action
    if choice == 'P':
        doBoulders()
    elif choice == 'S':
        doStructure()
    elif choice == 'B':
        doBeeping()
```

```
    elif choice == 'R':
        doRun()
```

This version of `doStart()` is much cleaner. It displays text, gets a choice, and then acts on that choice. All of the prompting and input code has been moved out of the main function and has been replaced with one clear and clean line of code:

```
    choice=startChoice()
```

But is this actually better? Yes, the code is cleaner, but the `startChoice()` function is only useful for `doStart()`. As each location function has different options, we'd need a different function for each one—all almost the same. Ahhhhhh! Duplication! We're trying to de-duplicate code!

The truth is that the concept makes sense. Moving the choice code out of the location functions is a good idea, but this is definitely not the right implementation.

Designing a Reusable Component

How could we improve on this? We could create a general-purpose function: one that is not hard coded to specific options, one that can display all sorts of options.

Let's call our new function `getUserChoice()`. You'll pass `getUserChoice()` the available options as arguments. It could then display whatever options you passed, obtain a choice that is one of those options, and return it. That would give you the benefit of isolating the choice code while not necessitating lots and lots of functions. Perfect!

You know how to pass arguments to a function; we did that in Chapter 11. So what could a general-purpose `getUserChoice()` function definition look like?

We could try this:

```
def getUserChoice(letter, prompt):
```

This function would accept a letter and the text to display—for example, `getUserChoice("R", "Run!")`. The function could display the letter and the prompt as passed.

But that will only work if a location has a single option. What if another location had 2 options? Well, we could add more arguments, like this:

```
def getUserChoice(letter1, prompt1, letter2, prompt2):
```

Great, that handles 2 options. But what if other locations had 3, or 5, or even 12 options? And for that matter, what of the location that needed just 1? The function would throw an error if too few arguments were passed.

We need a better and more flexible way to pass arguments. Any ideas?

Maybe we can use a variable that can store as many (or as few) options as we need. Anything?

A variable that can store *lists* of values? <nudge> <wink>

You know what it is, right? Yes, lists. We can use lists!

We could define the function like this:

```
def getUserChoice(options):
```

And then pass it options in a list, like this:

```
options=["E", "Explore", "R", "Run!"]
getUserChoice(options)
```

This way, you can pass as many options as needed, adding two items to the list for each option. The code can then loop through the list. Within the function code, `options[0]` will be the first allowed letter, and `options[1]` will be its matching prompt; `options[2]` will be the next allowed letter, and `options[3]` will be its matching prompt; and so on.

This is actually a really good solution. But, we can make it a little better.

Back in Chapter 6 we explored lists, and we mentioned in passing that you can create lists of lists. Yep, a list containing lists.

The best way to explain lists of lists is to look at an example. Create a file named `List7.py`. (You'll probably want to put it in your main Python code folder as it is not part of the adventure game.) Here's the code:

```
# Create a list of lists
options = [["P","Examine boulder pile"],
           ["S","Go to the structure"],
           ["B","Walk towards the beeping"],
           ["R","Run!"]]

# Some test prints
print(options)
print(len(options))
print(len(options[0]))
print(options[0])
print(options[1])
print(options[1][0])
print(options[1][1])
```

TIP

Line-breaks In Lists Long lists, like the ones here, can be broken over multiple lines which makes them so much easier to read. Just make sure that lines end with a comma.

We know this list looks strange. We'll get to that. For now, save it and run it, and you'll see output that looks like this:

```
[['P', 'Examine boulder pile'], ['S', 'Go to the structure'], ['B', 'Walk towards the beeping'], ['R', 'Run!']]
4
2
['P', 'Examine boulder pile']
['S', 'Go to the structure']
S
Go to the structure
PS C:\Users\ben\Documents\Python> 
```

There's a lot to digest here, so let's look at the code.

Ok, so what is this code doing?

```
print(options)
```

This is pretty simple: It displays the whole list.

What does this display?

```
print(len(options))
```

`options` is a list with 4 items, so `len(options)` returns `4`, so the code prints 4.

As you will recall, lists go inside of square brackets, so `[1,2,3]` would be a list with three items in it. This code also creates a list with three items. This is the first:

```
["P","Examine boulder pile"]
```

The four items are separated by commas:

```
options = [["P","Examine boulder pile"],
           ["S","Go to the structure"],
           ["B","Walk towards the beeping"],
           ["R","Run!"]]
```

But here the items are <drumroll> lists! Yep, each item is another list containing two items, so each item is enclosed within square brackets.

It looks a little funky, we know, which is why we separated it onto multiple lines to make it easier to read. The list starts and ends with two square brackets. Why? The first `[` creates the outer list. The second `[` creates the first inner list. Same at the end: The second `]` closes the outer list, and the `]` in front of it closes the final inner list.

These arrows help explain things:

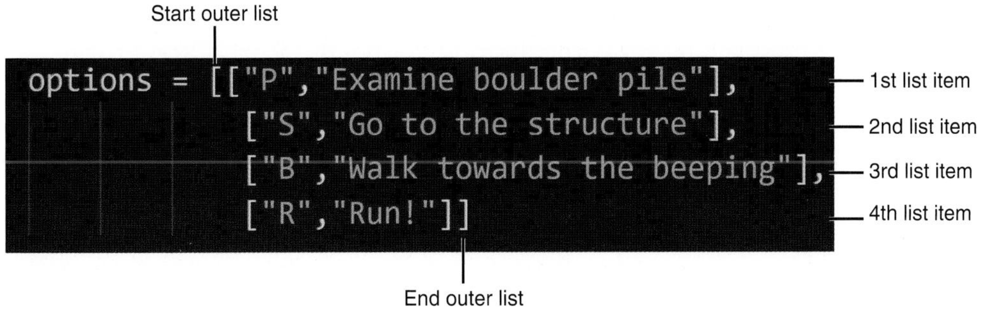

Start outer list

```
options = [["P","Examine boulder pile"],       — 1st list item
           ["S","Go to the structure"],        — 2nd list item
           ["B","Walk towards the beeping"],   — 3rd list item
           ["R","Run!"]]                       — 4th list item
```

End outer list

So, how do you access individual list items?

len() and Lists of Lists

How long are the lists in our example? `len(options)` will return 4, as there are four items in `options`. Yes, the items are lists; each list is just one item. `len(options[0])` will return 2, as list `options[0]` (like list `options[1]` and list `options[2]`) contains two items—the letter and prompt text.

Lists of Lists of Lists of...

You've seen lists, and you've seen lists of lists. And, yes, you can create lists of lists of lists. And more!

In some languages, lists of lists are referred to as *two-dimensional arrays*, and lists of lists of lists are called *three-dimensional arrays*. And you can even go out of our spatial world into more than three dimensions!

You know that you use `[index]` notation to access list items. `options[0]` returns the first item in a list, right? So here it returns the first item in `options`, which is `["P","Examine boulder pile"]`. Similarly, `options[1]` returns the second item, which is the list `["S","Go to the structure"]`. This can be seen in the `print()` statements.

So, if `options[1]` refers to the entire second list, how can we access the individual items in that list? Like this:

```
print(options[1][0])
print(options[1][1])
```

The first `print()` displays `S` as that is item `0` inside of item `1`. `options[1]` means item `1` in `options`, `options[1][0]` means item `0` within item `1` in `options`. The second `print()` displays item `1` within item `1`, which is `Go to the Structure`.

This is a fun and powerful way to use lists, but the syntax can be tricky at first. Play with the code in `List7.py`, change what is being printed, and try different options to get a feel for how to use `[index][index]` syntax.

Using lists of lists is a great way to pass options to our `getUserChoice()` function. This format will make it easy to add options (each of which is a list of two items—letter and prompt). It can handle as many options as needed. And it'll make the actual UDF code really clean, too.

Plus, added bonus: As you know, you can use the append() function to add items to lists. How could this be useful? Imagine a scenario where your game has three options. But, if the user has an item—perhaps a key they found—then there is a fourth option to unlock a door. You could create your basic options list and then have an if statement that checks to see if the user has the key, and if yes, use append() to add the Unlock door option. Nice, huh?

Creating the User Options Function

Ok, so let's create the getUserChoice() function. We know that it will accept a single argument (the options formatted as a list of lists), and it will return whatever the user selected.

This function could have uses outside of this game, so let's put it in its own file. Create a new file (in your Adventure folder) named Utils.py. We'll use this file for all sorts of utility functions, starting with getUserChoice().

Here's the code:

```
############################################
# Utils.py
# Utility functions
############################################

# getUserChoice()
# Displays a list of options, prompts for an option, and returns it
# Pass it a list of lists in format [["Letter","Display Text"]]
# Example: [["A","Option A"],["B","Option B"],["C","Option C"]]
# Returns selected letter
def getUserChoice(options):
    # Create a variable to hold valid inputs
    validInputs=""
    # Loop through the options
    for opt in options:
        # Add this one to the valid letters list
        validInputs+=opt[0]
        # And display it
        print(opt[0], "-", opt[1])
```

```
    # Create the prompt
    prompt="What do you want to do? [" + validInputs + "]: "
    # Initialize variables
    choice=""
    done=False
    # Main loop
    while not done:
        # Get a single upper case character
        choice=input(prompt).strip().upper()
        # If the user entered more than 1 character
        if len(choice) > 1:
            # Just use the first
            choice=choice[0]
        # Do we have 1 valid input?
        if len(choice) == 1 and choice in validInputs:
            # We do, outa here!
            done = True
    # Return the selected option
    return choice
```

You can't test this code as is. Well, actually, you can. If you save the code and run it, though, nothing will happen.

Well, that is not quite true. Something did happen. When the code ran, it defined a function. But that's it. The function was defined but never actually executed. No code executed? Then no output.

#####

What's with the line of # symbols at the top of `Utils.py`? As you know, # starts a comment; anything after the # is ignored by Python. So that whole block at the top of the file is one big comment. What's it for? Coders like to start their files with information about what the file is, what it does, who wrote it, and so on. The line of pound signs above and below the comments are just to make the comment stand out.

To test the function, add some text code beneath the function—something like this:

```
choices = [["A", "Option A"],
           ["B", "Option B"],
           ["X", "Option X"],
           ["3", "And a numeric one, just because"]]

choice = getUserChoice(choices)
print(choice)
```

Now if you save and test the code, it will display options, prompt for input, and then display what the user chose.

So, what does our `getUserChoice()` function do?

It starts with a few lines of comments to explain what the function is, what to pass to it, and what it returns.

The function definition is pretty simple. It accepts a single argument:

```
def getUserChoice(options):
```

The function needs to restrict user input to only the valid options. But what are the valid options? That depends on what gets passed to the function. That means the code to check for valid options can't be hard coded. Instead, we need to build a set of valid options that will be used to validate user input. We start with an empty variable, like this:

```
    # Create a variable to hold valid inputs
    validInputs=""
```

Then we loop through all the options with a `for` loop:

```
    # Loop through the options
    for opt in options:
```

Within each iteration, `opt` will contain an option—a list with two items; `opt[0]` will contain the letter, and `opt[1]` will contain the text prompt.

The code within the loop does two things with each option:

```
        # Add this one to the valid letters list
        validInputs+=opt[0]
```

This line of code adds the letter to `validInputs`. The variable was empty at first. Using the above test code, it'll be `"A"` on the first iteration, `"AB"` on the second, then `"ABX"`, and then `"ABX3"`. These, and only these, are all of the allowed inputs, and we'll use this variable later in the function.

Then the code displays the option:

```
        # And display it
        print(opt[0], "-", opt[1])
```

The first item in the test code (the first loop iteration) is list `["A","Option A"]`. Within the list, item `[0]` is `"A"`, and item `[1]` is `"Option A"`. So this will print `A - Option A`.

Once the options have been displayed, we use `input()` to prompt the user for their selection. We want the `input()` prompt to display the available options, which are now in variable `validInputs`, so we create a prompt like this:

```
    # Create the prompt
    prompt="What do you want to do? [" + validInputs + "]: "
```

In our example, this will create a variable named `prompt` containing `What do you want to do? [ABX3]:`.

Next, we initialize a couple of variables:

```
    # Initialize variables
    choice=""
    done=False
```

`choice` will store the user choice. `done` is a boolean value, it can only ever be `True` or `False`, and we set the flag to `False` now; when the user selection is complete, we'll set it to `True`.

Next comes a while loop with input() code, much like you've seen many times before:

```
# Main loop
while not done:
```

We initialized done to False, and this while loop will keep running until done becomes True.

By the way, that line of code could have been written like this:

```
# Main loop
while done == False:
```

The end result is the same thing. But while not done feels so much cleaner. Right?

Within the while loop, we do this:

```
    # Get a single upper case character
    choice=input(prompt).strip().upper()
    # If the user entered more than 1 character
    if len(choice) > 1:
        # Just use the first
        choice=choice[0]
    # Do we have 1 valid input?
    if len(choice) == 1 and choice in validInputs:
        # We do, outa here!
        done = True
```

The code first uses input() to get a choice and then strips extraneous spaces and converts it to uppercase.

It then checks to ensure that the user only entered one letter. If there are more than one, then choice=choice[0] replaces the user selection with the first character, effectively ignoring the ones the user should not have typed.

And finally, the code checks to make sure that the user typed something by checking the length of choice and then checks to see if choice is in validInputs. If the length is right and choice is in validInputs, the code sets done to True, which then forces the while to stop looping.

Once the user makes a valid selection, the function simply returns `choice`:

```
    # Return the selected option
    return choice
```

Test your new function with different options. Add items to the list, edit and remove some, test all sorts of combinations to make sure it is working properly.

And when you are done testing it all, remove the test code you added below the function.

Updating Your Code

Now that you have a new `Utils` file with a wonderful new `getUserChoice()` function, how do we use it in our adventure game?

The code is now in three files: `Main.py` is the main game, `Strings.py` processes externalized strings, and `Utils.py` contains `getUserChoice()`. For code in `Main.py` to use functions that are in `Utils.py`, we need to import `Utils.py` into `Main.py`, just like we did `Strings.py`. So now your `import` statements at the top of `Main.py` should look like this:

```
# Imports
import Strings
import Utils
```

Combining `import` Statements

Python lets you import multiple libraries on one line. So the code:

```
import Strings
import Utils
```

could be shortened to:

```
import Strings, Utils
```

The end result is the same thing, so use whichever syntax you prefer.

Now you can modify your functions to use the new `getUserChoice()` function. Here is the updated version of the `doStart()` function:

```
# Location: Start
def doStart():
    # Display text
    print(Strings.get("Start"))
    # What can the player do?
    choices = [
        ["P", "Examine pile of boulders"],
        ["S", "Go to the structure"],
        ["B", "Walk towards the beeping"],
        ["R", "Run!"]
    ]
    # Prompt for user action
    choice = Utils.getUserChoice(choices)
    # Perform action
    if choice == 'P':
        doBoulders()
    elif choice == 'S':
        doStructure()
    elif choice == 'B':
        doBeeping()
    elif choice == 'R':
        doRun()
```

Save and run your code. It is functionally the same as it was before. (Remember, we are refactoring here.) So what changed?

We have a variable named `choices`, which is a list of lists that define all of the possible choices available to the player:

```
    choices = [
        ["P", "Examine pile of boulders"],
        ["S", "Go to the structure"],
        ["B", "Walk towards the beeping"],
        ["R", "Run!"]
    ]
```

And then we use our new `getUserChoice()` function to actually get the choice:

```
# Prompt for user action
choice=Utils.getUserChoice(choices)
```

As `getUserChoice()` is in the `Utils` library, we invoke it as `Utils.getUserChoice()`. The `choices` list (of lists) gets passed as an argument. The function returns the user choice, which is saved to the `choice` variable.

The rest of the code in `doStart()` is the same as before.

So, what did we achieve with all of this?

- The actual game code is cleaner as the user input loop has been removed.
- We now have a clean and flexible way to handle options that vary during game play.
- User choice input is now an external function—one that will be used everywhere we need to prompt the user for options. If we want to change how that works (add color, create buttons, anything at all), we just update that one function, and every instance of its use will be updated, too. Actually, you can try this. Look at the `getUserChoice()` function. It contains the code `print(opt[0], "-", opt[1])`, which is used to display each option. Change that hyphen to an equals, or a colon, or anything else. One little change, and every single menu option will be updated. Perfect!

CHALLENGE 14.1

You know what the challenge is this time: Refactor your game. Update every single location function in your game to use the new `getUserChoice()` function.

CHALLENGE 14.2

Back in Chapter 11, you created a wonderful `inputNumber()` function. That will be useful in your game, so copy it into `Utils.py`.

CHALLENGE 14.3

You know what else would make a great function? You are often going to need to ask the user to make a yes-or-no choice. Things like `Do you want to pick up the weapon?` or `Do you give up?` or `Do you need help?`

You could have a `while` loop in your code and use `input()` to get a `Y` or `N` from the user. But, nah. You could also probably use `getUserChoice()`. But that's a little convoluted.

So, create a new function in `Utils.py` called `inputYesNo()`. You'd call it like this:

```
pickUpGun=inputYesNo("Do you want to pick up the gun?")
```

`inputYesNo()` would display the passed text, prompt the user, and return a result.

You can use `inputNumber()` as a starting point for this one.

Summary

Refactoring is all about gradually and continuously improving your code. In this chapter and the previous one, we looked at a couple of ways to do this: identifying code that can be refactored for reuse and externalizing strings. Our application now is made up of multiple files, and we'll be adding more in the next chapters as we introduce additional functionality.

CHAPTER 15

Carrying (and Using) Stuff

In Chapters 13 and 14, we took a break from coding our game to clean up our code. We are going to continue doing that in this chapter, this time focusing on how to carry and use items.

Planning the Inventory System

Every adventure game requires that the player obtain and use items. Maybe you need to collect coins to buy an item from a story. The coins you collect are items, as is whatever you buy. Or perhaps you encounter a door that is locked, and it'll only open if you have found a particular item: a key. Items can be maps, food, potions, weapons, you name it.

In your game, for example, the structure has a door. It won't open yet. Try to open the door, and you see this:

```
What do you want to do? [SDBR]: d
The door appears to be locked.
You see a small circular hole. Is that the keyhole?
You move your hand towards it, it flashes blue and closes!
Well, that didn't work as planned.
```

The game doesn't actually tell the player to find a key. That's implied, and they'll need to do so to continue.

Working with items requires that your code have a way to store and access them during game play. And that's the job of an inventory system.

The question is how to store this information? You could create a bunch of variables:

```
# Inventory
coins = 0
sonicKey = False
jetPack = False
food = 100
```

This way, as players get more coins, you can just add them to the `coins` variable. If they were to find the key or jetpack, you'd set those flags to `True`. And `food` starts with `100` and gets used over time (so you subtract from the `food` variable) unless the user finds more (in which case you add to the variable).

That could work, but dealing with lots of individual variables isn't ideal. You couldn't easily loop through them all, saving and restoring would be onerous, and you'd always run the risk of accidentally overwriting variables.

Ok, so what about using a list?

```
# Inventory
inv = [0, False, False, 100]
```

This way, you could refer to `inv[0]` for the coins and `inv[1]` for the key.

Um, nope, that won't work. It's way too easy to make a mistake by referring to the wrong item. Lists are perfect for collections of the same type of thing (such as animals, as we saw in Part I of the book). Lists are not well suited for collections of related items of different types.

So, what to do?

Creating a Dictionary

Turns out that Python has another data type for just this purpose. Dictionaries are similar to lists in that they can store multiple values of different types, but unlike lists, they are stored using names.

Let's look at an example. Create a file named `Dict1.py` (which you'll probably want in your main `Python` folder, not in your `Adventure` folder). Here's the code:

```
pet = {
    "animal":"Iguana",
    "name":"Iggy",
    "food":"Veggies",
    "mealsPerDay":1
}
```

If you run the code, it won't display anything. So wait a moment before doing so.

This code creates a variable named `pet`. You'll notice that `pet` contains multiple values within curly braces (the { and } characters). Those curly braces tell Python that this is a dictionary.

{} or []

Don't confuse square brackets with curly braces. `pet = []` creates a list, and `pet = {}` creates a dictionary.

Oh, and `pets = [{},{}]` creates a list of dictionaries!

Each item in a dictionary is defined as a key:value pair. The key is the name of the item, and it is always a string enclosed within quotes. The value is any value; it can be strings and numbers, as we used here, but can potentially be lists, dictionaries, and more, too.

This pet dictionary contains four items. You can verify this by adding this code to Dict1.py:

```
print(len(pet))
```

Save and run the code, and it'll print 4, the value returned by len(pet).

If you want to access a specific item in the dictionary, you must refer to it by its key. For example:

```
pet = {
    "animal":"Iguana",
    "name":"Iggy",
    "food":"Veggies",
    "mealsPerDay":1
}

print(pet["name"], "the", pet["animal"])
print("eats", pet["mealsPerDay"], "times a day")
```

Save and run this updated code. What does it display?

pet["animal"] means get the value for key "animal", which is Iguana. pet["name"] means get the value for key "name", which is Iggy. And so on.

So the code will display:

```
Iggy the Iguana
eats 1 times a day
```

Working with Dictionaries

As you can see, dictionaries are perfect for grouping different but related information.

The `update()` Method

You can update dictionary items by just assigning new values, like this:

```
pet["mealsPerDay"] = 2
```

In addition, you can also use the `update()` function to do this:

```
pet.update({"mealsPerDay": 2})
```

Why would you ever want to use `update()` when a simple assignment works? `update()` can be used to update multiple name:value pairs at once.

Updating dictionary files is easy. This is the code for file `Dict2.py`:

```
pet = {
    "animal":"Iguana",
    "name":"Iggy",
    "food":"Veggies",
    "mealsPerDay":1
}

pet["mealsPerDay"] = 2

print(pet["name"], "eats", pet["mealsPerDay"], "meals")
```

This code creates the same dictionary as before but then updates the `mealsPerDay` item. Run this code, and it'll display: `Iggy eats 2 meals`.

Some other dictionary functions you may find useful are:

Function	Description
`clear()`	Remove all items from a dictionary.
`copy()`	Make a copy of a dictionary.
`keys()`	Return a list of all dictionary keys.
`values()`	Return a list of all dictionary values.

Lists of Dictionaries

Create a new file named `Dict3.py`. Here's the code:

```
pets = [
    {
        "animal":"Iguana",
        "name":"Iggy",
        "food":"Veggies",
        "mealsPerDay":1
    },
    {
        "animal":"Goldfish",
        "name":"Goldy",
        "food":"Flakes",
        "mealsPerDay":3
    }
]

for pet in pets:
    print(pet["animal"], "-", pet["name"])
```

Save and run the code. It will display:

```
Iguana - Iggy
Goldfish - Goldy
```

What is `pets` in this code? It's obviously a list because it is defined using square brackets. But what is in the list? Two items, and each is a dictionary defined using curly braces.

The `for` loop loops through list `pets`, and on each iteration, it creates a dictionary variable named `pet` whose values are then displayed.

The Inventory System

Ok, so now you know how to use dictionaries. And, yes, they are ideal for our inventory system. We could create an inventory like this:

```
inv = {
    "StructureKey": False,
    "Coins": 0
}
```

This way, for example, we could check `inv["StructureKey"]` to see if the player has the key and respond accordingly. And when the user finds the key, we just need to set `inv["StructureKey"] = True`.

That works, but we can improve things a little bit by providing *wrapper functions*.

> **NEW TERM**
>
> **Wrapper Function** A *wrapper function* is a function whose purpose is just to call some other code. It wraps the code, and thus the name.

What does that mean? Look at this code snippet:

```
inv = {
    "StructureKey": False,
    "Coins": 0
}

def takeStructureKey():
    inv["StructureKey"] = True

def hasStructureKey():
    return inv["StructureKey"]
```

This code creates the inv dictionary and two supporting functions. When the player finds the key, you just call takeStructureKey() to add it to the inventory; doing so sets the StructureKey value to True. And you can use hasStructureKey() any time to execute code only if the user has the key, like this:

```
if hasStructureKey():
```

hasStructureKey() returns True or False, which makes it really useful in if statements like this one.

These wrapper functions are entirely optional. After all, you can always access dictionary items directly. But, wrappers can make the code much easier to use and read.

Creating an Inventory

Ok, let's create our inventory system. We actually only need the key for now but will add the code for the coins, too, so we have it ready for future use.

In the Adventure folder, create a new file named Inventory.py. Here's the code:

```
#############################################
# Inventory.py
# Inventory system
#############################################

inv = {
    "StructureKey": False,
    "Coins": 0
}

# Add key to inventory
def takeStructureKey():
    inv["StructureKey"] = True

# Remove key from inventory
def dropStructureKey():
    inv["StructureKey"] = False
```

```
# Does the player have the key?
def hasStructureKey():
    return inv["StructureKey"]

# Add coins to inventory
def takeCoins(coins):
    inv["Coins"] += coins

# Remove coins from inventory
def dropCoins(coins):
    inv["Coins"] -= coins

# How many coins does the player have?
def numCoins():
    return inv["Coins"]
```

The code starts by defining the inventory dictionary, a variable named `inv`. It has two items in it: `StructureKey` keeps track of whether or not the player has the key (we initialize it to `False`), and `coins` tracks how many coins the player has (that one is initialized to `0`).

Then come the wrapper functions. For each item, you typically can do three things: get the item, drop the item, and check the status of the item. So, three wrapper functions per item, and you have two items, so six wrapper functions in all.

For inventory items that are `True` or `False` (like your key), you'd want a function that gets the item (sets the flag to `True`), a function that drops the item (sets the flag to `False`), and a way to check if the player has the item (just return the flag).

The Most Common Inventory Types

You are obviously not limited to Boolean and integer items in your inventory, but these tend to be the most used types. That's why we picked these two items for this example. That way, you can use the code as the basis for any future items and wrapper functions.

For inventory items that the player can accumulate multiple times (like your coins), you'd want a function that gets items (it'll increment the value) and drops items (decrement the value), as well as a way to return how many are in the inventory.

When your game necessitates additional items, you simply need to add a key:value pair to the dictionary and then create the wrapper functions.

Plugging In the Inventory System

Now that you have an inventory system, let's add it to our code. How? Another `import`. Change your `Main.py` so that the imports look like this:

```
# Imports
import Strings
import Utils
import Inventory as inv
```

That last `import` needs explaining.

As you will recall, when you execute functions in a library, you need to provide the fully qualified function name, like this:

```
Inventory.takeStructureKey()
```

`Inventory` is a good name for the file, but it is a long word to type over and over. So what do we do? We give it an alias:

```
import Inventory as inv
```

This tells Python to import the `Inventory` library but to refer to it by the shorter name `inv`, like this:

```
inv.takeStructureKey()
```

Much better!

Using the Inventory System

We're going to need some more strings, so add them to the `get()` function in `Strings.py`.

We already have messages for the structure door and trying to open the door with no key. Now we need a message for when the player tries to open the door with the key. Here's the `elif` you need to add:

```
elif id == "StructureDoorKey":
    return ("You look at the key you are holding.\n"
            "It is flashing blue, as is the keyhole.")
```

Now, how does the player find the key? Well, keep this to yourself, but it'll be hidden among the boulders. Add this `elif`:

```
elif id == "BouldersKey":
    return ("You look closer. Was that a blue flash?\n"
            "You reach between the boulders and find ...\n"
            "It looks like a key, it occasionally flashes blue.")
```

Now we need to let the player find the key. For now, it'll be easy: Just go to the boulders, and it'll be there. We'll make this harder in the next chapter, when we add the ability to track progress. For now, this is the updated `doBoulder()` function:

```
# Location: Boulders
def doBoulders():
    # Does the player have the key?
    if not inv.hasStructureKey():
        # No, display text
        print(Strings.get("BouldersKey"))
        # Add key to inventory
        inv.takeStructureKey()
    else:
        # Yes, so display regular boulder message
        print(Strings.get("Boulders"))
    # Go back to start
    doStart()
```

This updated function now first uses the `inv.hasStructureKey()` wrapper function to see if the player has the key or not. If not, it displays the new message telling the player that they found the key. And then it adds the key to the inventory, using this code:

```
# Add key to inventory
inv.takeStructureKey()
```

If the user has the key already (meaning they came back to the boulders a second time), then the old boulder text is displayed.

Ok, so now the player can find the key. Next, we need to change the structure door code. Previously, if the player went to the door, they saw a message about needing a key—and that was it. Now the code needs to respond differently based on whether the player has the key or not. Here is the updated `doStructureDoor()` function:

```
# Location: Structure door
def doStructureDoor():
    # Display text
    print(Strings.get("StructureDoor"))
    if inv.hasStructureKey():
        print(Strings.get("StructureDoorKey"))
    else:

print(Strings.get("StructureDoorNoKey"))
    # What can the player do?
    choices = [
        ["S", "Back to structure"],
        ["R", "Run!"]
    ]
    # Does user have the key?
    if inv.hasStructureKey():
        # Yep, add unlock to choices
        choices.insert(0, ["U","Unlock the door"])
    # Prompt for user action
    choice = Utils.getUserChoice(choices)
```

```
    # Perform action
    if choice == 'S':
        doStructure()
    elif choice == 'R':
        doRun()
    elif choice == 'U':
        doEnterStructure()
```

Ok, this is a fun one. The code first displays the basic door message. It then checks to see if the player has the key or not and uses this code to display one message if yes and another if no:

```
    # Display text
    print(Strings.get("StructureDoor"))
    if inv.hasStructureKey():
        print(Strings.get("StructureDoorKey"))
    else:

print(Strings.get("StructureDoorNoKey"))
```

Then come the user choices, like before. But the code now adds a choice if the player has the key:

```
    # What can the player do?
    choices = [
        ["S", "Back to structure"],
        ["R", "Run!"]
    ]
    # Does user have the key?
    if inv.hasStructureKey():
        # Yep, add unlock to choices
        choices.insert(0, ["U","Unlock the door"])
```

`choices` starts with the same two choices as before. If the player has the key, it adds an item to the `choices` list. The `Unlock the door` option is important; we want it to be the first item in the list. So rather than use `append()` to add `["U","Unlock the door"]`, we use `insert()` and place it at position `0` (making it the first choice).

And finally, this code is added to respond to the door being unlocked:

```
    elif choice == 'U':
        doEnterStructure()
```

Obviously, to run this code, you need a `doEnterStructure()` function, but you get the idea.

Now you see the value and power of our `getUserChoice()` function. The ability to change options dynamically based on inventory or other criteria is critical to making the game dynamic.

Ok, save the code and test it. The game starts as before:

```
You step outside. Nothing is familiar.
The landscape is dusty, vast, tinged red, barren.
You notice that you are wearing a spacesuit. Huh?
You look around. Red dust, a pile of boulders, more dust.
There's an odd octagon shaped structure in front of you.
You hear beeping nearby. It stopped. No, it didn't.
P - Examine pile of boulders
S - Go to the structure
B - Walk towards the beeping
R - Run!
I - Inventory
What do you want to do? [PSBRI]: 
```

Enter `S` to go to the structure and then `D` to open the door:

```
The door appears to be locked.
You see a small circular hole. Is that the keyhole?
You move your hand towards it, it flashes blue and closes!
Well, that didn't work as planned.
S - Back to structure
R - Run!
What do you want to do? [SR]: 
```

The player doesn't have the key, so the door doesn't open.

Enter S to go back to the structure, S again to go back to the start location, and then P to look at the pile of boulders:

```
You look closer. Was that a blue flash?
You reach between the boulders and find ...
It looks like a key, it occasionally flashes blue.
You look around. Red dust, a pile of boulders, more dust.
There's an odd octagon shaped structure in front of you.
You hear beeping nearby. It stopped. No, it didn't.
P - Examine pile of boulders
S - Go to the structure
B - Walk towards the beeping
R - Run!
I - Inventory
```

The player now has the key. And, yep, that was too easy. We'll change that soon enough.

Enter S to go back to the structure and then D to try the door again:

```
The door appears to be locked.
You see a small circular hole. Is that the keyhole?
You look at the key you are holding.
It is flashing blue, as is the keyhole.
U - Unlock the door
S - Back to structure
R - Run!
What do you want to do? [USR]: _
```

This time, the code responds differently because the key is in the inventory. Nice!

Oh. Go back to the boulder again, and you'll see this:

```
Seriously? They are boulders.
Big, heavy, boring boulders.
```

We now have a functioning inventory system, and the game can respond differently, depending on inventory contents.

Displaying the Inventory

One last point about inventories: Most games give you a way to check what you are holding. This is pretty easy to do. Add this function to the end of Inventory.py:

```
# Display inventory
def display():
    print("*** Inventory ***")
    print("You have", numCoins(), "coins")
    if hasStructureKey():
        print("You have a key that flashes blue")
    print("*****************")
```

This code is pretty simple. It defines a function named display(), which prints the current inventory contents. Notice that it uses the wrapper functions as opposed to accessing inv dictionary items directly. This is the preferred way to do things. Why? Well, imagine that you wanted to format coins a specific way or needed to perform any calculations (temporary multipliers on food or energy, for example). Always accessing items the same way ensures that you'll always execute the code you want.

So, how do we display the inventory? Just call the display() function. For example, if you added this to the choices in doStart():

```
        ["I", "Inventory"]
```

You could then add this to the processing:

```
    elif choice == "I":
        inv.display()
        doStart()
```

This way, if the user selects I, you display the inventory and then redisplay the doStart() options.

Yes, doStart() is calling doStart(). That's allowed, and it's called *recursion*.

NEW TERM

Recursion *Recursion* is when code calls itself—for example, a function named `doStart()` calling `doStart()`. Recursion is allowed, and, when used properly, is super powerful.

CHALLENGE 15.1

You now have everything you need to define a complete inventory system. Identify places in your game where you'll use additional inventory items. Add them to the inventory and create the appropriate wrapper functions.

Summary

In this chapter, you've learned how to use Python's dictionaries to store related items. You've used a dictionary and wrapper functions to create an inventory system. And you've seen how to work with the inventory inside of your game.

CHAPTER 16

Keeping It Classy

You now have a functioning inventory system that allows players to obtain, carry, and use items. And your game can adapt based on inventory items. The next thing you need is a player management system. To create this, we'll introduce you to classes, which are the focus of this chapter.

The Player System

In Chapter 15, you used a dictionary to create an inventory system. We used that to hide a key that the player needed to find in order to unlock the door.

But, let's be honest, we did a pretty lousy job of hiding the key. A player can just go to the boulders, and—ta-da!—there it is. In a real game, you'd typically create some sort of puzzle that must be solved before the key would be discoverable; you might require another item, like a shovel, to be found first, or make the key appear only after a series of steps are performed in order, or make it available via an in-game trade.

For our game, we'll make the key discoverable after multiple visits to the boulders. And to do that, we need a way to track visits, and that's where a player system comes into play (pun intended!).

A player system tracks player actions, statuses, and more. What type of things? Places visited, lives left, energy used, time played, points accumulated, and so on. These are not things you pick up and use, so they don't belong in an inventory system, but they do need to be tracked, and thus, a player system

And to create our player system, we are going to introduce you to a new type of Python object: the class. The truth is you've used classes already. For example:

```
name="Shmuel"
```

That variable `name` is a class of type `str` (Python's string class). If you were to display the variable's type, like this:

```
print(type(name))
```

you'd see `<class 'str'>` displayed.

And when you use functions like `upper()`:

```
name=name.upper()
```

you are actually calling a method named `upper()` in that `str` class.

So, yep, you've used lots and lots of classes. But you've not created one of your own. Yet.

Classes or Dictionaries?

We used a Python dictionary for our inventory system and are using a Python class for our player system. Why? Well, the truth is, we could have used classes or dictionaries for both systems. But we want you to know how to use both dictionaries and classes, so we have you use one of each. In your own code, you are free to use whatever you prefer.

Oh, and by the way, dictionaries are actually classes, too! Yep, a dictionary is a class, of type `dict`.

Creating a Player Class

Ok, so what actually is a class? In programming, a class is an object, much like variables are objects. But classes are special because of what they can do. We'll use lots of classes in Part III of this book. For now, the important thing we need you to understand about classes is that they can contain both data and functions.

What does that mean? Well, think about the lists and dictionaries we've created. What do they contain? Data, just data. They are variables that can contain variables. Dictionaries and lists can't contain functions, just data.

Classes, on the other hand, can contain data (called *properties*) and functions (called *methods*). For example, the `str` class we just referred to contains data (the text stored in the variable) and methods (like the `upper()` function).

This is important because by storing both data and the functions that access that data, classes are perfectly suited for writing highly reusable self-contained code.

There's a lot more to classes, as we'll see in Part III (where you'll be using lots of them). But, with this basic introduction, let's proceed with creating our player class.

Creating the Class

We'll create our class in its own file. So, create a new file named `Player.py` in your `Adventure` folder. Here's the code you need:

```
############################################
# Player.py
# player class
############################################
```

```
# Define player class
class player:
    pass
```

You can save and execute the code if you'd like, but you won't see any output. This code simply creates a class by using the `class` keyword followed by the name of the class and a colon.

The class code needs to be indented beneath this class statement (just like with `if` and `while` and `def`). We have nothing in your class yet, so we put a `pass` statement in there just so Python wouldn't throw error messages.

Now that you have a class, let's make it do something useful.

Defining Properties

As we explained earlier, classes can store data, and data in classes are called *properties* (or *attributes*).

> **NEW TERM**
> **Attributes** Data in classes are properties. This is true in just about every programming language. But Python also uses the term *attributes* to refer to all the data in classes, including properties, and also other information about the class. That said, in this book, if you see *attributes*, just think properties.

How do you create properties? Properties are variables, so you create them just like you'd create any other variables. Here's the updated code:

```
############################################
# Player.py
# player class
############################################

# Define player class
class player:
```

```
    # Properties
    name = "Adventurer"
    livesLeft = 3
    boulderVisits = 0
```

We removed the pass statement, as that is not needed anymore, and we added three properties.

name stores the name of the player, so you can personalize messages in the game, and we initialized it with the default value "Adventurer".

We also created a property to keep track of how many lives the player has left and initialized that to 3.

And, finally, the property we need to hide the key is boulderVisits, which we initialized to 0. (This property will be incremented each time the player visits the boulders.)

> TIP
>
> **Always Initialize Properties** You should always initialize properties with default values. This way, code will always work, even if you don't set property values explicitly in your code.

Save your changes.

If you'd like to test the class, you can add code like this beneath it:

```
p=player()
print(p.livesLeft)
```

What does this code do?

The first line creates a variable named p, which is an instance of the player class. Notice that we added parentheses after the class name. The truth is that p=player would have worked, too, but you'll usually want to include those parentheses so that you have the option of passing arguments to the class, if needed.

NEW TERM

Instance When a variable of a class type is created, we say that we've created an *instance* of that class. The act of creating an instance is called *instantiation*. So, you don't actually create a class variable; you *instantiate* an *instance* of the class.

Yes, we are helping you speak programmer-ese.

The second line displays the value in the `livesLeft` property inside of the `p` class.

So what would this code display? `3`, the value of `livesLeft`.

Test the other properties. And when you are done, remove your test code from the file.

It is important to note that when you create a class, you are actually creating a new type of variable. If you were to use `print(type(p))`, you'd see that `p` is a variable of type `class player`. And the class you create is just as much a class as any of Python's built-in classes—and can be used the same way.

Properties Can Be Any Type

We created simple text and numeric properties in our class. But, properties can be as simple or as sophisticated as needed, and can be lists, dictionaries, even other classes.

Displaying All Class Properties

If you want a list of all the properties in a class, you can use the `dir()` function. If your class instance is named `p`, you can use `dir(p)` to obtain a list of attributes. And because `dir()` returns a list, you can use a `for` loop to loop through each property. Here's an example:

```
p=player()
for att in dir(p):
    print (att, getattr(p, att))
```

The `for` loop loops through the list returned by `dir()` and creates a variable named `att` for each attribute in the list. `print()` then prints the attribute name and uses the `getattr()` function to get the attribute value.

Note that this code won't just display class properties; it'll display all class attributes (including lots of built-in ones), too.

Creating Methods

Now that our class has the properties we need, let's create our methods. Here's the code to add to your class:

```
# Get name property
def getName(self):
    return self.name

# Get number of lives left
def getLivesLeft(self):
    return self.livesLeft

# Player died
def died(self):
    if self.livesLeft > 0:
        self.livesLeft-=1

# Is player alive
def isAlive(self):
    return True if self.livesLeft > 0 else False

# Get number of times boulders were visited
def getBoulderVisits(self):
    return self.boulderVisits

# Player visited the boulders
def visitBoulder(self):
    self.boulderVisits += 1
```

Most of this code should be self-explanatory. Just like how you create functions, `def` is used to define methods (which, as you will recall, are functions).

What's different about these functions is the argument `self`. What is this? When you create methods in a class, those methods need to be able to access the class itself. `self` is simply a reference to the instance of the class, and by passing `self`, your method can access class properties.

So, to get the player name, we use this method:

```
# Get name property
def getName(self):
    return self.name
```

The `getName()` method gets passed a reference to the class instance, and it uses that to return `self.name`, meaning the `name` property in the current class (`self`).

If that sounds odd, um, yeah, it kinda is. We know. But, go with it. Make sure that `self` is the first argument to any class method, and you'll be good to go.

Let's look at another example:

```
# Get number of lives left
def getLivesLeft(self):
    return self.livesLeft
```

This one is pretty simple: `getLivesLeft()` returns the `livesLeft` property, so you can know how many lives your player has left.

Where methods get a bit more interesting is when they do more than just return properties. Look at this example:

```
# Is player alive
def isAlive(self):
    return True if self.livesLeft > 0 else False
```

Your code could check if a player is alive by simply checking how many lives they have left. But rather than do that `if` calculation all over the place, we created a method called `isAlive()`, which your code can call. It returns `True` if there are lives left (`livesLeft > 0`) or `False` if there are no lives left (meaning the player is dead). This way, you can use code like this in your game:

```
if p.isAlive():
```

Does Not Need to Be `Self`

Actually, you can name the first argument of a class method anything you'd like. Python coders have adopted `self` as the standard name, so you'll see that used in most Python code. But if you want to use another name, go for it.

Inline `if` Statements

Did you notice anything different about the return statement in the `isAlive()` method? That's an inline `if` statement—an `if` statement with an `else` in a single line of code. Technically, this is called a *ternary conditional operator*. (Yeah, that's why we called it an inline `if` statement.)

This code:

```
return True if self.livesLeft > 0 else False
```

is functionally equivalent to this code:

```
if self.livesLeft > 0:
    return True
else:
    return False
```

Either syntax works. We used the inline `if` because it is just so much cleaner, and it looks so much more professional (and we love looking very professional).

Nice, huh?

Oh, one important thing to note: The `isAlive()` method is defined as `def isAlive(self):`, with the `self` argument. In the `if` statement we just looked at, we called `isAlive()` with no arguments. So, what about that `self`? Well, turns out you don't have to worry about it. Python deals with that one for you; you just call the method (passing arguments, if needed) but ignore the `self` argument when you are calling class methods.

Methods that simply return properties are great. But where classes become super useful is when you create super useful methods that do whatever processing they need to return super useful results.

Back to our boulders and the methods we'll need to hide the key and eventually make it discoverable. First this method:

```
# Player visited the boulders
def visitBoulder(self):
    self.boulderVisits += 1
```

Every time the player visits the boulder location, we'll call this `visitBoulder()` method. All it does is increment the `boulderVisits` property so we can keep track of how many times the location has been visited.

To get the visit number, our code can call this method:

```
    # Get number of times boulders were visited
    def getBoulderVisits(self):
        return self.boulderVisits
```

This one is self-explanatory (we hope!).

Initializing the Class

Before we move on to using our class, there's one additional topic we should discuss.

When instantiating classes, it is sometimes necessary to execute some default code. This is often done to initialize properties, which we don't need to do here (as we did this with simple assignments right inside of the class definition). But there are other reasons to do so, too.

When you create a class, you can define a *constructor*—a method that will automatically be executed.

NEW TERM

Constructor A *constructor* is a method in a call that gets called automatically when a class is instantiated.

We don't actually need a constructor in your class, but you need to know what constructors are and what they look like, so here we go:

```
    # Initialize class and properties
    def __init__(self):
        self.name = "Adventurer"
        self.livesLeft = 3
        self.boulderVisits = 0
```

In Python, constructors are always named __init__ (that's two underscore characters before and after the word init). If a method with that name exists, Python will execute it. Simple.

In this code snippet we're demonstrating how you could use the constructor to initialize properties. But, as already noted, we don't need to do that as we've initialized them already.

If you want to add this code to your class, you can. Your choice.

Using Our New Class

We now have a class for your player system. So let's plug it into the game and update the boulder and key-finding code.

The first thing we need to do is import the new Player file. So, update your import statements like this:

```
# Imports
import Strings
import Utils
import Inventory as inv
import Player
```

Next, we need to create an instance of our new class. Add this code to the top of Main.py. You can put it right after the import statements:

```
# Create player object
p = Player.player()
```

The player class is in the Player library, so we refer to it as Player.player().

Now when you run the game, the code will immediately instantiate the player class, and we can use this new instance (named p) in our code.

Oh, we need one more block of text for our game. We have text that gets displayed when the player looks at the boulder, and we have text that gets displayed when they find the key. Let's add one more block of text that will be displayed on the second and subsequent visits. Add this to the get() function in Strings.py:

```
    elif id == "Boulders2":
        return ("What's with you and boulders?\n"
                "They are still big, heavy, boring boulders.")
```

Great. Now all we have to do is update the `doBoulder()` function. Here is the updated code:

```
# Location: Boulders
def doBoulders():
    # Track this visit
    p.visitBoulder()
    # Display text
    if p.getBoulderVisits() == 1:
        print(Strings.get("Boulders"))
    elif p.getBoulderVisits() == 3:
        print(Strings.get("BouldersKey"))
        inv.takeStructureKey()
    else:
        print(Strings.get("Boulders2"))
    # Go back to start
    doStart()
```

Let's review the updated function. We need to know how many times the player has visited the boulders, so the first thing the code does is this:

```
    # Track this visit
    p.visitBoulder()
```

As you know, the `visitBoulder()` method in the `player` class simply increments the `boulderVisits` property. So, the first time the user goes to the boulders the count will be incremented to `1`, the next time it'll be incremented to `2`, and so on.

Then comes an `if` statement. If this is the first visit, then the `Boulders` message is displayed. If this is the second visit, then the `else` will display the `Boulders2` message. If this is the third visit, then the `elif` will display the `BouldersKey` message and also take the key and add it to the inventory, using this code:

```
        inv.takeStructureKey()
```

If the user visits again, the `else` will show the `Boulders2` message.

That should do it! Ok, let's test it.

The game starts. Enter `I` to display the inventory. There is nothing in the inventory:

```
*** Inventory ***
You have 0 coins
*****************
```

Enter `P` to look at the pile of boulders:

```
Seriously? They are boulders.
Big, heavy, boring boulders.
You look around. Red dust, a pile of boulders, more dust.
There's an odd octagon shaped structure in front of you.
You hear beeping nearby. It stopped. No, it didn't.
P - Examine pile of boulders
S - Go to the structure
B - Walk towards the beeping
R - Run!
I - Inventory
What do you want to do? [PSBRI]:
```

The first boulders message is displayed. No hints here. Will the player figure it out?

Enter `P` to go to the boulders again:

```
What do you want to do? [PSBRI]: p
What's with you and boulders?
They are still big, heavy, boring boulders.
You look around. Red dust, a pile of boulders, more dust.
There's an odd octagon shaped structure in front of you.
You hear beeping nearby. It stopped. No, it didn't.
P - Examine pile of boulders
S - Go to the structure
B - Walk towards the beeping
R - Run!
I - Inventory
What do you want to do? [PSBRI]:
```

This time, the second boulders message is displayed. That's a subtle hint. If the player is paying attention, they'll notice that the text changed a bit, hinting at the fact that different things happen on return visits.

Enter P to go to the boulders a third time:

```
You look closer. Was that a blue flash?
You reach between the boulders and find ...
It looks like a key, it occasionally flashes blue.
You look around. Red dust, a pile of boulders, more dust.
There's an odd octagon shaped structure in front of you.
You hear beeping nearby. It stopped. No, it didn't.
P - Examine pile of boulders
S - Go to the structure
B - Walk towards the beeping
R - Run!
I - Inventory
What do you want to do? [PSBRI]: _
```

Bingo! The player has found the key. Enter I to check the inventory:

```
*** Inventory ***
You have 0 coins
You have a key that flashes blue
*****************
```

That worked! The player found the key, and it is in the inventory, exactly as planned.

What happens if the player goes back to the boulders?

```
What do you want to do? [PSBRI]: p
What's with you and boulders?
They are still big, heavy, boring boulders.
You look around. Red dust, a pile of boulders, more dust.
There's an odd octagon shaped structure in front of you.
You hear beeping nearby. It stopped. No, it didn't.
P - Examine pile of boulders
S - Go to the structure
B - Walk towards the beeping
R - Run!
I - Inventory
What do you want to do? [PSBRI]:
```

All future visits will show the second boulders message.

And now the player can proceed to the structure and unlock the door.

CHALLENGE 16.1

Our `player` class has a `name` property that you can use to personalize the game. Update your `doWelcome()` function to ask the player for their name and save it to the `player` class. You can do something as simple as `p.name=input()`, or you can create a method in `player` to `setName()`. Either way works.

Then use `p.getName()` in your code to display personalized messages.

Oh, you'll also want to personalize the text returned by `get()` in `Strings.py`, too. One simple way to do this is to pass `p.getName()` as a second argument to the `get()` method, and use that when you construct the text to be displayed..

CHALLENGE 16.2

When a player runs, they die (method `doRun()`). Change the code so that when they run, they lose a life. (Hint: we have a method in the class that does just this.) Then use `isAlive()` in an `if` statement. If the player is still alive, send them to `doStart()` to continue playing; if not, use `gameOver()`.

Summary

In this chapter, you learned how to create and use classes. You created a class for the game's player system and introduced new functionality by combining this new system with the inventory system created in Chapter 15.

CHAPTER 17

Color Your World

You now have the beginnings of a functioning game. And it looks boring. Plain old black-and-white text. Blah! In this chapter, we'll show you how to install and use third-party Python libraries, and we'll use one to introduce a splash of color to our game.

Installing Third-Party Libraries

We mentioned third-party libraries way back in Chapter 3. Python comes with all sorts of built-in libraries, and you've used many of them. third-party libraries are created by Python developers, and you can use them just as you would the built-in libraries.

Of course, before you can use libraries, you need to install them. To add color to our game's output we'll be using a popular third-party Python library called Colorama. The truth is that you can add color to your output without any libraries by adding codes like `ESC [ 31 m` to your output. (That's red text, by the way.) But, by using Colorama, you can actually use sensible text (like the word `RED`), which is much easier.

So how do you install libraries in Python? When you installed Python back in Chapter 1, a series of tools and utilities were installed, too. One of them is called PIP, and its job is to install (and update and remove) third-party libraries.

You use PIP right inside the Terminal window (where application output is usually displayed). Yep, when your code isn't running, you can type terminal commands in that window. To install Colorama, the command is:

- **Windows users:** `pip install colorama`
- **Mac and Chromebook users:** `pip3 install colorama`

After issuing the command, you see this:

```
Collecting colorama
  Using cached colorama-0.4.4-py2.py3-none-any.whl (16 kB)
Installing collected packages: colorama
Successfully installed colorama-0.4.4
```

PIP

PIP is an acronym that stands for Pip Installs Packages or Pip Installs Python. And, yes, the first word is the acronym PIP! That's programmer humor for you.

Alternatively, some have suggested that PIP stands for preferred installer program. But we like the other acronym.

Don't worry if you see a different version number. The version will change as the library developer makes changes and updates. The key here is the last line. So long as it says `Successfully installed`, you're good to go.

Using Colorama

To color text in the Terminal window, you need to embed special codes (called *escape sequences*) in the output. Rather than deal with obscure codes, Colorama lets you use English color names, which it converts to the necessary codes.

So, to display text in red, you'd do something like this:

```
print(colorama.Fore.RED+"Hello, this is in red")
```

Easy enough.

Importing and Initializing the Library

Before we can use Colorama, we need to import the library. You know how to do that:

```
import colorama
```

`colorama` is a long name. You can shorten it with an alias, as we did back in Chapter 15 with the `Inventory` file:

```
import colorama as col
```

This way, you can shorten the above code to:

```
print(col.Fore.RED+"Hello, this is in red")
```

This is all syntax you've seen before.

But there is another way to use `import` that you've not seen yet. Look at this `import` statement:

```
from colorama import Fore
```

This import is a little different. It imports just the Fore part of the colorama library and lets us access Fore without needing to fully qualify the name. What does that mean? We could do this:

```
print(Fore.RED+"Hello, this is in red")
```

Now the code is even shorter!

You can use any syntax you want. We'll use this new one just so you can get used to it.

The two parts of the colorama library we need are init (which initializes the library) and Fore (which has the codes for foreground colors). So, your updated import code block should look like this:

```
# Imports
import Strings
import Utils
import Inventory as inv
import Player
from colorama import init, Fore
```

The last thing we need to do before using Colorama is to initialize it. Add this code to the top of your Main.py (either before or after the player class instantiation):

```
# Initialize colorama
init()
```

Test your app to make sure nothing's broken. You'll not see any color just yet, but things should just work exactly as they did previously. If they do, then all is good, and we can move on to adding color to your output.

Coloring Your Output

You have pretty limited color options in the Terminal window. Basically, you can use BLACK, RED, GREEN, YELLOW, BLUE, MAGENTA, CYAN, and WHITE as text colors.

Foreground color means the color of the text itself. Colorama also supports background colors (so you can have red on yellow, for example), but we'll just use foreground colors here to keep things simpler. And you'll want to pick different colors for different parts of the text.

We've decided to use `GREEN` for the main game text, `YELLOW` for menus (as they need to be bright and clear), `RED` for when something goes wrong, and `CYAN` for the inventory.

To use these colors, we simply need to add the right codes to the `print()` functions. For example, this is the updated `doWelcome()` function:

```
# Welcome the player
def doWelcome():
    # Display text
    print(Fore.GREEN+Strings.get("Welcome"))
```

All that has changed is the inclusion of `Fore.GREEN` that has been prepended into the display text. That's all you need to do.

When the player tries to open the door, we'll display prompts in the standard `GREEN`, unless there's an error (you can't open the door, sorry), in which case we display the text in `RED`. Here's a snippet from the `doStructureDoor()` function:

```
# Location: Structure door
def doStructureDoor():
    # Display text

print(Fore.GREEN+Strings.get("StructureDoor"))
    if inv.hasStructureKey():

print(Fore.GREEN+Strings.get("StructureDoorKey"))
    else:

print(Fore.RED+Strings.get("StructureDoorNoKey"))
```

As you can see, this is all pretty simple.

Custom Output Functions

Rather than stick color instructions all over the place, you may want to create your own utility functions (put them in `Utils.py`). You could have one called `printGreen()`, so that any text passed to it prints with a `Fore.GREEN` prefix, and so on.

Or you could create functions like `printMessage()`, `printErrorMessage()`, `printMenuText()`, etc., and use the colors you want inside of those.

There is no right or wrong way to do this. It's all about how you, as the coder, want to organize your code.

See how much power you have?

Where things get less simple is coloring the menus or inventory display. Why? Open `Inventory.py` and try adding `Fore.CYAN`. VS Code underlines `Fore`, as you can see here:

```
# Display inventory
def display():
    print(Fore.CYAN+"*** Inventory ***")
    print(Fore.CYAN+"You have", numCoins(), "coins")
    if hasStructureKey():
        print(Fore.CYAN+"You have a key that flashes blue")
    print(Fore.CYAN+"*****************")
```

Why did this happen? Because the code in `Main.py` knows about Colorama, but the code in `Inventory.py` does not. You'll need to add the import to this file, too.

Add this to the top of `Inventory.py`:

```
# Imports
from colorama import Fore
```

We don't need to initialize Colorama again, so we just need `Fore` this time. With this change, things will work.

Oh, you'll need to do the same for `Utils.py` if you want to color the choices in those `print()` statements.

Save your code and run the game. Depending on the colors used, you should see output like this:

```
*** Inventory ***
You have 0 coins
*****************
You look around. Red dust, a pile of boulders, more dust.
There's an odd octagon shaped structure in front of you.
You hear beeping nearby. It stopped. No, it didn't.
P - Examine pile of boulders
S - Go to the structure
B - Walk towards the beeping
R - Run!
I - Inventory
What do you want to do? [PSBRI]: s
You examine the odd structure.
Eerily unearthly sounds seem to be coming from inside.
You see no doors or windows.
Well, that outline might be a door, good luck opening it.
And that beeping. Where is it coming from?
S - Back to start
D - Open the door
B - Walk towards the beeping
R - Run!
What do you want to do? [SDBR]: d
The door appears to be locked.
You see a small circular hole. Is that the keyhole?
You move your hand towards it, it flashes blue and closes!
Well, that didn't work as planned.
S - Back to structure
R - Run!
What do you want to do? [SR]:
```

This looks much better. You can use as much or as little color as you'd like. Just keep in mind:

- Pick colors that make sense. By that we mean don't use green for errors or warnings.
- Be consistent in color use, with all menus one color, all messages one color, and so on. That helps orient players, as the color helps them identify what they are seeing.

- For greater impact, you can use background colors, too. If you want to do so, you'll need to add `Back` to the `import` line, and then you can do things like `Back.WHITE+Fore.RED`.
- Remember that colors are sticky. What does that mean? If you don't set a color in a `print()`, then the last color you set will be used. Setting a color basically turns it on, and it remains the active color until you change it. So if something isn't coloring as expected, you probably didn't exactly provide a color, and the previously chosen color is being used. This applies to setting background colors, too.
- You'll also want to set colors back when your application finishes running. If you don't, the last color used will remain the Terminal text color. So, in the `gameOver()` function, you should probably set the color back to `Fore.WHITE` when you are done.

TIP

You Can Auto Reset If you don't want colors to be remembered, change your `init()` to `init(autoreset=True)`. This way, colors will be applied to the current `print()` only.

CHALLENGE 17.1

Now that you know how to color your output, go ahead and color the whole game.

Summary

In this chapter, you learned how to install and use third-party Python libraries. You use the fun Colorama library to color your game's output.

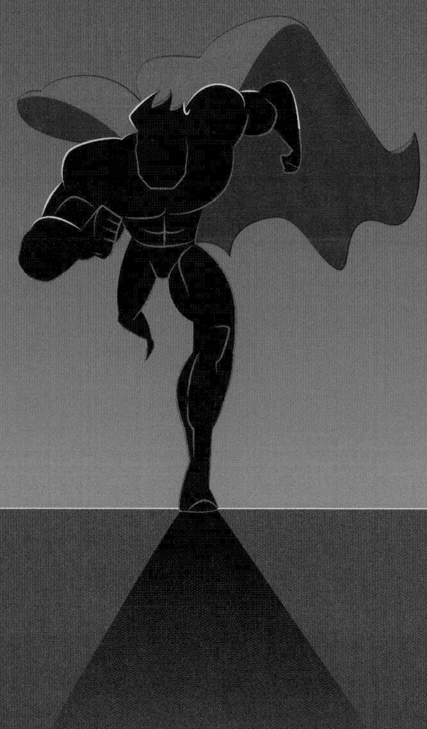

CHAPTER 18

Keep Going

You now have a functioning (albeit limited) text-based adventure game. Using libraries and functions, lists and dictionaries, and classes, you have everything you need to really build a complete and comprehensive game. In this chapter, we'll give you some ideas about where to go next and pointers to help you get there.

Health and Lives

Many games track player lives. When players *die*, they lose a life and continue playing. The game is over when no lives are left. Our `player` class has properties and methods for using lives, and you can use them in your game.

Newer games also track player health and often combine doing so with tracking lives. How could you do this in your game?

For starters, you'd need to update the `player` class with a couple of properties. Here's what our updated class looks like:

```
# Properties
name = "Adventurer"
livesLeft = 3
boulderVisits = 0
maxHealth = 100
health = maxHealth
```

You'll see that two properties have been added: `maxHealth` and `health`.

`maxHealth` stores the maximum amount of health a player can have at any time. We'll need this value for all sorts of calculations, and rather than hard code the value all over the place, we do so once, in a property that other code can refer to. This way, if we needed to change the value, we'd do so once, in one place only. Here `maxHealth` is `100`, but you can change it to whatever value your game needs.

`health` stores the current player health level. When the game starts, the player needs to be at full health, so the `health` variable is initialized to `maxHealth`. Of course, if your game works differently—maybe the player starts at half health and has to locate items to increase health—you change the initialization as needed.

Now we need methods to work with lives and health. We'll start with methods to add and remove lives.

If your game allows a player to add lives (maybe by finding an item, using a potion, buying a heart, etc.), you'll need a way to update the player system with this information. This `addLives()` method gets added to the `player` class:

```
    # Add lives
    def addLife(self, lives=1):
        # Increment lives
        self.livesLeft += lives
        # And fill up health
        self.health = self.maxHealth
```

When executed, the addLife() function does two things. The first line increases the value of the livesLeft property, effectively giving the player another life. Many games also restore player health when a life is added, and the second line in the function restores player health back to maxHealth. If you don't want this to happen, just remove that second line.

As this function is a method in a class, the first argument is always self (as we discussed in Chapter 16).

But look at that second argument. Does it look different to you? What does lives=1 mean? That =1 provides a default value for argument lives (which actually makes the lives argument optional).

In our game we only need to add a single life at a time, so we could have simply written addLife() like this:

```
    def addLife(self):
        self.livesLeft += 1
        self.health = self.maxHealth
```

Call addLife(), and it increments livesLeft by 1 (that's what += 1 does). Simple.

But what if at some point in the future we needed the code to allow users to add multiple lives at once? We'd need another function that accepted the number of lives to add as an argument. Something like this:

```
    def addLives(self, lives):
        self.livesLeft += lives
        self.health = self.maxHealth
```

True, we may not need this functionality now, but at some point we may, and then we'd have two very similar functions.

Write Flexible Methods

This `addLife()` function is a good example of how you should write all your methods. Wherever possible, plan for future needs and capabilities and make your code as flexible as possible. This will make your code more reusable and future safe. And this can be done with any function, not just methods within classes.

Anticipating possible future needs, we created a single `addLife()` function that supports both use cases. How does it do this? By accepting an optional argument—one that has a default value that is used if no explicit argument value is passed. So, if your code called the method like this:

```
p.addLife()
```

without passing a value for `lives`, then Python would use the default value of `1` for that argument value. But if the code did this:

```
p.addLife(3)
```

then the passed value of `3` would be used.

We may never need the ability to add multiple lives. But, with barely any extra code, we can support that use case, and we've added no complexity to how the function gets called either (`p.addLife()` works perfectly). So, why not?

Now we need a method to remove a life:

```
    # Lose lives
    def loseLife(self, lives=1):
        # Decrement lives
        self.livesLeft -= lives
        # Make sure didn't go below 0
        if self.livesLeft < 0:
            # It did, so set to 0
            self.livesLeft = 0
        # If no lives
        if self.livesLeft == 0:
            # No health either
            self.health = 0
```

```
        # If lives left
        elif self.livesLeft >= 1:
            # Reset health to full
            self.health = self.maxHealth
```

loseLife() looks more complicated, but it really isn't.

Like the addLife() function, it accepts an optional number of lives, and it defaults to 1.

The first thing it does is decrement the livesLeft property. But, unlike when we add lives, when we subtract lives, we'll want to make sure we didn't inadvertently go below 0. This code addresses that:

```
        # Make sure didn't go below 0
        if self.livesLeft < 0:
            # It did, so set to 0
            self.livesLeft = 0
```

Now if livesLeft goes below 0, it gets set back to 0. Now users can't have negative lives! Phew!

The rest of the code sets health as needed. Each time the player starts using a new life, health is reset back to maxHealth. But if there are no lives left, then we set health to 0.

We can now add and delete lives as needed. Next, we need to do the same for health. Let's start with a method to get the current health value:

```
    # Get health value
    def getHealth(self):
        return self.health
```

getHealth() is a simple function: It just returns the current value of the health property.

So, on to adding and losing health. Here are the two new methods:

```
    # Add health
    def addHealth(self, health):
```

```
        self.health += health
        # Make sure not over maxHealth
        if self.health > self.maxHealth:
            # Went too high, reset to max
            self.health=self.maxHealth

    # Lose health
    def loseHealth(self, health):
        self.health -= health
        # Make sure not < 0
        if self.health < 0:
            # Lose a life
            self.loseLife()
```

`addHealth()` accepts an argument that tells the function how much health to add. It then uses `self.health += health` to add the passed `health` amount to the `health` property. An `if` statement then makes sure that `health` isn't larger than `maxHealth` (which could happen if `health` were at `75` and the user did some action that added `50`, for example). If `health` is greater than `maxHealth`, it gets reset to `maxHealth`.

`loseHealth()` does the opposite: It subtracts from the `health` property. If doing so makes `health` go below `0`, then the function calls `loseLife()` (which, as you saw previously, handles decrementing `livesLeft` and sets `health` as needed).

With these properties and methods, you have everything you need to support lives and health in your game. So what should you do next?

- Modify your game code to give players ways to add and lose lives.
- You also need ways to use and gain health.
- You previously added a way to display inventory contents, and you'll probably want to do the same to display life and health status.
- If you really want to up the sophistication level, you can display a health meter. You'll want to write a function that accepts a meter maximum and the current level—the two things you'll need in order to display a progress meter. You could even color the meter: green if the current level is 50% or more of the meter maximum, yellow if it is between 25% and 50%, and red if the value is less than 25%.

Watch Variable Names

The `addHealth()` and `loseHealth()` functions are good examples of how *not* to write code. Yes, they work, but naming an argument the same as a property is asking for trouble. If the property is named `health`, it's safer to use anything but the name `health` for the argument name.

Shopping for Items

Buying items is a popular and common game feature. Some items may be required (meaning the game can't be finished without having procured them), and some may be optional (they improve the game experience but are not required to complete the game). Allowing players to buy items is a good way to add variability to a game. By buying different items, players can impact game play.

We added support for coins in our inventory system. But we never added any way to do anything with the coins.

So, how could you support shopping in your code? There are a few things you'll need to do:

- Players need a way to obtain coins. You can perhaps give them coins when they solve a puzzle. Or enemies can drop coins when they are beaten. You can hide coins in various locations and add them to the player's inventory when found. (If you do this, you need to decide what happens if the player revisits that location. Do they get more coins, or is it a one-time deal?)
- You need to decide if the store is always available as an option or whether it's in specific game locations.
- You need a way to display a list of things available for purchase.
- And, finally, when the player purchases an item, you need to remove those coins from the inventory and add the item they bought.

There is no single way to implement these tasks, but we'll show you one way to create a list of items for purchase and how to display them to the player.

This is the code for `Items.py`:

```
############################################
# Items
# Items that may be purchased
############################################

items = [
    {
        "id":"health",
        "description":"Health restoration potion.",
        "key":"H",
        "cost":100
    },
    {
        "id":"blaster",
        "description":"Laser blaster.",
        "key":"B",
        "cost":250
    },
    {
        "id":"grenades",
        "description":"3 Space Grenades.",
        "key":"G",
        "cost":300
    },
    {
        "id":"shield",
        "description":"Shield which halves enemy damage.",
        "key":"S",
        "cost":500
    },
    {
        "id":"life",
        "description":"Additional life.",
        "key":"L",
        "cost":1000},
]
```

When creating a list of items that can be purchased you'll want to think about how this information will be used. You'll need to check that the player has enough money to buy an item, so you'll need to access the cost. You'll want a clear description of the item. And so on.

To this end, you create a list of dictionaries. Each item in a dictionary is one item that can be purchased. If you need to add more items to the game, you just add items to this dictionary. And then you write supporting functions. Here's one example, which gets the items that are available for purchase:

```
# Get available items
# Return in format used by getUserChoice()
def getItems():
    # Variable for result
    result = []
    # Loop through items
    for item in items:
        # Create empty list
        i=[]
        # Add key
        i.append(item["key"])
        # Add description + cost
        i.append(item["description"]+" ("+str(item["cost"])+")")
        # Add this item to the result
        result.append(i)
    # Return it
    return result
```

`getItems()` is an interesting function. As you will recall from Chapter 14, the `getUserChoice()` function expects choices to be passed as a list of lists. Your list of items to be purchased is a list of dictionaries. So, `getItems()` loops through the items and creates the list of lists that `getUserChoice()` expects. How does it do this?

The function starts by creating an empty list to store the result, like this:

```
result = []
```

It then uses a for loop to loop through the items. Each time it loops, it creates another temporary list variable to store this particular item, like this:

```
# Create empty list
i=[]
```

It then needs to add two items into this list. The first is the menu letter (what the player enters to select a menu option), and the second is the menu text. To add the first, we do this:

```
# Add key
i.append(item["key"])
```

The append() function adds an item to a list, and here it adds the value key for the current item.

The menu text is comprised of the description and the cost, like this:

```
# Add description + cost
i.append(item["description"]+" ("+str(item["cost"])+")")
```

Again, append() adds this to the temporary list. When done, the list (for the first item) will look like ['H', 'Health restoration potion. (100)'], which is exactly what we need.

This item is then added to the result:

```
# Add this item to the result
result.append(i)
```

This continues for each item, and then the completed result is returned.

Now the list of items can be displayed using the existing menu function, perhaps like this:

```
# Display shopping list menu
choice=Utils.getUserChoice(Items.getItems())
```

Clever, huh?

If you plan to implement items and shopping, here are some things to consider:

- Give players ways to obtain coins. (We'll show you one idea next.)
- Decide how the player displays the store and items.
- Possibly put shopping in a loop so that the player can keep buying things until they are done.
- You may want to limit the shopping to show only items the player can afford. You could modify `getItems()` to accept the number of coins the player has, and then, when you loop to build the list of items, have an `if` statement that checks the cost and only append ones the player can afford.
- Some items purchased will need to be added to the inventory. If the player buys health or lives, you call the appropriate `player()` methods instead.

Random Events

You may want your game to be linear, meaning that things happen in a specific order every time the game is played. Or you may want to introduce variability into the game, so that each time it is played, things are a little different. There is no right or wrong way to implement game play. You, as the coder, get to decide what your game does.

If you do want to introduce variability, you can employ random events. You know how to use the `random` library; we did that together way back in Chapter 3. You can use `random` anywhere you want to introduce a random event. For example, code like this would *find* 100 coins on the ground and would add them to the inventory:

```
# 100 coins show up 1 in 4 times
if random.randrange(1, 5) == 1:
    # Tell player
    print("You see 100 coins on the ground.")
    print("You pick them up.")
    # Add to inventory
    inv.takeCoins(100)
```

This code would find coins about one in four times. How? Because the `random.randrange(1, 5)` returns a random number from 1 to 4 (the 5 is not included, as you will recall). This means that approximately a quarter of the time the code will return 1, a quarter of the time it'll return 2, and so on. The `if` statement checks to see if `randrange()` returned 1, which it does about one in four times, and if yes, the coins are found and picked up. So, a quarter of the time that this function runs, the user will get coins. Want it to be one in three times? Just change the range to be `1, 4`.

If you do this often enough, you might want to write a function to determine if a random event should occur or not. Look at this function (which could be added to `Utils.py`):

```
# Should a random event occur?
# Pass it a frequency, 2=1 out 2, 3=1 out of 3, etc.)
def randomEvent(freq):
    return True if random.randrange(0, freq)==0 else False
```

`randomEvent()` accepts a single argument, which tells the function how often the event should occur. Pass it 4, and it'll return `True` one in four times and `False` the other three times. Pass it 2, and half the time it'll return `True` and half the time it'll return `False`. The logic is the same as in the previous example, but this time it is put into a user-defined function.

By using this function you don't really have less code than you'd have by using `randrange()` right inside your app. But using a user-defined function like this is still a good idea. For starters, it keeps your code cleaner. In addition, it allows you to easily change how randomness works; just change one function rather than lots of individual pieces of code.

So how would you use the function? Like this:

```
# 100 coins show up 1 in 4 times
if Utils.randomEvent(4):
    # Tell player
    print("You see 100 coins on the ground.")
    print("You pick them up.")
    # Add to inventory
    inv.takeCoins(100)
```

As you can see, the result is the same, but the code is a bit cleaner. `Utils.randomEvent(4)` returns `True` approximately one in four times, and when that happens, the code under `if` is executed, and the player gets the coins.

And you can add even more randomness if you'd like. Look at this example:

```
# 1-100 coins show up 1 in 4 times
if Utils.randomEvent(4):
    # Pick a random number of coins
    coins=random.randrange(1, 101)
    # Tell player
    print("You see", coins, "coins on the ground.")
    print("You pick them up.")
    # Add to inventory
    inv.takeCoins(coins)
```

Now there is a one in four chance of finding a random number of coins (between 1 and 100). Randomness is a great way to make your game more interesting.

Battling Enemies

Battling enemies is another common game feature. Unfortunately, this one is a bit trickier to implement. That said, we'll give you some pointers to get you started.

Like items, enemies have properties. So you'll want an `Enemies.py` file, perhaps something like this one:

```
############################################
# Enemies
# Defines enemies, supporting functions
############################################

# List of enemies
# Each needs a short name, a description,
# strength (higher number = need to do more damage to kill),
# and defense (lower number = easier to hit)
```

```
enemies = [
    {
        "id":"slug",
        "description":"Space slug",
        "strength":10,
        "damageMin":1,
        "damageMax":3,
        "defense":2
    },
    {
        "id":"eel",
        "description":"Radioactive eel",
        "strength":50,
        "damageMin":10,
        "damageMax":15,
        "defense":1
    },
    {
        "id":"alien",
        "description":"Green tentacled alien",
        "strength":25,
        "damageMin":5,
        "damageMax":10,
        "defense":3
    }
]
```

This code defines and organizes enemies. Each has an `id` and a `description`, and then there is data that describes the enemy's abilities and behavior. `strength` is how much damage the player must inflict to kill the enemy. `damageMin` and `damageMax` are the range of values for the amount of damage the enemy can inflict on the player. (We wanted a range so that each time the enemy attacks, the actual damage inflicted will be random using that range, but you could easily change it to a fixed damage value.) `defense` is how well the enemy can avoid attacks from the player; `"defense":3` means that there is a one-in-three chance of the enemy dodging an attack.

You get the idea. You don't have to use these specific settings, and you can make any setting fixed or a range, as needed. The key is that all enemy data needs to be cleanly defined and organized.

Your code could then get a specific enemy by using the `id` key. Or if you wanted a random enemy, you could do something like this:

```
# Get a random enemy
def getRandomEnemy():
    # Return a random enemy
    return random.choice(enemies)
```

That said, that's the easy part. The trickier part is the actual battle mechanics. There are lots of ways to do this, and a popular one is turn-based battling, kinda like Pokémon battles. To do this:

- One side goes first (you could randomize that if you'd like), and then each side takes turns launching an attack.
- You could allow users to pick which weapon to attack with, based on what they have in their inventory. Different weapons would inflict different amounts of damage, and some may be single-use weapons (use it and then it's gone from the inventory).
- You may want to allow the player to use potions or somehow improve their health mid-battle.
- Based on weapons used, range of damage inflicted, and ability to dodge, eventually one side will win. If the enemy `strength` is reduced to `0`, then the player wins. If the player runs out of health (or lives), then the enemy wins.
- What happens when the battle is over? That's up to you. Beating the enemy may be part of the player's journey that allows the user to progress (basically walking past the enemy). Or the enemy may drop items for the user to pick up and put in the inventory. Or, well, you're the coder, so you decide!

As we said, this one is tricky. Not all games need battling enemies. If yours does, you'll want to spend time carefully planning.

Saving and Restoring

Some games let players save their progress and then restore it later. You might do this when the game is too long for players to complete all at once. Or players may want to save their progress before trying something new (like battling an enemy) so that if they die, they can restore back to where they were.

So long as your game data is well organized (in dictionaries and classes, for example, as opposed to scattered in variables all over the place), then you'll find that Python makes this quite easy. And the magic is a Python library named `pickle`.

How does saving and restoring work? To save your game, you need to do the following:

1. Create a single variable that contains all of the data you need to save.
2. Data gets saved in a file on the computer, so pick a file name to use.
3. Use `pickle` to serialize the data and save it to the file.

Restoring your game is the reverse:

1. Read data from the saved file.
2. Deserialize it with `pickle`.
3. Save the data back to the right variables.

NEW TERM

Serializing In Python, *serializing* data means taking an internal Python object (variables, lists, classes, dictionaries, etc.) and turning it into a string of bytes that can be stored. *Deserializing* is the opposite: turning a string of bytes back into a Python object.

Pickle? Really?

Yes, the Python library that you use to save and restore data is `pickle`. The name may sound funny, but there is actually a good (or at least sensible) reason for this. When you pickle foods like cucumbers or onions, what you are doing is preserving them. The Python `pickle` library is also used to save (and thus preserve) data.

Ok, so let's see how this works. Look at this code:

```
# Imports
from os import path
import pickle

# Data file
saveDataFile = "savedGame.p"
```

The first import is the library used to access files on your computer. You need that to actually save and read the saved file. The second line imports the pickle library. Then you create a variable named saveDataFile, which contains the name of the file that will actually hold the saved game data.

As for saving data, look at this code:

```
# Create a data object to store both data sets.
db = {
    "inv":inv,
    "player":player
}

# Save it
pickle.dump(db, open(saveDataFile, "wb"))
```

When you save game data, you want all of the data in one big variable. Here we create a dictionary named db (for database), and inside it we save our inv and player variables (assuming that these are the names we are using).

The next line of code actually saves the data. pickle.dump() gets passed the data to save (the db variable) and the open file to save it to. The "wb" argument tells dump() to write binary data (as opposed to simple text data). That's all there is to it. Game data saved!

To restore game data, we just do the opposite:

```
# Now read back saved file
if path.isfile(saveDataFile):
    db = pickle.load(open(saveDataFile, "rb"))
    inv = db["inv"]
    player = db["player"]
```

This code first uses `path.isfile()` to verify that the saved game file exists. If it does, it uses `pickle.load()` to read and deserialize the data and then puts the restored data back in the original `inv` and `player` variables. Here we use an `"rb"` argument which tells `dump()` to read binary data.

As you can see, saving and restoring data in Python is really easy. We mean that. We've done this in other programming languages, and most can't do this in just a few lines of code.

If you do want to support save and restore, here are some things to keep in mind:

- What we did here—copying all objects to be saved into a single save variable—is the cleanest and easiest way to save data. You don't want to be saving and restoring lots of variables. Trust us on this one.
- The variable you save should contain everything you need to restore the game to a specific state.
- Decide if you want a single save file or multiple files. A single file is simpler to work with but will only let you restore to a specific point in game play. Multiple save files will let players restore as they need, but you'll need a way to let them pick which to restore.
- You may want to check to see if there are any saved games at game startup. If you detect a saved game, ask the user if they want to restore it.

Summary

In this chapter, we've introduced lots of ideas and techniques that you can use to really take your text-based adventure game to the next level. In Part III, we'll use these skills as we tackle graphics-based games.

Part III
RACING AROUND

CHAPTER 19

Crazy Driver

In Part II you created a text-based adventure game, and, in the process, learned lots of skills and techniques. In this section we're going to kick things up a notch and create a graphical game. And just like we did with our text-based adventure, we'll start with the basics and add functionality in each chapter.

Introducing Pygame

Writing graphical games can be complicated. Unlike text-based games, where you simply print text, graphical games need to manage images on the screen, movement, interactions between objects, keyboard or mouse input, audio, and more—and all concurrently (meaning lots of things happening simultaneously). You can't just use an `input()` and wait. Stuff—lots of stuff—happens while you are waiting, too. Yeah, it's a lot (which is why we introduced text-based gaming first).

The good news is that most game developers don't start from scratch. Rather, they build their games on top of trusted and proven gaming engines. This allows them to focus more on their games and less on the low-level details needed for lighting, animation, movement, physics, and so on.

Pygame is a gaming engine written for Python developers. It's powerful, easy-to-use, and free (released as open source). All that makes it perfect for our game.

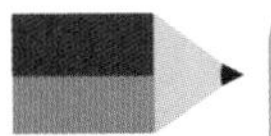

NEW TERM

Open Source *Open source* software is code that is designed to be publicly available; anyone can see it, modify it, and use it—for free. There's a bit more to it than that; there are different open source licenses that allow different uses. But for now, open source means you can use it for free to create your game.

Prepping the Game

Before we get coding, let's review the game we'll be creating and get set up.

Game Concept

Crazy Driver is a simple car racing game. You're driving a car along a busy road. But, you are driving the wrong way—right into oncoming traffic! You crazy driver, you! (Don't ever do this in real life, duh!)

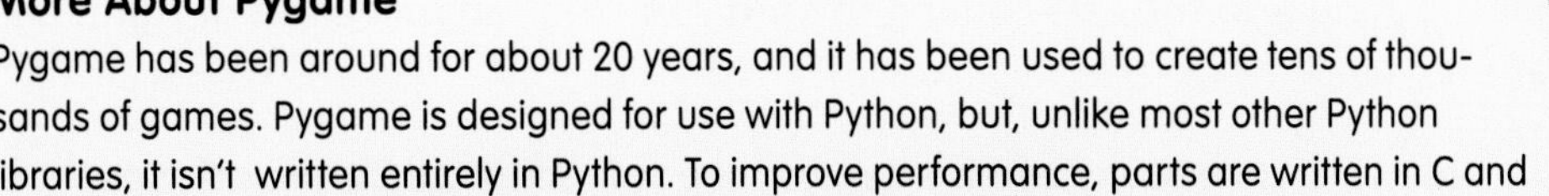

More About Pygame

Pygame has been around for about 20 years, and it has been used to create tens of thousands of games. Pygame is designed for use with Python, but, unlike most other Python libraries, it isn't written entirely in Python. To improve performance, parts are written in C and Assembler, which can run more than 100 times faster than Python.

As is often the case with large projects like Pygame, it was built on top of another popular and powerful library, called SDL (for Simple DirectMedia Layer), which provides access to audio, keyboard, mouse, joystick, GPU, and more. SDL itself is used by gaming luminaries including Valve Software.

The point of all of this is that Pygame is powerful and trusted. While we'll be building a rather simple game, Pygame can be used to build really sophisticated games, too. And some not very sophisticated ones, actually (including Flappy Bird that was all the rage a few years ago).

If you want to learn more about Pygame, visit pygame.org, where you'll also find lots of great examples that demonstrate what the library can do.

This is a top-down view game (also called an overhead perspective game). This means that the game appears as if you were above it looking down, like this:

The objective is simple: You are at the bottom of the screen, and you need to avoid crashing into the cars coming toward you. You can move left or right, and that's it.

Each time you successfully avoid a car, you'll get a point. Oh, and each time you successfully avoid a car, the game will get a little faster.

Installing Pygame

Pygame is not included with Python, so you'll need to install it. To do so, you'll do exactly the same thing you did when you installed Colorama back in Chapter 17:

- **Windows users:** `pip install pygame`
- **Mac and Chromebook users:** `pip3 install pygame`

```
Collecting pygame
  Using cached pygame-2.0.1-cp39-cp39-win_amd64.whl (5.2 MB)
Installing collected packages: pygame
Successfully installed pygame-2.0.1
```

As before, don't worry if you see a different version number or even different text. Just focus on the last line. So long as it says `Successfully installed`, you're good to go.

Creating Work Folders

Create a new work folder for our game. Move your mouse over the VS Code Explorer panel. Hover over the **PYTHON** section to display the toolbar. Click the **New Folder** icon, which is second from the left. Enter a folder name (`CrazyDriver` would work) and press **Enter**. You now have a new folder that is your main game folder (also called the *application root folder*).

Graphical games often need supporting files. At a minimum, you'll need image files, and you may also need audio files, music files, and more. In general, these should not all be stored in the same folder as your code. Rather, you'd create a separate subfolder for each. Our game uses graphic images, so create a folder inside of your new folder named `Images`. (The folders may look odd in VS Code until you have files in them. Don't worry if that's the case.)

You now have a main game folder and a subfolder to store game image files. When you create new code files, make sure you have clicked on the right folder in the Explorer panel first. Your code needs to go in the main game folder (not the `Images` subfolder).

Obtaining Images

Graphical games use graphics. (That is obvious, right?) At a minimum, you'll need graphics for the cars and background—usually PNG files.

Images are not created in Pygame. You need to create them using a tool like Photoshop. We'd love for you to create your own graphics, but to help you get started, we've created some graphics you can use. You can download them from the book web page or by scanning this QR code.

When you download the images ZIP file, you'll want to extract the images from it. You can usually do this by double-clicking on the file in your computer's file browser. Copy the images from the ZIP file into the `Images` folder that you just created. And if you opt to create your own images, they'll go in the `Images` folder, too.

Getting Started

We're going to build our game incrementally. That means that you'll be able to run it to test code and changes, but it won't be playable for a little while. And we're going to start by defining the game play space.

Downloadable Code

You are going to be updating and refining the game code file (which you are about to create) in every chapter in this part of the book. It's not a lot of code, so type away if you'd like. Or you can download the code from the book web page by scanning this QR code. To make things easier for you, we've posted the code as it would look at the end of each chapter.

Initializing Pygame

Create a new file in your game root folder. As this is the main game file, name it `Main.py` (or any name of your choice, actually). Here's the code:

```
# Imports
import pygame

# Game colors
BLACK = (0, 0, 0)
WHITE = (255, 255, 255)
RED   = (255, 0, 0)

# Main game starts here
# Initialize Pygame
pygame.init()

# Initialize frame manager
clock = pygame.time.Clock()
# Set frame rate
clock.tick(60)

# Set caption bar
pygame.display.set_caption("Crazy Driver")
```

If you save and run this code, it'll look like nothing happened. Don't panic! That's what is supposed to happen, for now.

Let's review the code. We start by importing the Pygame library. Simple enough.

Next, we define variables for a few colors that we'll need in the game. Colors are specified as RGB values separated by commas, like this:

```
# Game colors
BLACK = (0, 0, 0)
WHITE = (255, 255, 255)
RED   = (255, 0, 0)
```

ALL CAPS

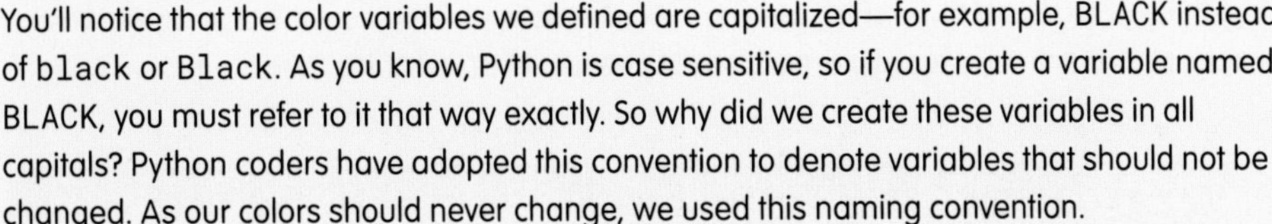

You'll notice that the color variables we defined are capitalized—for example, BLACK instead of `black` or `Black`. As you know, Python is case sensitive, so if you create a variable named BLACK, you must refer to it that way exactly. So why did we create these variables in all capitals? Python coders have adopted this convention to denote variables that should not be changed. As our colors should never change, we used this naming convention.

We've frequently used mixed case for variable names; for example, `lightGreen`. If the variable is all caps, it will make it hard to separate words, as in `LIGHTGREEN`. For this reason, coders often use an underscore (_) to separate words, as in `LIGHT_GREEN`.

RGB Values

Colors on a computer screen are created by mixing different amounts of red, green, and blue light. Yep, when your screen displays yellow, it is actually displaying lots of red and green and no blue. Seriously!

Because all colors are created using combinations of red, green, and blue, a color value is called an RGB value (R for red, G for green, B for blue), and it is made up of three numbers that specify how much of each color is present. The amount of each color is a number between 0 (for none of that color at all) and 255 (for all of that color).

This means that `255, 0, 0` will display red; the R value is `255` (full intensity), and the G and B are `0` (no light at all). Magenta (or purple) will be `255, 0, 255`: full red and blue and no green. Black is `0, 0, 0`: all three with no light at all. White is `255, 255, 255`: all three at full intensity.

Partial values can be used, too. Which means that there are over 16 million (that's 256 to the power of 3) color combinations possible.

Colors provided to code (including Python) as well as graphic and illustration software all use RGB values like this.

Next comes the actual library initialization. Before Pygame can be used, it must be initialized (just like the Colorama library that we used in Chapter 17). This is done with a single line of code:

```
# Initialize Pygame
pygame.init()
```

Tuple

Look at the code for the three color variables. Do they look different to you? Look again. They look a bit like lists that we've used many times already—but not quite. Lists are defined like this:

```
RED = [255, 0, 0]
```

with values separated by commas surrounded by square brackets. Right?

Here we used parentheses instead:

```
RED   = (255, 0, 0)
```

RED looks like a list, but it obviously isn't one. So, what is it?

It's actually a *tuple*, another Python type that is very similar to a list, but with one big difference. Unlike lists, tuples can never be changed. You can't add items, you can't edit items, you can't make any changes at all.

This makes tuples really useful for variables that should never change, like our colors.

Graphical game screens need to be updated constantly—many times a second. The rate at which the screen is updated is called the *frame rate*.

NEW TERM

Frame Rate When we look at a screen, perhaps watching a movie or playing a video game, it appears as though images are changing all the time. The truth is that they are not. Screens get updated many times a second—faster than the human eye can readily notice. That creates the illusion of constant changes.

Screens update many times a second. The update speed is measured in *frames per second* (or *FPS*), and that value is called the *frame rate*.

Higher frame rates make the video changes look more fluid and realistic, but they also use more processing power.

Managing frame rates involves keeping track of time, so we create a clock object that does exactly that, providing the game with a way to track when frames need to be updated:

```
# Initialize frame manager
clock = pygame.time.Clock()
```

`Clock` is defined inside of the Pygame `time` library, so we use the fully qualified `pygame.time.Clock()` to instantiate our `clock` object.

Now that we have a `clock` object, we can use it to set the game frame rate, like this:

```
# Set frame rate
clock.tick(60)
```

`clock.tick(60)` tells Pygame to update the display no more than 60 times per second (or 60 frames per second).

The last thing the code does is update the caption bar, which is the bar at the top of the game play area. (You can see it at the top of the game, earlier in this chapter.) Here's the code:

```
# Set caption bar
pygame.display.set_caption("Crazy Driver")
```

The Pygame `display` library is used to manage anything that gets displayed on the screen. Here we use the `set_caption()` method to set the caption text to `Crazy Driver`. Later we'll add code so that the caption keeps updating to show the current game score.

That's all the code does, which is why it won't do very much if you run it.

The next thing we need to do is to tell Pygame the size of the game window, so add this to the bottom of your code:

```
# Initialize game screen
screen = pygame.display.set_mode((500, 800))
```

Games created in Pygame can run in different modes, including full screen or in a window. This line tells Pygame that our game runs in a window, and it sets the window size to 500 pixels wide and 800 pixels high. The `set_mode()` method returns the game area, which we save to a variable named `screen`.

Now if you were to save and run the code, you'd see a black box (exactly 500 pixels wide and 800 pixels high) briefly flash on the screen.

We're making progress!

Displaying Stuff

We now have a game area (called a *surface*) to work with. Everything that happens in the game—displaying items, moving them, and so on—happens on the game surface.

NEW TERM

Surface A *surface* is an object that represents an area of the screen where you display images, text, and more. You place items on the surface, and then Pygame can display them.

Let's update the game area. The surface is accessed via the `screen` variable we created. We can fill the background with a solid color. In this case, we'll make it white, using the `fill()` method. Add this to the bottom of your file:

```
# Set background color
screen.fill(WHITE)
```

Pixel

A pixel (short for *picture element, pix* = picture, *el* = element) is the smallest item that can be displayed on a screen. Each pixel is a tiny dot that is entirely one RGB color. Larger images or videos are actually made up of lots and lots of pixels. When pixels are super small and there are lots of them, you don't notice the individual pixel dots and just see the combined image.

This is why 1080 images look better than 720 images. 1080 has more pixels in the same space as a 720 image, and the individual pixels are smaller and less apparent. 4K has far more pixels than 1080, which is why 4K images look even smoother.

As its name suggests, `fill()` fills the screen with a color, and here we are passing it the `WHITE` color we previously defined. Note that `WHITE` only works because we created it. If you tried to use `BLUE` now, you'd get an error as we have not defined `BLUE`.

Save and run the code. Well, that didn't work. The box briefly flashed on the screen, but it was still black. What happened to our `fill(WHITE)`?

Well, here's the important thing to know about gaming engines—and this is true of all gaming engines, not just Pygame: Graphical games typically update the display a lot, and they do it very frequently. And often there are lots of changes that need to be made all at once. Updating the display takes time, so game engines typically remember all the changes that need to be made, but they don't actually make them until you tell them to do so. It's an extra step for you, but it makes for much faster and more responsive games.

And that's what happened here. We told Pygame to set the background color using `fill(WHITE)`, and Pygame updated its own internal list of changes with that color change. But we never told Pygame to update the display, so, well, it didn't.

How do we update the display? Add this below the `fill()` method:

```
# Update screen
pygame.display.update()
```

Save and test the code. This time, the box that flashes on the screen will be white.

`display.update()` does exactly what you'd expect: It updates the display with any pending changes.

The Game Loop

Our game (yeah, we know calling it a game right now is a bit of a stretch) starts and then quits right away. That's because, as you will recall, Python executes your code line by line, and once it has processed the final line of code, the application terminates.

To keep the game running (until the game is over), we need a loop, much like the loops we've used so many times in prior chapters. And the entire game goes inside of a loop. When the loop ends, the game is done.

So, what goes in the loop? In our game, we'll need code for the player to move left and right, oncoming cars will need to appear and move toward the player, we'll need to track the score and adjust game speed, and more. All of that goes inside of the game loop.

Let's add a simple game loop. You can add this to the bottom of `Main.py`:

```
# Main game loop
while True:
    # Check for events
    for event in pygame.event.get():
        # Did the player quit?
        if event.type == pygame.QUIT:
            # Quit pygame
            pygame.quit()
            sys.exit()

    # Update screen
    pygame.display.update()
```

Save the changes and run the game. This time, the game screen will display (with a white background), and the box will remain on the screen until you manually close it (by clicking on the Close icon at the top of the screen or clicking the X on the game window).

So what does this code do? It starts with a strange-looking loop:

```
# Main game loop
while True:
```

This is a `while` loop, much like the ones we used previously, but this one has a condition of `True`. On each loop iteration, Python will check to see if the condition is `True`, and it always will be. That makes this an endless loop. Usually that's a bad thing, but it works for us as it keeps the game running.

Next comes a `for` loop, which checks to see if any events have occurred that we need to respond to in our game. What are events? They could be a key pressed or a mouse button clicked. If those occurred, your code would need to respond accordingly. The only event we need to respond to right now is the `QUIT` event, which means the player closed the game window.

`pygame.event.get()` returns a list of events that need to be responded to (if there are any), and that gets passed to a `for` loop, which iterates through those events, like this:

```
for event in pygame.event.get():
```

Within the `for` loop, a variable named `event` will contain the details of an event to be responded to. We need to check for the `QUIT` event, so we use this `if` statement:

```
# Did the player quit?
if event.type == pygame.QUIT:
```

If the player did indeed quit, then we need to shut down Pygame and close the computer window it was running in. That's what these two lines do:

```
# Quit pygame
pygame.quit()
sys.exit()
```

The second line of code uses the `sys` library, which contains methods used to work with the environment Python runs in. To use this, you'll need add an `import` to the top of your code:

```
import sys
```

And finally, the last line of code in the game loop should always be a display update, like this:

```
# Update screen
pygame.display.update()
```

Our game loop doesn't update anything, so the `update()` method won't really do anything. But, as a general rule, you'll always want to update the display at the end of each game loop iteration, so we added it here for future use.

One more tweak before we wrap this chapter. And to make it easier to see what's going on, here is the complete `Main.py`:

```
# Imports
import sys
import pygame
from pygame.locals import *

# Game colors
BLACK = (0, 0, 0)
WHITE = (255, 255, 255)
RED   = (255, 0, 0)

# Main game starts here
# Initialize Pygame
pygame.init()

# Initialize frame manager
clock = pygame.time.Clock()
# Set frame rate
clock.tick(60)

# Set caption bar
pygame.display.set_caption("Crazy Driver")

# Initialize game screen
screen = pygame.display.set_mode((500, 800))

# Set background color
screen.fill(WHITE)

# Update screen
pygame.display.update()
```

```
# Main game loop
while True:
    # Check for events
    for event in pygame.event.get():
        # Did the player quit?
        if event.type == QUIT:
            # Quit pygame
            pygame.quit()
            sys.exit()

    # Update screen
    pygame.display.update()
```

So what changed here? Two things.

As you know, coders love clean, tight code and always look for ways to simplify what they write. When using Pygame, you'll find yourself referring to events like `pygame.QUIT` repeatedly. It would be cleaner to just be able to refer to `QUIT`, without specifying the library as a prefix. The above code uses `QUIT` this way in the `if` statement:

```
if event.type == QUIT:
```

`QUIT` is a local variable defined in the `pygame` library. So how can we use `QUIT` without specifying the `pygame` library name? The answer is that we can import the variables in `pygame` directly into our code. Look at the `import` statements at the top of the file:

```
# Imports
import sys
import pygame
from pygame.locals import *
```

The first two `import` statements are ones you are very familiar with. The third one is new. It tells Python to import all of the local variables (that's what `locals` means) from `pygame`, making them available in our code as if they were our own local variables. Neat, huh? Now we can refer to `QUIT` as if it were a local variable.

CHALLENGE 19.1

Try changing the window size passed to `set_mode()`. Make it bigger, smaller, wider...you get the idea.

We defined three colors. Try changing `fill()` to use `RED` instead of `WHITE`. And then create your own color variables and use them. Remember, you can use any values between `0` and `255` for each of the RGB values. You may want to use just `0` and `255` as you play with the colors. (That still gives you 8 combinations to try.)

Summary

In this chapter, you've learned what Pygame is and installed it. You've also created the basic game structure, which is now ready to display graphics in the next chapter.

CHAPTER 20

Image-ine the Possibilities

Now that you have a basic Pygame application set up, it's time to actually make it look like a game. In this chapter, we'll place images on the game surface and learn how to work with files and folders, too.

Files and Folders

Our Crazy Driver game right now is made of a single file named `Main.py`, which contains Python code. But that's about to change. Real games are made up of lots of files, and not all of them are code. You'll have image files at a minimum, and possibly video, music, and other files, too. And you'd not want all of those files in the same folder. That would get unruly and unmanageable.

Our game just uses images (and in Chapter 19 we guided you through saving them in an `Images` folder). If you had video files, sound clips, music files, etc., you'll probably want to save them in their own appropriately named folders, too. A more complete game may have a folder structure that looks something like this:

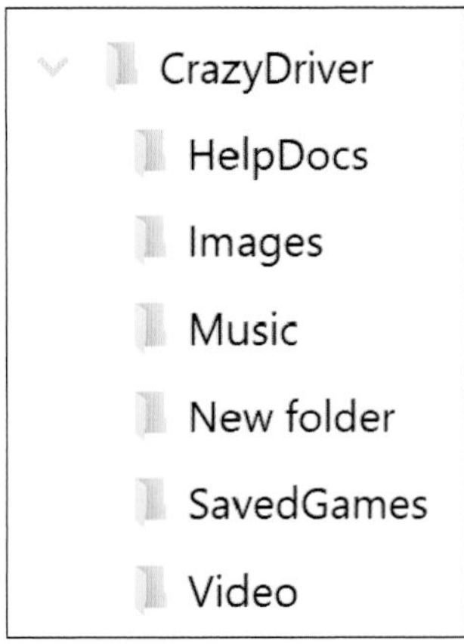

The challenge, however, is that your code needs to know where to find these files when it needs them. And you do not want to hard code file paths. Why? Because depending on the operating system used and which folder the app is being run from, the exact path to the files and folders could change. What works on your computer may not work on someone else's.

NEW TERM

Path Files on your computer are stored in folders. And folders can be inside of other folders. The exact location of a file, taking into account the folders, is called a *path*.

The solution? Build paths to the folders dynamically. When the game starts, it checks to see where it is running and then creates variables for the paths to the necessary folders. Your code uses these variables to access files. It's only a few extra lines of code, and it makes your app safer and more *portable*.

> NEW TERM
>
> **Portable** When code is written in a way that ensures that it'll execute safely on different computers, devices, or operating systems, it is said to be *portable*. Portability is a good thing, and coders always try to write code that is as portable as possible.

How do we get the path to the code that is running? Python makes this really easy. Create a test file and type this code:

```
print(__file__)
```

Save and run the code. You'll see the full path to the file being executed displayed in the Terminal window.

How does this work? `__file__` is a special built-in variable that contains the full name of the currently executing code—exactly what we need. Pay attention to that variable: It has two underscores before and after the word `file`.

Now we have the path to the code. Next, we need to extract just the folder name portion, as that will tell us which folder the code file is in. That folder is our game root folder. To extract the folder (also called a directory) from a fully qualified path, change the code to look like this:

```
import os
print(__file__)
print(os.path.dirname(__file__))
```

Save and run the code. This time, you'll see two lines in the output: first the full path to the code and then the code directory.

TIP

Work Like a Pro Libraries, both built-in ones and third-party ones like Pygame, tend to have lots of modules with lots of methods. You don't need to memorize them. Type part of a name, and VS Code will help you find what you need. And if that doesn't work, just do what the pros do and Google it. If you search for "Python get file path," you'll see code much like what we used here, and other solutions, too.

The `os` library contains functions for working with your operating system, including files. `os.path.dirname()` accepts a path and extracts just the folder portion, which is what we need.

With this, we can easily create variables for our game paths. Here's the updated code:

```
import os

# Build game paths
GAME_ROOT_FOLDER=os.path.dirname(__file__)
IMAGE_FOLDER=os.path.join(GAME_ROOT_FOLDER, "Images")

print("Game root:   ", GAME_ROOT_FOLDER)
print("Image folder:", IMAGE_FOLDER)
```

Save and run this code. It'll print two lines of output, reporting the game root and image folder.

The code is pretty simple. The first path variable is created like this:

```
GAME_ROOT_FOLDER=os.path.dirname(__file__)
```

This simply saves the extracted folder path to the variable `GAME_ROOT_FOLDER`.

The next line saves the path to the image folder, which is inside the game root. To do this, it uses a function called `os.path.join()`, like this:

```
IMAGE_FOLDER=os.path.join(GAME_ROOT_FOLDER, "Images")
```

The `join()` function is used to add to the path in a way that is safe for all computer operating systems. This code creates a variable named `IMAGE_FOLDER` that is constructed dynamically using `GAME_ROOT_FOLDER` and adding the `Images` folder to it. (We previously created this folder, so we know it's there.) And we don't have to worry about slash or backslash characters (which you need in file paths); `join()` takes care of that for us.

We'll use this code to access the images we'll be placing on the surface shortly.

CHALLENGE 20.1

We're only using images right now, and thus we have just an `Images` folder. But it's good to plan for the future. Assume that you have `Sound` and `Videos` folders and create variables for each of those. You should be able to create each with a single line of code.

Setting the Background

In the last chapter, we created a game window and set the background to white. Let's now update the code to display the road image as the background. The road image is in the `Images` folder and is appropriately named `Road.png`. When done, your game screen will look like this:

That looks way better than a white background!

Here's the updated `Main.py`:

```
# Imports
import sys, os
import pygame
from pygame.locals import *

# Game colors
BLACK = (0, 0, 0)
WHITE = (255, 255, 255)
RED   = (255, 0, 0)

# Build game paths
GAME_ROOT_FOLDER=os.path.dirname(__file__)
IMAGE_FOLDER=os.path.join(GAME_ROOT_FOLDER, "Images")

# Main game starts here
# Initialize Pygame
pygame.init()

# Initialize frame manager
clock = pygame.time.Clock()

# Set frame rate
clock.tick(60)

# Set caption bar
pygame.display.set_caption("Crazy Driver")

# Load images
IMG_ROAD = pygame.image.load(os.path.join(IMAGE_FOLDER, "Road.png"))

# Initialize game screen
screen = pygame.display.set_mode(IMG_ROAD.get_size())

# Main game loop
while True:
```

```
    # Place background
    screen.blit(IMG_ROAD, (0,0))

    # Check for events
    for event in pygame.event.get():
        # Did the player quit?
        if event.type == QUIT:
            # Quit pygame
            pygame.quit()
            sys.exit()

    # Update screen
    pygame.display.update()
```

Save and run the code. This time, the game window displays the road background until you close the window.

Okay, so what changed? Let's walk through the code.

We made one change to the imports:

```
# Imports
import sys, os
import pygame
from pygame.locals import *
```

As you just saw, `os` is what we use to work with file paths, so we need to `import` it.

Combining `import` Statements

As previously notes, we can place each `import` on its own line, like this:

```
import sys
import os
```

Python also lets you combine these lines, as we did in our code, like this:

```
import sys, os
```

The end result is the same thing, so use which format you prefer.

Next come the game color definitions, like before.

Then we create the two folder variables, as discussed previously. `GAME_ROOT_FOLDER` stores the computer path to our game, and `IMAGE_FOLDER` stores the path to where the game image files are.

After that comes Pygame initialization, frame manager and frame rate, and caption bar text, unchanged, so no explanation needed.

Then comes this code:

```
# Load images
IMG_ROAD = pygame.image.load(os.path.join(IMAGE_FOLDER, "Road.png"))
```

To use an image in Pygame, it needs to be loaded into a variable and placed on a surface. Here we want to load the road image; that's the file `Road.png` in the `Images` folder. As we did before, we use `os.path.join()`to safely (and portably) create the file path to the file we need. `pygame.image.load()` then retrieves the specified image and draws it on a surface named `IMG_ROAD`.

It is important to note that loading an image doesn't actually display it. To display the image, we need to copy this new surface to our main game surface and then update the display. We'll get to that in a moment.

Next, we initialize the game screen, as we did before. But there's an important change here. Previously we gave `set_mode()` an exact hard-coded screen size (500 pixels by 800 pixels). Not anymore. Look at this revised line of code:

```
# Initialize game screen
screen = pygame.display.set_mode(IMG_ROAD.get_size())
```

We previously loaded `Road.png` into the `IMG_ROAD` surface. `IMG_ROAD` knows all about the image, including how big it is. So, rather than hard code the size (hard code = bad, right?), we use `IMG_ROAD.get_size()`. This way, the game window will be sized to match the road background image size (which, coincidentally, just happens to be 500 pixels by 800 pixels). And if we used a different sized image, the window would adjust accordingly.

There is one more super-important change. We removed the code that makes the background white and added this to the game loop in its place:

```
# Place background
screen.blit(IMG_ROAD, (0,0))
```

This line of code is what puts the road image onto the game screen. Remember, we have two surfaces now: the main game surface (which we called `screen`) and the background image surface (which we called `IMG_ROAD`). The `blit()` function copies a passed surface and copies it onto another surface. Here it copies `IMG_ROAD` onto `screen`.

`blit()` takes two arguments: the image being copied and where to copy it to. Why is that second argument needed? Surfaces are two dimensional. Think of them as squares (or rectangles). When you copy an image onto a surface, you need to tell the surface where to place the image by using an x,y coordinate—a pair of numbers that identifies a location on the target surface. `0,0` refers to the top-left corner of the screen, which is exactly where we want our background placed so that it fills the entire `screen`.

NEW TERM

x,y Coordinate An x,y coordinate (also called an x,y axis) marks a location on a plane. The x number is the horizontal position starting from the left, and the y number is the vertical position starting from the top. And, as you'd expect, in Python these values start from `0`. This means that position `0,0` is the top-left corner, `100,50` would be 100 pixels from the left and 50 from the top, and so on.

NEW TERM

Blit Blit is a strange word, right? It actually stands for *block transfer*, which is what actually happens when you blit: You copy (transfer) a block of information from one location to another.

Placing the Cars

Now that you have the background image placed, let's add the two cars to the screen: the player car and the oncoming car (we'll call it the *enemy*). The cars won't move yet. We'll add that functionality in the next chapter. For now let's just place them, much like we did the background.

Here's the updated code for `Main.py`:

```
# Imports
import sys, os, random
import pygame
from pygame.locals import *

# Game colors
BLACK = (0, 0, 0)
WHITE = (255, 255, 255)
RED   = (255, 0, 0)

# Build game paths
GAME_ROOT_FOLDER=os.path.dirname(__file__)
IMAGE_FOLDER=os.path.join(GAME_ROOT_FOLDER, "Images")

# Main game starts here
# Initialize Pygame
pygame.init()

# Initialize frame manager
clock = pygame.time.Clock()

# Set frame rate
clock.tick(60)

# Set caption bar
pygame.display.set_caption("Crazy Driver")

# Load images
IMG_ROAD = pygame.image.load(os.path.join(IMAGE_FOLDER, "Road.png"))
IMG_PLAYER = pygame.image.load(os.path.join(IMAGE_FOLDER,
"Player.png"))
```

```
IMG_ENEMY = pygame.image.load(os.path.join(IMAGE_FOLDER,
"Enemy.png"))

# Initialize game screen
screen = pygame.display.set_mode(IMG_ROAD.get_size())

# Create game objects
# Calculate initial player position
h=IMG_ROAD.get_width()//2
v=IMG_ROAD.get_height() - (IMG_PLAYER.get_height()//2)
# Create player sprite
player = pygame.sprite.Sprite()
player.image = IMG_PLAYER
player.surf = pygame.Surface(IMG_PLAYER.get_size())
player.rect = player.surf.get_rect(center = (h, v))

# Enemy
# Calculate initial enemy position
hl=IMG_ENEMY.get_width()//2
hr=IMG_ROAD.get_width()-(IMG_ENEMY.get_width()//2)
h=random.randrange(hl, hr)
v=0
# Create enemy sprite
enemy = pygame.sprite.Sprite()
enemy.image = IMG_ENEMY
enemy.surf = pygame.Surface(IMG_ENEMY.get_size())
enemy.rect = enemy.surf.get_rect(center = (h, v))

# Main game loop
while True:
    # Place background
    screen.blit(IMG_ROAD, (0,0))

    # Place player on screen
    screen.blit(player.image, player.rect)

    # Place enemy on screen
    screen.blit(enemy.image, enemy.rect)
```

```
    # Check for events
    for event in pygame.event.get():
        # Did the player quit?
        if event.type == QUIT:
            # Quit pygame
            pygame.quit()
            sys.exit()

    # Update screen
    pygame.display.update()
```

Save and run the code. You'll see two cars placed on the screen. The player car will be centered at the bottom, and the enemy car will be at some random location at the top. Your display will look something like this, and each time you run it, the enemy car should be in a different location:

The game is starting to take shape. Let's look at what changed in our code.

We added our favorite `random` library to the `import` statements. We need that to randomly place the enemy car.

We updated the code that loads our images to also load the two cars we need:

```
# Load images
IMG_ROAD = pygame.image.load(os.path.join(IMAGE_FOLDER, "Road.png"))
IMG_PLAYER = pygame.image.load(os.path.join(IMAGE_FOLDER,
"Player.png"))
IMG_ENEMY = pygame.image.load(os.path.join(IMAGE_FOLDER,
"Enemy.png"))
```

Just like we did with `IMG_ROAD` previously, `IMG_PLAYER` loads the `Player.png` car, and `IMG_ENEMY` loads the `Enemy.png` car. Now we have three images loaded onto surfaces and ready to use.

Then comes something new. We created *sprites*, a kind of image object that can be placed on a surface, moved, rotated, removed, and more.

NEW TERM

Sprite In computer graphics, a *sprite* is a two-dimensional image that is placed onto a larger image. Sprites can be displayed or hidden, moved, rotated, and transformed in all sorts of ways. Sprites are key to creating the illusion of animation and movement in games, animated movies, and more.

Because our cars need to move, we make them sprites. Here's the code for the player car sprite:

```
# Calculate initial player position
h=IMG_ROAD.get_width()//2
v=IMG_ROAD.get_height() - (IMG_PLAYER.get_height()//2)
# Create player sprite
player = pygame.sprite.Sprite()
player.image = IMG_PLAYER
player.surf = pygame.Surface(IMG_PLAYER.get_size())
player.rect = player.surf.get_rect(center = (h, v))
```

This looks more complicated than it actually is, so let's go through it together.

When sprites are placed on a surface, we need to define exactly where they are to be placed. We want the player car to be centered at the bottom of the screen, so we'll position the sprites by figuring out their centers (unlike when we placed the background at an exact fixed position). Determining the center requires a little bit of math, and that's what the first two lines of code do:

- The horizontal position is exactly half of the width of the road (which, as you will recall, is the size of the game screen). We save `IMG_ROAD.get_width()//2` to a variable named `h` (for horizontal).
- The vertical position is a little trickier. If we just used the height of the road, the center of the car would be at the bottom of the screen, so only the top half of the player car (the half above the center point) would be displayed. To display the whole player car flush on the bottom, we subtract half of the height of the car from the screen height by using the code `IMG_ROAD.get_height() - (IMG_PLAYER.get_height()//2)`. This is saved to variable `v` for vertical.

This image helps explain player car positioning:

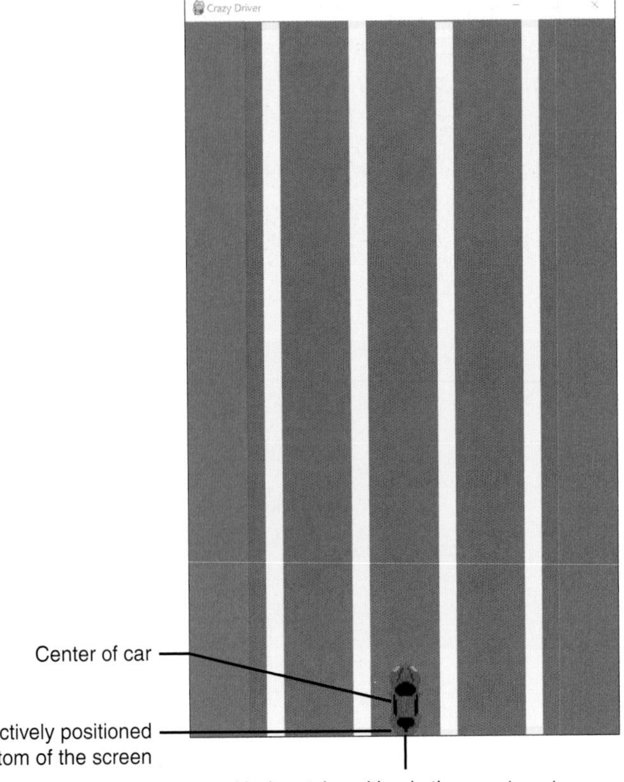

Now we have two variables, which contain the horizontal and vertical center positions for the player sprite.

The code then creates the sprite and names the variable `player` and sets the sprite image to `IMG_PLAYER` (the player car image we just loaded). Note that this looks like initializing a class because—surprise!—`Sprite()` is a class!

The sprite object needs to know how big the image is. Rather than hard code values, we use `get_size()` to get the actual image size (just like we did when we set the game screen size based on the background image size).

And, finally, we define the rectangle that will hold the sprite. This is used to place the sprite in the correct position on the game surface, using the two position variables we just calculated.

Placing the enemy car works similarly:

```
# Calculate initial enemy position
hl=IMG_ENEMY.get_width()//2
hr=IMG_ROAD.get_width()-(IMG_ENEMY.get_width()//2)
h=random.randrange(hl, hr)
v=0
# Create enemy sprite
enemy = pygame.sprite.Sprite()
enemy.image = IMG_ENEMY
enemy.surf = pygame.Surface(IMG_ENEMY.get_size())
enemy.rect = enemy.surf.get_rect(center = (h, v))
```

Again, we first calculate the sprite positions. And again, this involves a little math:

- Actually, we don't need math for the vertical position. We want the enemy to start at the top of the screen with only half the car showing. (The full car will appear as it drives toward the player.) Variable `v` is the vertical position, so we set `v=0`.

- The horizontal position is a bit more interesting. Unlike the player sprite, which we want centered, the enemy sprite needs to be placed at a random horizontal position. As you know, picking a random number requires that we provide the minimum and maximum for a range of values. So we calculate the leftmost allowed position (which will be the range minimum) and save it to variable `hl` (for horizontal left) and the rightmost position (which will be the range maximum) and save it to variable `hr` (for horizontal right). We then use `randrange()` to pick a random number between `hl` and `hr` and save it to `h`.

This figure will help explain this:

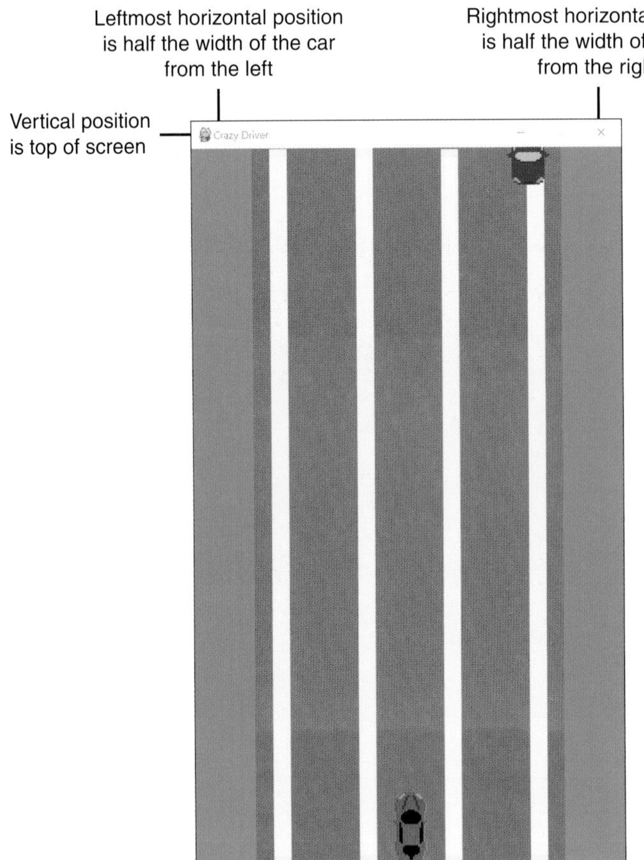

The rest of the code is the same as the player sprite code but using the enemy image instead of the player image.

We now have two sprites ready to use.

Can All Be Inline

We calculated sprite positions and saved the results to variables. We then passed those variables to `get_rect()` to position the sprites. The variables we created are only ever used by `get_rect()` in the very next lines of code. As such, we could have just done the math right inside of `get_rect()` and not created the variables. And, in fact, that's what most developers would have done, and if you were to look at code examples and tutorials online, that's what you'd typically see. We isolated the calculations and saved their results to variables to make the code easier to explain and understand. You can do what we did here, or you can put the calculations right inline. The end result is the same, so it's up to you.

The only other change is in the game loop itself:

```
# Place player on screen
screen.blit(player.image, player.rect)

# Place enemy on screen
screen.blit(enemy.image, enemy.rect)
```

As we did with the road image, the player and enemy cars are blitted onto the screen, using the sprite rectangle as the location.

And now we have three images placed on the screen. In the next chapter, we'll make them move.

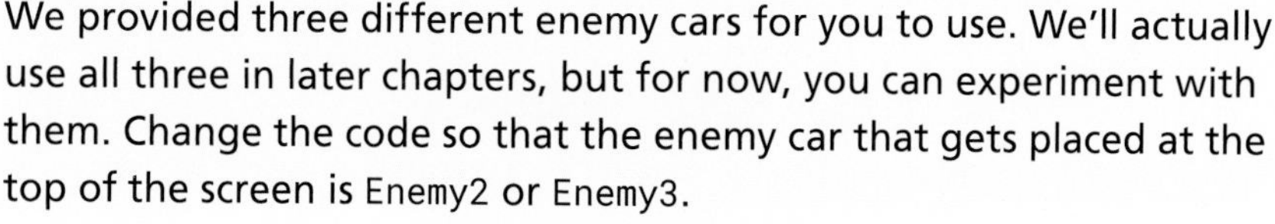

CHALLENGE 20.2

We provided three different enemy cars for you to use. We'll actually use all three in later chapters, but for now, you can experiment with them. Change the code so that the enemy car that gets placed at the top of the screen is `Enemy2` or `Enemy3`.

Summary

In this chapter, you've learned how to load images in Pygame and how to place them on the screen for display. Next up, moving them!

CHAPTER 21
We Like to Move It

Our game is starting to look like, well, a game. The only problem is that the cars are just sitting there, not moving at all. In this chapter we'll change that.

Moving the Enemy

We now have a game screen with a road background and an enemy car that appears at random locations along the top of the screen. Now we'll make the enemy move.

As you will recall, the enemy is driving toward you (going the right way—and you are the one driving the wrong way!). To make the enemy move, we simply need to move the sprite down the screen.

How fast will the enemy move? That's up to you. If it moves 1 pixel at a time, it'll move really slowly; if it moves 100 pixels at a time, it'll move really quickly. We'll start by making it move 5 pixels at a time, and later we'll make it move faster as the game progresses.

Open `Main.py` and add this code near the top of the file, right before or after the color definitions would be a great location:

```
# Game variables
moveSpeed = 5
```

This code creates a variable named `moveSpeed` and initializes it to `5` (the number of pixels we'll move by). We'll use this variable when we move sprites.

Oh, this variable truly is variable. We'll soon add code to change midgame play, so we didn't use capital letters for the name this time.

Now for the fun part. Go to the game loop and find the code that blits the `enemy` on to the screen. Right after that line, add this code:

```
    # Move enemy downwards
    enemy.rect.move_ip(0, moveSpeed)
```

`move_ip()` moves a sprite. It takes two arguments. The first is the number of pixels to move horizontally; we don't want to change horizontal positioning, so that value is `0`. The second is the number of pixels to move vertically. We pass it `moveSpeed` (which we initialized to `5`), so `enemy` will move `5` pixels down the screen.

Save and run the code. You'll see the enemy start at a random location along the top and then drive down the screen toward the player. And then...oh no!...it drives right off the screen!

Up, Down, Left, Right

We're moving our sprite in one direction, passing a vertical value but not a horizontal one. We could pass both, which would effectively move the sprite diagonally. We could also pass negative values: -5 for the first value would move left 5 pixels, and -5 for the second value would move up 5 pixels.

Why is this happening? move_ip() keeps moving the enemy by 5 pixels, exactly as coded. It doesn't care if the sprite is visible or not. The enemy keeps going and going off into nonvisible space.

What should happen is that when an enemy reaches the bottom of the screen, we move it back to the top. That way, it'll look like one car has passed us and a new one is heading our way. To do this, we'll need to check the position of the enemy each time we move it to see if it has reached the bottom of the screen.

We can do this with a simple if statement. Add this code right after the move_ip() line:

```
    # Check didn't go off edge of screen
    if (enemy.rect.bottom > IMG_ROAD.get_height()):
        # At bottom, so move back to top
        enemy.rect.top = 0
```

Save and run the code. The enemy car drives down the screen, and when it reaches the bottom, it moves back to the top.

How does this work? You will recall that sprites have rectangles around them that Pygame uses to keep track of where they are. Each time we call move_ip(), Pygame updates the rectangle so that enemy.rect always contains the exact location of the enemy sprite. enemy.rect.bottom contains the exact location of the bottom of the enemy sprite. The if statement simply checks to see if the bottom of enemy is greater than the height of the road. If yes, then we've gone off the screen, and the code then sets enemy.rect.top to 0, which moves it back to the top of the screen.

Pretty cool, huh?

The only problem is that when the enemy reappears at the top of the screen, it is in the same horizontal position as before. Why? Because we are changing the vertical position but not the horizontal position.

Let's change that. We used math and `randrange()` to pick an initial random horizontal position for the enemy. We can do exactly the same thing again each time we put the enemy back at the top. Remove the code that moves the `enemy` to the top of the screen and replace it with this code:

```
        # Calculate new random location
        hl=IMG_ENEMY.get_width()//2
        hr=IMG_ROAD.get_width()-(IMG_ENEMY.get_width()//2)
        h=random.randrange(hl, hr)
        v=0
        # And place it
        enemy.rect.center = (h, v)
```

This is the same code that we used to place the `enemy` sprite initially. It calculates the range minimum and maximum, uses `randrange()` to pick a horizontal location, and sets the vertical location to `0`. (`0` is the top of the screen, remember?)

Save and run the code. Now the `enemy` car will drive to the bottom of the screen, and then a new `enemy` will appear, starting from a random location.

What happens if the enemy crashes into your player car? Nothing yet. In fact, you can't even move out of the way yet! We'll fix that next.

Duplicated Code?

We know what you are thinking. We've gone on and on about how coders hate duplicated code, and we just duplicated the code that calculates the enemy positions.

Oh, the shame!

Well, the truth is that this is temporary code. We're going to replace it in a future chapter when we add support for multiple enemy images. As this is essentially throwaway code, we took the lazy option and, yes, duplicated code.

But this is the exception, really. We mean it. As a rule, no duplicated code!

Moving the Player

The `enemy` sprite moved automatically. On each frame refresh, it moved 5 pixels down the screen.

The `player` sprite can't move automatically. It needs to move only when the player tells it to do so. How will players do this? Our game will use the left and right arrow keys on the keyboard; press left to go left, right to go right. This obviously requires that we check if those keyboard keys have been pressed. And, once again, Pygame makes this really easy.

In your game loop, find the line of code that blits the `player` sprite. Add this right after that line of code:

```
# Get keys pressed
keys = pygame.key.get_pressed()
# Check for LEFT key
if keys[K_LEFT]:
    # Move left
    player.rect.move_ip(-moveSpeed, 0)
#  Check for RIGHT key
if keys[K_RIGHT]:
    # Move right
    player.rect.move_ip(moveSpeed, 0)
```

`key.get_pressed()` returns a list of all the available keys, and each will be `True` if pressed or `False` if not. We save the returned list in a viable named `keys`, which we can then check. If `keys[K_LEFT]` is `True`, then we know the left arrow key has been pressed, and so on.

All Sorts of Key Options

As you have seen, `key.get_pressed()` returns a list of all the possible keys that could be pressed, with each set to `True` or `False`. In our game, we only care about the left and right arrow keys. But other games might want to test for key combinations (Ctrl+A, or left arrow and up arrow pressed at the same time), and this is easily done by checking multiple values from the returned list.

What do we do if the player presses the left or right arrow key? We use the `move_ip()` function to move the `player` sprite, just as we did the `enemy` sprite:

- If the right arrow key was pressed, we execute `player.rect.move_ip(moveSpeed, 0)`, which moves the player `5` pixels to the right (and `0` pixels vertically).
- If the left arrow key was pressed, we move by `-moveSpeed`, which moves the player `5` pixels to the left (but not vertically). Notice the minus sign there: `moveSpeed` is `5`, so `-moveSpeed` is `-5`, as we explained previously.

Save the changes and run the game. You can now move your player left and right.

And you can move them right off the screen! It's the same problem we had with `enemy` going too far.

So, what to do? With `enemy`, we moved the sprite back to the top of the screen. But that doesn't make sense for the `player` sprite. What would that do? Move the `player` sprite back to the center? Nah! You could do it Pac-Man style: Go off one side of the screen and reappear on the other.

But, for us, a better option is to not let the `player` sprite go too far in the first place.

Update the `if` statement that checks for the left arrow key as follows:

```
if keys[K_LEFT] and player.rect.left > 0:
```

Now the `if` statement checks to see if the left arrow key was pressed and determines whether the `left` side of the `player` rectangle is greater than `0`. If `left` is `0`, then the player is already all the way to the left and won't be able to move further.

What about the right arrow key? Change that `if` statement, too:

```
if keys[K_RIGHT] and player.rect.right < IMG_ROAD.get_width():
```

This code checks the `right` side of the `player` rectangle to make sure that it has not gone beyond the width of the road (the width of the game screen).

This is better: The player can no longer fall off the edge of the screen. But we are not quite done. As coders, we need to anticipate how our code will be used and plan for every scenario. And here's one that may not have happened yet but inevitably will at some point.

When the player presses the left or right arrow key, we move the `player` sprite by 5 pixels. And we make sure that the player can't go too far off the screen. Right? But what if the current position is pixel 3 horizontally? When the player presses the left arrow key, our code will check to see if the position is less than 0, and as it isn't, it'll allow the sprite to move. Where will it move to? 5 pixels left of pixel 3 is –2, which means that part of the car will be over the edge of the screen. That's less than ideal.

There are a couple of ways to address this. We could change the code to check how many pixels there are left to move and use a number less than 5, if needed. Or we could just move the `player` sprite, and if we move it too far just nudge it back.

Let's go with the latter option. Here is the updated `player` sprite movement code:

```
# Get keys pressed
keys = pygame.key.get_pressed()
# Check for LEFT key
if keys[K_LEFT] and player.rect.left > 0:
    # Move left
    player.rect.move_ip(-moveSpeed, 0)
    # Make sure we didn't go too far left
    if player.rect.left < 0:
        # Too far, fix it
        player.rect.left = 0
#  Check for RIGHT key
if keys[K_RIGHT] and player.rect.right < IMG_ROAD.get_width():
    # Move right
    player.rect.move_ip(moveSpeed, 0)
    # Make sure we didn't go too far right
    if player.rect.right > IMG_ROAD.get_width():
        # Too far, fix it
        player.rect.right = IMG_ROAD.get_width()
```

Let's walk through this together.

We start by using `key.get_pressed()` to check if left or right arrow key was pressed.

If the left arrow key was pressed and we're not too far to the left, `move_ip()` moves the `player` sprite 5 pixels to the left. This is the same code that we used before. What changed is what comes next. An `if` statement checks to see if the `left` edge of the `player` rectangle is less than `0`, which would mean we've moved too far. If that happens, we set `player.rect.left = 0`, which puts the `player` sprite exactly on the left edge.

The code then does the same thing for the right arrow key. If the `right` edge of the `player` sprite is greater than the road width, then we've gone too far. If that happens, we set `player.rect.right = IMG_ROAD.get_width()`, which aligns the sprite as far right as it can go.

Much better. Our cars now all move, and they can't end up where they shouldn't be.

Although nothing happens when you crash into oncoming cars. We'll fix that next.

Making Lots of Little Changes

In our code, we move the `player` sprite and then correct the position if we allow it to move too far.

So, question: Is this really a good option? Won't it look weird to the player if their car moves slightly offscreen and then nudges back?

And the answer is...nope! Not at all. In fact, the player will have no idea.

You can make as many changes as you want to the display— change colors, add or remove sprites, move items, do whatever you want—and the player will see none of those changes while they are happening.

Why? As explained previously, Pygame doesn't actually update the display until you call `pygame.display.update()`. This means you can move sprites, adjust them, do whatever you need, without the player knowing. They'll see the changes you made only when you want them to.

And that's why we put `pygame.display.update()` at the very bottom of the game loop. Pretty smart, huh?

CHALLENGE 21.1

Game speed is controlled by the `moveSpeed` variable. It specifies how many pixels the `enemy` should advance by and how many pixels the `player` sprite moves with each left or right arrow key press.

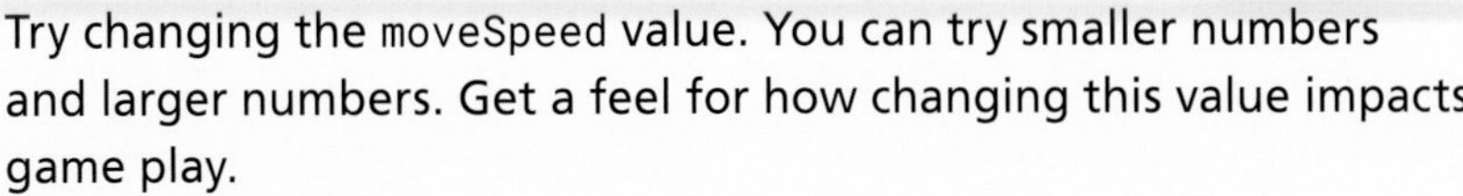

Try changing the `moveSpeed` value. You can try smaller numbers and larger numbers. Get a feel for how changing this value impacts game play.

CHALLENGE 21.2

We used the left and right keys to move the `player` sprite. You don't have to use those keys; you can pick your own. Many games use A and S, for example. Update the code to use those keys. You'll want to check for `K_a` and `K_s`.

Or allow both sets of keys, letting players use left arrow or A to go left and right arrow or S to go right. Here's a hint: You can do this easily with an `or` in your `if` statement. If you do this, be careful to group your conditions correctly with parentheses because you'll have an `and` and an `or`.

Summary

You now have cars that move. Nice. They can even move until they should crash—but then they don't. They kinda pass through each other. As cool as that ghostly effect is, we need to actually handle crashes properly. Fortunately, handling collisions is the subject of the next chapter.

CHAPTER 22

Crash, Bang, Boom

You now have a playable game—well, playable as in a game that you can never win or lose. So, yeah, maybe not so playable. In this chapter we'll fix that, and we'll also add score tracking and incrementally increasing game difficulty.

You Crashed, Game Over

Enemies drive toward you (or is it you driving toward them? Hmmm.). You move left or right to avoid them. That's how things work now.

What happens if you crash into oncoming traffic? Right now nothing, but what should happen is game over. And that means we need to be able to *detect collisions* and then respond when a collision occurs.

Collision Detection

In our game, a crash is literally a collision. But that's not what *collision detection* means. In game engines, *collision detection* is the process of determining if object boundaries have overlapped. And that's important. If your game allows you to drop bombs, then you need to know if a bomb hit a target, even if the game engine has no idea what a bomb even is. If your player approaches a door, the game engine needs to let you do something, even though it doesn't know what doors are. Same for jumping to bump into a mushroom or tossing a Poké Ball. From the game engine's perspective, the actual action being performed is not important. What is important is that items come into contact with each other (bomb and target, character and mushroom, etc.). The game engine's collision detection system is responsible for knowing when things come into contact with each other, and it does that by checking object boundaries to see if they overlap. If, for example, the character's boundary overlaps the mushroom's boundary at all, then there has been a *collision*, and the game engine will let you know so you can respond as appropriate for your game (and that will double your height for some reason).

Pygame keeps things simple. It uses rectangles for all sprites, and a collision occurs when any part of the rectangles overlap. Other game engines support more sophisticated collision detection options that can work with irregular shapes, too.

We need to make two changes to our code. Let's start with the code that will get executed when a collision occurs. We'll create a user-defined function named `GameOver()`. For now it'll just quit the game; we'll add more functionality later.

Here's the code, which you can add to your `Main.py` (just remember that user-defined functions must be defined before they are used, so a good place to put the function would be after the game variables are initialized but before the main game code):

```
# Game over function
def GameOver():
    # Quit Pygame
    pygame.quit()
    sys.exit()
```

This code is really simple. In fact, you've seen similar code before. Back in Chapter 19, we added code to the main game loop to allow players to quit the game. That code simply quit Pygame and exited the operating system environment. That's exactly what this code does. Call `GameOver()`, and the game will quit.

So how do we call `GameOver()`? We need to add collision detection. And this is super complicated stuff. Not!

Add this code in your game loop. It can go anywhere in the game loop, but ideally it should go after all sprite movement. So a good location would be right before or after the code that checks for the `QUIT` event. Here's the code:

```
    # Check for collisions
    if pygame.sprite.collide_rect(player, enemy):
        # Crash! Game over
        GameOver()
```

Save and test the game. Avoid oncoming cars, and the game will keep playing. But as soon as you collide, game over.

The magic here is the `collide_rect()` function. You simply pass it two objects, and it compares the rectangles defined by their boundaries. If the rectangles overlap in any way, the function will return `True`. Otherwise, it'll return `False`.

Here we are passing our two sprites, `player` and `enemy`, to `collide_rect()`. So long as you avoid oncoming cars, the two sprites won't overlap, so no collision occurs, and the function returns `False`. But if (or should that be when?) you crash, the sprites will overlap, and the function will return `True`. When that happens, the `GameOver()` function is called, and the game quits.

That was easier than you expected, right? That's the beauty of game engines: Once you have the basics in place, they take care of all the hard stuff for you.

We'll make our `GameOver()` function more interesting in the next chapter.

Tracking Score

Right now in the Crazy Driver game, you can avoid oncoming traffic until you crash. To make things more interesting, we should add scoring so you earn a point for each enemy you've successfully avoided. We need to make three changes to our code:

- We need a way to track the score.
- Scores have to be updated each time a vehicle has been avoided.
- And we need a way to show the score.

Let's tackle these one at a time.

Tracking scores is easy: We just need a variable that we'll increment as needed. We have one game variable already, and now we add a second. Here's the updated game variables section:

```
# Game variables
moveSpeed = 5
score = 0
```

Simple enough.

Now how do we increment the score during game play? The score needs to go up each time a car is avoided. Or, put differently, when an oncoming car reaches the bottom of the screen, then it's been avoided—and the score needs to go up.

Does that sound familiar? We already have code that gets executed when a car reaches the bottom of the screen. Our game loop contains this `if` statement:

```
    # Check didn't go off edge of screen
    if (enemy.rect.bottom > IMG_ROAD.get_height()):
```

The code under that `if` statement handles `enemy` sprite position. We can use the same `if` statement to update the score. Add this code to the bottom of the `if` statement:

```
        # Update the score
        score += 1
```

Now each time an `enemy` reaches the bottom of the screen, it'll move to the top, and the `score` variable will be incremented by `1`. (As a reminder, `score += 1` is a shortcut for `score = score + 1`.)

The last thing we need to do is to display the score. Back when we started building the game, we set the caption bar, like this:

```
# Set caption bar
pygame.display.set_caption("Crazy Driver")
```

The caption bar can be updated whenever needed, so we can use it to display the score. Add this code to your game loop. You may want to put it right at the top of the loop, before the sprite code (as captions are not affected by screen updates):

```
# Update caption with score
pygame.display.set_caption("Crazy Driver - Score " + str(score))
```

This code updates the game caption on each game loop. `str(score)` converts `score` to a string, as you saw previously, and we use that to build the caption text. Before any car is avoided, the caption will be `Crazy Driver - Score 0`, and the caption will update as `score` changes.

Save and try it out. Your screen should look something like this, with the score displayed in the caption bar:

Increasing Difficulty

Our game is too easy. To make it more challenging, we'll gradually increase game speed so that each time a car is avoided, the game will get a little quicker.

And you're going to love how easy this is to do.

The game speed is controlled by a variable named `moveSpeed`. We initialized it to `5`, so, when the game starts, cars move toward you 5 pixels at a time. Similarly, the `player` sprite moves left and right 5 pixels at a time.

To make the game go faster, we just need to change that `moveSpeed` variable. And as we want to do so each time a crash is avoided, we can use the same `if` statement as the one we just used to increment the score.

Add this code (you can put it right after the score incrementing code):

```
        # Increase the speed
        moveSpeed += 1
```

Save and run the game. You'll see that things get faster each time you avoid a car.

How does this work? `moveSpeed` was initialized to 5, but as soon as you avoid a car, `moveSpeed` will be incremented to 6, which means oncoming cars now advance 6 pixels at a time. Then they advance 7 at a time, and so on.

You'll find that the game speed picks up quickly, and at some point, it'll move too fast to even see properly. Is that okay? Sure, if that's what you want. But you may want to set an upper limit—a max speed that the game won't go over. If you want to do this, add one more variable to the game variables section:

```
maxSpeed = 10
```

And then change the code that increments the speed to do so only if `moveSpeed` is less than `maxSpeed`, like this:

```
        # Increase the speed
        if moveSpeed < maxSpeed:
            moveSpeed += 1
```

That'll do it.

Yeah for No Hard Coding

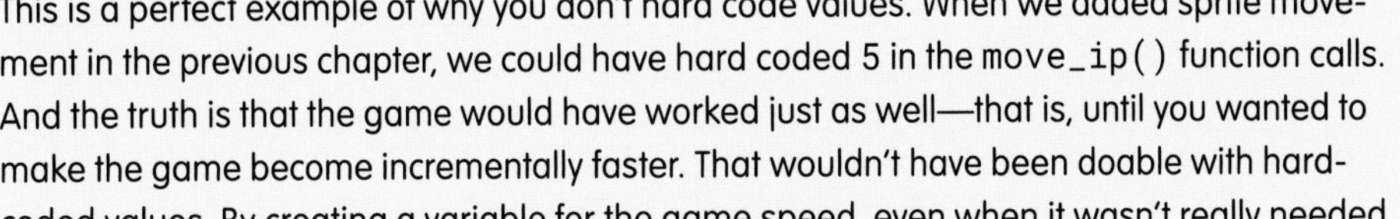

This is a perfect example of why you don't hard code values. When we added sprite movement in the previous chapter, we could have hard coded 5 in the `move_ip()` function calls. And the truth is that the game would have worked just as well—that is, until you wanted to make the game become incrementally faster. That wouldn't have been doable with hard-coded values. By creating a variable for the game speed, even when it wasn't really needed, we set ourselves up to easily make changes and add functionality.

Make It Yours

Feel free to change any of this. You can make `score` increment by `.5` so it ramps up more slowly. Or you can make it exponential by updating `score` with `moveSpeed *= 1.1` (which will multiply the score by 1.1, so increases will be slower at first and faster as the game progresses). You can also set `maxSpeed` to any value you want, or you can have no `maxSpeed` at all. Just be aware that if it gets so fast that it's jumping pixels greater than the height of the player car, it may never collide since the cars will never actually touch.

This is your game, so make it your own.

CHALLENGE 22.1

The game gets faster (and thus harder) the longer you play. But the scoring stays the same: 1 point per car avoided. Can you change that so that once the game doubles in speed, players get 2 points per car avoided?

Summary

We now have a real playable game. You can avoid cars, and the score (and speed) will increase. And if you crash, game over. In the next chapter, we'll add some finishing touches to our masterpiece.

CHAPTER 23

Finishing Touches

Our Crazy Driver game is fully functional. Not bad for 100 or so lines of code! In this chapter, we'll add some finishing touches—some little details that will make the game shine.

Game Over Revisited

When our game ends, it just ends: no display, no message, no anything. You can't even view your score. Let's change that. We created a `GameOver()` function that gets called when the game is over. Right now, it just does cleanup, like this:

```
# Game over function
def GameOver():
    # Quit Pygame
    pygame.quit()
    sys.exit()
```

We'll update this function to display a text message for a few seconds before the game ends, like this:

Pausing for a few seconds requires us to use the `time` library, which contains a `sleep()` function that pauses. So add `time` to your `import` statements:

```
# Imports
import sys, os, random, time
import pygame
from pygame.locals import *
```

Displaying text with Pygame is a little more involved than using the print() function we so know and love. Anything placed on a graphical screen needs to be turned into a graphic that can be blitted.

And you need to explicitly pick fonts and sizes. We'll use variables for our font details (no hard coding!). So add these two lines to your code's variables declarations:

```
textFonts = ['comicsansms','arial']
textSize = 48
```

textFonts is a list of fonts we want to use to display our text. Pygame will let you use any fonts installed on your computer, and we'll use Comic Sans because it's such a terrible font that it's perfect for a Crazy Driver game.

But what will happen if someone plays our game on a computer that doesn't have comicsansms installed? To address this potentiality, we specify additional fonts, including ones that will pretty much always be present, like the safe (and boring) arial. Pygame will try the fonts in the order specified, so it will prioritize comicsansms and will use that if it is installed. But, if comicsansms is not available, Pygame will fall back to arial.

textSize is the font size we want. Duh!

Okay, so on to our updated GameOver() function. Here's the code:

```
# GameOver function
# Displays message and cleans things up
def GameOver():
    # Game Over text creation
    fontGameOver = pygame.font.SysFont(textFonts, textSize)
    textGameOver = fontGameOver.render("Game Over!", True, RED)
    rectGameOver = textGameOver.get_rect()
    rectGameOver.center = (IMG_ROAD.get_width()//2,
                           IMG_ROAD.get_height()//2)
    # Black screen with game over text
    screen.fill(BLACK)
    screen.blit(textGameOver, rectGameOver)
    # Update the display
    pygame.display.update()
```

```
    # Destroy objects
    player.kill()
    enemy.kill()
    # Pause
    time.sleep(5)
    # Quit pygame
    pygame.quit()
    sys.exit()
```

You can save the code and try the game. When you crash, you'll see a black screen with a bright red Game Over! message.

Let's look at the code.

We start by creating a font object (named `fontGameOver`) and passing it the font name and size variables.

Then the `render()` method is used to draw text on a new surface, which we named `textGameOver`. `render()` accepts the text to be drawn, an *antialiasing* flag that we set to `True` to smooth out font lines, and the text color, which we set to `RED` (using the color variables we created way back when). `render()` can also accept an optional text background color, but we skipped that as we'll be filling the entire window with background color anyway.

NEW TERM

Antialiasing When lines (including lines that make up text) are drawn using pixels, the edges can look jagged. *Antialiasing* is a technique used to smooth out those edges.

Next, we get the object's rectangle and set the sizes, just like we did with all of the image and sprite objects. We need to do this because we're going to blit it, just like the cars and the background.

The background is then painted black with `fill()`, just like we did in Chapter 19, and the text object is blitted onto the display. Our friend `display.update()` then updates the screen to display our background and text.

Next, we do some cleanup, destroying the `player` and `enemy` sprites that we created.

Killing Objects

Python is really good about cleaning up after itself. If you create objects and don't remove them, Python will do it for you. But coders generally like to control when objects are created and killed, which is why we explicitly cleaned up our sprites here.

We want the Game Over! text to be displayed for 5 seconds, so we pause using the `sleep()` function, like this:

```
# Pause
time.sleep(5)
```

And finally, we quit Pygame.

Pause

Some games allow players to pause and catch their breath. How could we do that in our game? If we set `moveSpeed` to `0`, then nothing will move, effectively pausing the game.

What makes this a little tricky is if you are going to set `moveSpeed` to `0`, you need to remember what the speed was before you paused so you can set it back once the game resumes.

Let's try that. We are using the left and right arrow keys to control the player, and we'll add support for pressing the spacebar. While the spacebar is pressed down, the game will pause. Release it, and the game will resume.

Create a game variable called `paused` and initialize it to `False`, which we'll use to track whether the game is paused or not:

```
paused = False
```

Now we need to modify the game loop. We need to respond to the user pressing the spacebar to stop all movement, and while paused, we'll also ignore left and right arrow keys. (We wouldn't want the player to be able to cheat by moving out of the way while the oncoming car is paused.)

We need to make some changes to the code that processes key presses, so here is the updated code:

```
    # Get keys pressed
    keys = pygame.key.get_pressed()

    # Are we paused?
    if paused:
        # Check for SPACE
        if not keys[K_SPACE]:
            # Turn off pause
            # Set speed back to what it was
            moveSpeed=tempSpeed
            # Turn off flag
            paused=False
    else:
        # Check for LEFT key
        if keys[K_LEFT] and player.rect.left > 0:
            # Move left
            player.rect.move_ip(-moveSpeed, 0)
            # Make sure we didn't go too far left
            if player.rect.left < 0:
                # Too far, fix it
                player.rect.left = 0
        #  Check for RIGHT key
        if keys[K_RIGHT] and player.rect.right < IMG_ROAD.
get_width():
            # Move right
            player.rect.move_ip(moveSpeed, 0)
            # Make sure we didn't go too far right
            if player.rect.right > IMG_ROAD.get_width():
                # Too far, fix it
                player.rect.right = IMG_ROAD.get_width()
        # Check for SPACE key
        if keys[K_SPACE]:
            # Turn on pause
            # Save speed
            tempSpeed=moveSpeed
```

```
        # Set speed to 0
        moveSpeed=0
        # Turn on flag
        paused=True
```

Save and run this code. You can now press the spacebar to pause the game and release it to continue game play.

The code first checks to see if the game has been paused or not. If paused is True, then the only key the code responds to is the spacebar (key K_SPACE). When keys[K_SPACE] becomes False, we know that the spacebar is no longer being pressed, so moveSpeed is restored, and paused is set to True.

If the game is not paused, then processing continues as usual. The code checks for the left and right arrow keys being pressed and moves the player accordingly. And it also checks to see if the spacebar was pressed. If pressed, the current moveSpeed is saved to a temporary variable so it can be restored later, and paused is set to True.

And that's one way to implement a pause.

CHALLENGE 23.1

We created a paused variable to track whether or not the game is paused: True if it is, False if not. Was this necessary? Actually, no, it wasn't. There is another way to know if we're paused or not: just look at moveSpeed, which will be 0 only if the game is paused. Modify the code to remove the paused variable, and use the existing moveSpeed variable to pause (and unpause) game play.

Varying Enemies

Let's make one more enhancement that is a bit more involved. (But you're a pro by now, so you have nothing to worry about.)

Right now the game has a single enemy that reaches the bottom of the screen and then reappears at the top. That works, but it is the same enemy image over and over. It would be way more fun if different enemy images were used at random.

And if different enemies were different sizes, well, that would make game play more interesting, as that would impact obstacle avoidance and collisions.

Yeah, multiple different enemy vehicles would be better, which is why we've provided three for you to use.

Changing our code to support multiple enemies is not hard. It's all stuff we've done before. But quite a bit of code has to change to make this work. We'll walk through the key changes here, and you are always free to download the code, too.

The game now has an enemy sprite that is created before the game loop, ensuring that it is always ready to use. We'll change the code to create and remove the `enemy` sprite as needed. So, the first thing we need is a way to track which enemy we have, if any. Add this to your list of game variables:

```
eNum = -1
```

`eNum` is the active enemy number, and it'll be `0` for the first enemy, `1` for the second, and so on. As `0` or higher could be valid enemies, we use `-1` to mean no enemy (as `-1` could never be a valid enemy number).

Next, we need to load our enemy images. We currently load just one, like this:

```
IMG_ENEMY = pygame.image.load(os.path.join(IMAGE_FOLDER,
"Enemy.png"))
```

Delete this line of code. That sounds scary, we know. But, yes, we are serious: Delete it. Or comment it out.

TIP

Comment Out Code Instead of deleting a line of code, you can comment it out by putting a # character in front of it, like this:

```
#IMG_ENEMY = pygame.image.load(os.path.join(IMAGE_
FOLDER, "Enemy.png"))
```

This way, you can easily add the line back, if needed. And when you are finished testing, you can delete the unneeded code.

IMG_ENEMY is a simple variable that can load and store a single image. That won't work anymore as we need to load multiple images, so we'll replace that variable with a list.

Here is the code to replace it with:

```
IMG_ENEMIES = []
IMG_ENEMIES.append(pygame.image.load(os.path.join(IMAGE_FOLDER,
"Enemy.png")))
IMG_ENEMIES.append(pygame.image.load(os.path.join(IMAGE_FOLDER,
"Enemy2.png")))
IMG_ENEMIES.append(pygame.image.load(os.path.join(IMAGE_FOLDER,
"Enemy3.png")))
```

We've replaced IMG_ENEMY with a list we brilliantly called IMG_ENEMIES. The list starts off empty, like this:

```
IMG_ENEMIES = []
```

Then we use the append() method to add each of the three images, as we discussed way back in Chapter 6.

So far, so good.

And now, we need to be brave...and delete more code.

Before the main game loop, we created player and enemy sprites. Right? The enemy location and sprite code looks like this:

```
# Enemy
# Calculate initial enemy position
hl=IMG_ENEMY.get_width()//2
hr=IMG_ROAD.get_width()-(IMG_ENEMY.get_width()//2)
h=random.randrange(hl, hr)
v=0
# Create enemy sprite
enemy = pygame.sprite.Sprite()
enemy.image = IMG_ENEMY
enemy.surf = pygame.Surface(IMG_ENEMY.get_size())
enemy.rect = enemy.surf.get_rect(center = (h, v))
```

Delete this entire block of code. We don't need it anymore, as we'll be creating sprites as we need them right inside of the game loop.

Let's do that next. Add this code inside of your game loop. You can put it right after where you blit the `player` sprite:

```
# Make sure we have an enemy
if eNum == -1:
    # Get a random enemy
    eNum = random.randrange(0, len(IMG_ENEMIES))
    # Calculate initial enemy position
    hl=IMG_ENEMIES[eNum].get_width()//2
    hr=IMG_ROAD.get_width()-(IMG_ENEMIES[eNum].get_width()//2)
    h=random.randrange(hl, hr)
    v=0
    # Create enemy sprite
    enemy = pygame.sprite.Sprite()
    enemy.image = IMG_ENEMIES[eNum]
    enemy.surf = pygame.Surface(IMG_ENEMIES[eNum].get_size())
    enemy.rect = enemy.surf.get_rect(center = (h, v))
```

We only create a new `enemy` if we don't already have one. This code uses an `if` statement to check to see if we have an `enemy` or not. If `eNum` is `-1`, then we have no enemy and need one.

If there is no `enemy`, we need to randomly pick one, like this:

```
    # Get a random enemy
    eNum = random.randrange(0, len(IMG_ENEMIES))
```

This code uses the very familiar `randrange()` function to return a number between `0` and `len(IMG_ENEMIES)`, which we save to our `eNum` variable. As we have three enemies in `IMG_ENEMIES`, `eNum` will be `0`, `1`, or `2`. (This is why we used `-1` to indicate no enemy.)

The rest of the code is exactly the same as before, with one important change. We replaced `IMG_ENEMY` with `IMG_ENEMIES[eNum]` as we are accessing a list item instead of a simple variable. The logic is all the same, but this way, we'll be using a randomly selected enemy.

The randomly generated enemy is still named enemy. This ensures that the rest of the code (including the code that moves the enemy and provides collision detection) still works. None of that needs to be changed.

But we do need to make one final code change. What happens when an enemy sprite reaches the bottom of the screen? Previously, we moved it back up to the top, at a new random location. We need to change that so that a new enemy will be generated.

Find the code that starts with this if statement:

```
    if (enemy.rect.bottom > IMG_ROAD.get_height()):
```

We're going to get rid of all the code used to move the enemy sprite. Instead, the code will look like this:

```
    # Check didn't go off edge of screen
    if (enemy.rect.bottom > IMG_ROAD.get_height()):
        # Kill enemy object
        enemy.kill()
        # No enemy
        eNum = -1
        # Increment the score
        score += 1
        # Increase the speed
        moveSpeed += 1
        # Increase the speed
        if moveSpeed < maxSpeed:
            moveSpeed += 1
```

When enemy reaches the bottom of the screen, we don't bother moving it but just kill the object, like this:

```
        # Kill enemy object
        enemy.kill()
```

And then we set eNum back to -1:

```
        # No enemy
        eNum = -1
```

Flags and Variables

Our code needs to know if we have an enemy or not. We created a variable named `eNum` (for enemy number) to keep track of this for us: `-1` means no enemy, and any other value is the index of the enemy we are using.

So, was this necessary? Couldn't we instead use a Boolean flag and set it to `True` if we have an enemy and `False` if not? Wouldn't the code be simpler that way?

Yes, we could indeed do so, and the code would be simpler. But coders need to anticipate what they'll be doing next. And the next enhancement we'll add will indeed require us to know not just that we have an enemy but what exact enemy we have. So, with the future in mind, we opted for a numeric variable over a Boolean one.

That's all there is to it. In the next game loop, the code will see that `eNum` is `-1`, and it will generate a new random `enemy` sprite, using the code we already created above.

Oh, and we removed the duplicated enemy code as promised, too!

CHALLENGE 23.2

Can you add additional vehicles to the game? You can create your own PNG files or try to find some online. Save the images to the `Images` folder and then add them to `IMG_ENEMIES`.

Ice Cubes

You can now display a variety of enemies. Crash into any one of them, and game over. This means that players need to avoid oncoming objects. Always.

But we can make things more interesting by introducing different objects that do different things, including objects that the player might want to hit. For example, imagine if there were random ice cubes on the road, like this:

Yes, it's silly, but we love silly in our games. So, ice cubes appear. Hit them, and the game will slow down back to the starting game speed (and then it'll start increasing speed again). Players would definitely want to hit the ice cubes, as doing so will let them play longer.

With the code we wrote to support multiple enemies, adding the ice cube functionality is pretty simple.

Let's add the ice cube to the enemy images:

```
IMG_ENEMIES.append(pygame.image.load(os.path.join(IMAGE_FOLDER,
"IceCube.png")))
```

Now there are four images loaded. If you run the game now, ice cubes will appear on the screen. Crashing into them will end the game. Why? Because our collision detection doesn't distinguish between enemy types. Hit any enemy, and game over.

Let's change that. But first, up top, where we defined game variables, we have this code:

```
moveSpeed = 5
```

Change this code to look like this:

```
startSpeed = 5
moveSpeed = startSpeed
```

`moveSpeed` changes as game play proceeds. Crashing into an ice cube will reset `moveSpeed` back to the original starting speed, so we need to save that value, as we did here.

We need one more code change. Find the collision detection code that looks like this:

```
    # Check for collisions
    if pygame.sprite.collide_rect(player, enemy):
        # Crash! Game over
        GameOver()
```

This code simply says that if there are any collisions, run the `GameOver()` function. We now need to treat ice cubes differently. So update the code so that it looks like this:

```
    # Check for collisions
    if eNum >= 0 and pygame.sprite.collide_rect(player, enemy):
        # Is it enemy 3?
        if eNum == 3:
            # It's the ice cube, reset the speed
            moveSpeed = startSpeed
        else:
            # Crash! Game over
            GameOver()
```

The code now checks collisions only if there is an active enemy (that is, if `eNum` is `0` or greater). If there is a collision, the code checks to see what enemy the player collided with. If it is enemy `3` (the 4th enemy in our list, Python starts counting from 0 as you know), then it is the ice cube, and the game speed is reset back to the starting speed. If it is any other enemy, then game over.

Save and run this code. You'll see the game plays as it did before, increasing speed with each vehicle avoided. If you hit an ice cube, the game slows back down to the original speed; if you avoid the ice cube, nothing changes.

Summary

In this chapter, we've added lots of bells and whistles to improve our game experience. We've added a Game Over! screen, giving players the option of pausing the game, and introduced random enemies and different enemy types. In the next chapter, we'll suggest other ideas for you to try.

CHAPTER 24

Keep Going

You have created a fun and functional game. Congratulations! But, coders are never satisfied with their creations and always look for cool new features to add. In this chapter, we'll present some ideas as next steps and give you hints or pointers to get started.

Splash Screen

Let's start with an easy one. Right now, the Crazy Driver game runs and starts. It has no introduction, no warning, no click-to-start. It just runs (because that's how we coded it). Most games start with a splash screen that displays the game name and maybe instructions (like telling players what keys to use) and the name of the creator (that's you, BTW).

So, how could you create a splash screen? Well, you could use the `GameOver()` code as a starting point. Copy it to a `GameStart()` function and call that function before your main game loop. You could use the same black background or any other color. Or, you could use the road image as the background.

You'll need to decide how the splash screen disappears and the game starts. Is it a timed pause like the Game Over! screen? Or should the user press a key or click a button to start the game? Either option works, and you get to decide which to use.

Scores and High Scores

The Game Over! screen just says Game Over! That's not very interesting. At a minimum, it should also display the player's score, perhaps like this:

There's one catch: Pygame can't display text with line breaks, so to create a display like this, you'll need a second set of objects: another `SysFont`, another `render()`, another rectangle, and so on. And then you'll blit the new text.

To make things easier, you can actually just make a copy of the game over block and change the object names (`fontGameOver2`, `textGameOver2`, etc., for example). That'll make for a more interesting (and useful) closing screen. (Just make sure you use different placement values, or your second line of text will be drawn over the first.)

But if you really want to up your game (bad pun intended), you could also display the high score, like this:

Doing this requires the following workflow:

1. The player plays the game.
2. When the game is over, check to see if there is a high score already saved.
3. If there is no high score saved, then the current game's score is the high score.

4. If there is a saved high score, read it from the save file and compare it to the current game score. If the current score is greater than the saved high score, then the current game score becomes the new high score.
5. Display the high score on the screen.
6. Save the high score to the save file so you have it for the next game.

Displaying the high score is much like displaying the current score. You need new font and text objects, which you can use to draw the text to the display.

How do you read and save high score files? Refer to the "Saving and Restoring" section in Chapter 18.

Oil Slick

In Chapter 23, you added an ice cube enemy. Hit it, and the game slows down.

Now add an oil slick enemy. We gave you an image named `Oil.png`. It's in your `Images` folder, and it looks like this:

To use it:

- Add a line of code to append `Oil.png` to the enemies list. If you add it last (after the ice cube), it'll be item 4.
- In your collision detection code, check for `eNum == 4` (meaning the player hit the oil slick) and do something devious.

As for what hitting an oil slick does, that's up to you. Here are some ideas:

- You could randomly move the player a few pixels to the left or right. You could even randomize how far they'll move.
- You could make the left and right keys not work for a couple of seconds.
- You could reverse the keys so the left key goes right and the right key goes left.
- You could make the whole screen go black for a few seconds, as if oil splashed the windscreen.

Hey, we weren't kidding when we said do something devious!

Oh, one more thing. Right now our code gives the player a point for every enemy avoided. That made sense when we only had car enemies. But now we have ice and oil; should avoiding those give the player points (and raise the speed)? Maybe. Or maybe not. You're the coder, it's up to you. If you'd like to only change score and speed if the enemy is a car, you'd want to add an if statement and necessary code in your collision detection to do that.

Multiple Enemies

Our game displays one enemy at a time. If you want to really up game play difficulty, you can display multiple enemies at a time, starting at different times and scattered randomly across the road. Dodging these will be much harder.

This is definitely a more complicated enhancement, so here are some notes and tips:

- You'll need to decide how often new enemies appear. Is it random? Every few seconds? Do you add an enemy each time the score increases by 5 (so 1 enemy until the score is 5, 2 until the score is 10, 3 until the score is 15, and so on)?

- Look at how we created and killed enemy objects (once we changed the code to support multiple image files). You can use the same technique to create enemies on demand.
- You can manipulate individual sprites, but that's a pain. A better option is to use sprite groups. You create a group like this:

  ```
  enemies = pygame.sprite.Group()
  ```

  And then, whenever you generate new enemies, you can add them to the group, like this:

  ```
  enemies.add(enemy)
  ```

  You can blit entire groups at once. You can also kill a group to kill all members.
- To move all group members you'd use a `for` loop and move each member, like this:

  ```
  for enemy in enemies:
  ```
- Sprite groups can also simplify collision detection. Instead of checking each sprite individually, you can use the `spritecollideany()` function, which checks if any sprites in a group collided.

As we noted, this enhancement is definitely more complicated. But with what you've learned thus far, it is quite doable.

And Then...

You now have the framework for a fun game—one with lots of room for you to be creative. So, do that: Create! Think of other features you could add. Here are some ideas:

- Put objects (mushroom perhaps?) on the road that temporarily change the `player` car size. A bigger car is more likely to crash an oncoming vehicle; a smaller one is less likely to do so.

- How about an invincibility potion? Hit that, and crashes won't kill you for a few seconds.
- Or how about temporary shields that deflect oncoming vehicles? When your shield is up, oncoming vehicles get nudged to the side so they don't hit you.
- Add firepower. Hit the right object, and you will be able to shoot away oncoming vehicles. And maybe doing so awards even more points.
- You could allow the player to move forward and backward for greater control. You can make that part of the core game, or available only as an unlock when a certain score is reached, or temporarily available when a specific item is hit.
- Another idea could be a jump button that allows you to leap over enemy cars. You'd need to decide how to show this, either changing the car image or growing it to simulate getting closer to the "camera."

So many ideas, all very doable, and all of which will make the game uniquely yours.

Summary

In this chapter, we've presented ideas that will really take our Crazy Driver game to the next level. And we've left you with lots of ideas about where to go next.

What Next?

Congratulations, you're a coder!

You've made it all the way to the end of our book, and along the way picked up critical coding skills that will continue to serve you well. And we hope you found the experience engaging and fun.

But, as we told you way back when we started on this journey together, coders are never really done—there's always more to learn (especially as technology keeps evolving).

So, before we say goodbye, we wanted to share some thoughts and ideas as to what to learn and do next.

Here goes.

There's a Lot More to Python

You learned a lot of Python in this book. And as you have discovered, Python is a fun and intuitive language. Python makes getting started simple, but don't let that simplicity fool you. Python is crazy powerful and capable, which is why it is one of the most used languages in the world.

So we want you to keep at it and dig into Python further:

- We worked with classes a bit, but not enough. If there is one area where we'd like you to really double down, that's what it is: classes. Actually, a great project would be to rewrite the Crazy Driver game using classes instead of one long block of code. In doing so, you'll actually find yourself writing more code, not less. But when you're done, you'll find that you can add functionality and complexity with much less effort. And, to get you started, we've posted a class-based version of the game for you to download from the book page.
- One topic we didn't get to is working with data and external data files. These types of projects tend to be less fun and games, which is why we didn't include them. But there is a huge demand for data scientists, and Python is one of the really popular ways to work with data. You can search online for project ideas. Look for data projects that involve XML files, JSON, and any large data sets. There are lots of these online, and lots of great examples to look at, too.

Web Development

Websites and web apps are fun projects, but they pose an interesting challenge by virtue of how many different languages and technologies you need to use to build them. So, what's involved in building websites?

- Web pages are created using HTML, which is a language; but it is not a programming language (so no if statements, no loops, no variables). Rather, it is a markup language, and it is used to lay out elements of a web page. HTML is read by your web browser (think Chrome, Safari, Edge, Firefox, etc.) which is how they know what to display. The good news is that HTML is super easy to learn. The bad news is that HTML by itself doesn't do much.

- You'll also need CSS (Cascading Style Sheets) which is the language used to design and format web pages and elements.
- Unlike HTML and CSS, JavaScript is indeed a programming language. It has been around for almost as long as the web because without it, the web would be a really boring place. JavaScript runs inside of the web browser, and it adds interactivity to pages. If you mouse over an item on a web page and something happens, that's JavaScript making that happen. JavaScript is a programming language, and it is not too hard to learn, especially as you'll tend to write lots of small blocks of code in it as opposed to full-blown applications. The key is that like HTML, JavaScript runs in the browser. For your web site or app to do anything more sophisticated, part of it needs to run on a server or in the cloud. And so:
- Pretty much every web application has a server backend. This is the glue that holds the whole app together, and it tends to be the largest part of any web application. What languages are used to write the backend of a web application? You'll be pleased to know that Python is a good and popular choice. Python itself doesn't really have any web-specific libraries or technology, but there are community-created third-party libraries that you can use. One very popular one is called Flask, which makes it easy to generate web pages and respond to them. In addition to Python, you can use Java, PHP, .NET, and more, for your website backend.
- Most websites need to store and access data (logins, items to purchase, user profiles, game scores, and so much more). This type of data lives in databases, and the language used to work with databases is called SQL. Fortunately, SQL is an easy language to learn (although it can take time to master).

> **TIP**
>
> **Learn SQL** If you want to learn SQL, we have a book suggestion for you. It's the best-selling SQL book out there, and it's written by our very own Ben. You can find it at https://forta.com/books/0135182794/.

Mobile App Development

The one thing Python really isn't well-suited for is mobile app development. For those you'll want to use other languages:

- To write apps for iOS (meaning they'll run on iPhone and iPad), you'll want to use a language called Swift. This is a pretty new language; it is easy to learn and use, and developers really like it. iOS apps are also written in Objective C (which is a variation of C, one of the most powerful languages out there, but a harder one to learn and master).
- Android apps are written in Java, one of the most used programming languages. Java has lots of other uses, too (often used for server side and backend code) and it is the preferred language for Android development.

Like web apps, your mobile apps will likely need backends, too. The options we mentioned for websites all apply to mobile apps, too.

Game Development

We used Pygame to create a graphical game in Part III. Pygame is fun, easy to use, and quite powerful. But it is not a full-blown gaming engine. If you really want to write games, take a look at Unity, the most widely used gaming engine and platform out there. With Unity you can write games for every major operating system, mobile device, and gaming platform (including Nintendo Switch, Sony PlayStation, and Microsoft Xbox).

Unity games are written in C#, which is a programming language based on C (and C++). Oh, and now that you're familiar with Visual Studio Code, you'll be pleased to know that Unity development is done with Visual Studio (VS Code's big brother), so the IDE will be familiar.

And Then…

And once you are done with all this, check out the book web page at **https://forta.com/books/0137653573** or scan this QR code. We've posted additional links and ideas there for you.

TIP

Chapter 25 Want access to a bonus Chapter 25? You'll find it online. Just use the link or QR code above.

And with that, thanks for joining us on this journey. We can't wait to see what you create!

Ben & Shmuel

INDEX

D

P

Q–R

S

T

X-Y-Z

VIDEO TRAINING FOR THE **IT PROFESSIONAL**

LEARN QUICKLY
Learn a new technology in just hours. Video training can teach more in less time, and material is generally easier to absorb and remember.

WATCH AND LEARN
Instructors demonstrate concepts so you see technology in action.

TEST YOURSELF
Our Complete Video Courses offer self-assessment quizzes throughout.

CONVENIENT
Most videos are streaming with an option to download lessons for offline viewing.

Learn more, browse our store, and watch free, sample lessons at **informit.com/video**

Save 50%* off the list price of video courses with discount code **VIDBOB**

*Discount code VIDBOB confers a 50% discount off the list price of eligible titles purchased on informit.com. Eligible titles include most full-course video titles. Book + eBook bundles, book/eBook + video bundles, individual video lessons, Rough Cuts, Safari Books Online, non-discountable titles, titles on promotion with our retail partners, and any title featured as eBook Deal of the Day or Video Deal of the Week is not eligible for discount. Discount may not be combined with any other offer and is not redeemable for cash. Offer subject to change.

Photo by izusek/gettyimages

Register Your Product at informit.com/register

Access additional benefits and **save 35%** on your next purchase

- Automatically receive a coupon for 35% off your next purchase, valid for 30 days. Look for your code in your InformIT cart or the Manage Codes section of your account page.
- Download available product updates.
- Access bonus material if available.*
- Check the box to hear from us and receive exclusive offers on new editions and related products.

**Registration benefits vary by product. Benefits will be listed on your account page under Registered Products.*

InformIT.com—The Trusted Technology Learning Source

InformIT is the online home of information technology brands at Pearson, the world's foremost education company. At InformIT.com, you can:

- Shop our books, eBooks, software, and video training
- Take advantage of our special offers and promotions (informit.com/promotions)
- Sign up for special offers and content newsletter (informit.com/newsletters)
- Access thousands of free chapters and video lessons

Connect with InformIT—Visit informit.com/community

Addison-Wesley • Adobe Press • Cisco Press • Microsoft Press • Pearson IT Certification • Que • Sams • Peachpit Press